WEBSTER'S
NEW W🌐RLD™

ROBERT'S RULES
of
ORDER
Simplified and Applied
Second Edition

WEBSTER'S
NEW WORLD™

ROBERT'S RULES

of

ORDER

Simplified and Applied

Second Edition

by Robert McConnell Production

Joyce M. Joseph
38 Fir Rd.
Rockland, MA 02370

Wiley Publishing, Inc.

Robert's Rules of Order: *Simplified and Applied*, 2nd edition

Copyright © 2001 by Robert McConnell productions

Published by Wiley Publishing, Inc., Indianapolis, Indiana

Published simultaneously in Canada

For general information on our other products and services or to obtain technical support please contact our Customer Care Department within the U.S. at 800-762-2974, outside the U.S. at 317-572-3993 or fax 317-572-4002.

Wiley also publishes its books in a variety of electronic formats. Some content that appears in print may not be available in electronic books.

Library of Congress Control Number: 2001092064

Manufactured in the United States of America

10 9

About the Author

Robert McConnell Productions is a multimedia company providing simplified information about parliamentary procedure in the form of videos, books, magazine articles, and a Web site: http://parli.com. The company published *Robert's Rules of Order: Simplified and Applied* in 1998, a book designed to take the complexity and the mystery out of Robert's Rules and to explain it to users in plain, easily understandable terms.

The company also makes special interest videos in its own production studio. To date, the company has made five videos about parliamentary procedure. *Parliamentary Procedure Made Simple: The Basics* is an 80-minute video produced in 1993. It has sold more than 12,000 copies worldwide so far. The next video, produced in 1996, is *All About Motions*, a 140-minute video covering all the motions in *Robert's Rules of Order*. The third and fourth videos are a 32-minute *How to Conduct a Meeting* and its Spanish companion version, the 46-minute *Como Conducir Reuniones*, the world's first video about parliamentary procedure made in Spanish. The fifth video is *Nominations & Elections*, a video designed to keep organizations out of trouble by showing them how to do the electoral process correctly.

The company markets these videos through a combination of direct mail brochures, targeted faxes, and a Web site, http://parli.com, which was the first Web site about parliamentary procedure on the Internet. The company also makes and markets videos about France, Russia, and Cuba, and produces custom-made videos for corporate clients.

Robert McConnell Productions has been in business since 1993.

Contents

Preface

This book is dedicated to people who want a clear, simple explanation of the rules of parliamentary procedure and strategies for saving time at meetings while preserving the democratic process. Most people are familiar with the rules of parliamentary procedure as they are presented in *Robert's Rules of Order*. The goal of this book is to help you understand and apply these rules for more effective and efficient meetings. We explain the principles and concepts behind each rule in everyday language so that you can understand why a particular rule is important and what its role is in maintaining the democratic process. Then, we show you, through scripts and everyday examples, how these rules can be applied in any meeting to bring order and help members get things done in a timely manner.

What makes this book unique? Several years ago an idea to produce videos to teach the basic rules of parliamentary procedure as exemplified in *Robert's Rules of Order* was born. These videos have sold thousands of copies worldwide. As technology progressed, we also created a Web site dedicated exclusively to helping people understand and apply the rules on a case-by-case basis and in an interactive way. This book takes the concept of teaching the rules through concise explanation of principles, everyday examples, and cases from our videos and Web site and puts it into book form. See the final page of this book for more information about these videos and our Web site.

We would like to thank the following people for their help in preparing the final manuscript for our first edition: Harold Corbin, Registered Parliamentarian, for reading the entire manuscript to ensure accuracy in conforming to *Robert's Rules of Order;* Jeanne Everett for reading the manuscript to ensure that it would make sense to the general reader and be free from errors in spelling, grammar, and punctuation; Sarah

McConnell for reading the manuscript in its early stages and offering constructive suggestions; and Faunette Johnston, Diana Francour, and the other editors at Macmillan Publishing for rendering the manuscript into its final form.

In the year 2000, a new official version of *Robert's Rules of Order, Newly Revised* was released. Because this book is based on that work, we approached our new publisher, Hungry Minds, Inc., to revise our book. It was important for us to keep up with the changes in current parliamentary law and electronic meetings. We also wanted to make the book more complete, so organizations can adopt it as their own parliamentary authority.

In this edition, you will find a new part on corporate charters, bylaws (including sample bylaws), rules of order, and standing rules. We discuss e-mail as a means of communication within the organization, how it should be used, and whether online meetings are valid ways of conducting business. We've included new information about nominations and elections, taking a recount, preventing election fraud, and motions relating to the polls. We've also added information about handling resignations, being excused from a duty, and adhering to open meeting laws. In carefully reviewing the 10th edition of *Robert's Rules of Order, Newly Revised,* we have decided *not* to change our book to comply with some of their changes. The reason is because the changes that were made in the 10th edition have made procedures more complicated, and our desire is to "keep it simple." We hope you will find this book useful, simple to understand, and easy to apply to meeting problems.

We want to thank Hungry Minds editors Joan Friedman and Billie A. Williams for their guidance and for making us keep difficult procedures simple to understand.

Robert McConnell Productions

Introduction

There are some basic principles and procedures that apply to all decision-making processes, whether you are a family trying to plan an outing, a manager trying to lead a work team, or an officer in an organization trying to conduct a meeting. These principles and procedures are referred to formally as *parliamentary procedure.* Parliamentary procedures are the rules that help us maintain order and ensure fairness in all decision-making processes. Robert's Rules of Order is one man's presentation and discussion of parliamentary procedure that has become the leading authority in most organizations today.

The basic principles behind Robert's Rules of Order are:

- Someone has to facilitate or direct the discussion and keep order.

- All members of the group have the right to bring up ideas, discuss them, and come to a conclusion.

- Members should come to an agreement about what to do.

- Members should understand that the majority rules, but the rights of the minority are always protected by assuring them the right to speak and to vote.

The following chapters first explain, in a simple way, the basic principles of Robert's Rules of Order. Then they show you how and when to apply the rules so that you can expedite your business quickly and efficiently while ensuring fairness and due process.

Webster's New World Robert's Rules of Order: Simplified and Applied, Second Edition includes several tools that will help you in this step-by-step process. "Scripting" of exactly what to say and when to say it appears throughout the book. The scripts are structured like the dialogue found in a play, and they begin by telling you who is to do the talking, followed by what should be said, and then any physical actions to be performed (which appear in brackets), such as rising to obtain the floor or rapping the gavel. Quick-reference boxes for each motion tell you at-a-glance the purpose of the motion; if it requires a second, is amendable, and is debatable; what kind of vote is required to adopt it; and what the result will be if adopted. Easy-to-read charts provide a quick visual guide to the ranking of each motion so that you can quickly determine the correct order of proceedings. And finally, the appendices provide an actual example of minutes, a script of an entire meeting, a guide to correct terminology, and a short history of Henry Robert and the development of parliamentary procedure as it is practiced today.

Part I

MEETINGS AND ORGANIZATIONS

1

The Basics

In a democratic society, we hold dear many principles of conduct and self-government. When people come together in their organizations and governments to conduct business, certain rules, referred to collectively as *parliamentary procedure,* must be applied correctly to maintain these democratic principles.

Organization members commonly make two mistakes: They do not know parliamentary procedure at all, and/or they misapply it because they don't understand the underlying democratic principles or they want to manipulate them. These mistakes invariably lead to confusion and, in the worst cases, can result in intimidation and the loss of members' rights. This chapter describes the fundamental democratic principles from which parliamentary procedure emerges and explains how these principles affect and apply to the structure of an organization. Parliamentary procedure is defined, followed by a discussion of its importance and application in protecting basic democratic principles. All members and their organizations must understand these principles to ensure the preservation of the democratic process.

STRUCTURE OF AN ORGANIZATION

There are basically two ways to structure an organization. One way is based on the *authoritarian model,* which favors the concentration of power in a leader or a small group of people who may or may not be responsible to the members. In the extreme form of this model, one person or a small group (such as a board of directors) may make all the decisions with no input or final approval from the membership.

The second way to structure an organization is based on the *democratic model,* which means that the people or the members govern. In the extreme form of this model, the members, not elected representatives, make all decisions. However, in most organizations, there is an agreed upon balance of power achieved between members and the officers they elect.

The democratic style of government is founded upon laws and the rights and responsibilities of all the members, not the whims of an unaccountable leadership. Abraham Lincoln defined democratic government as "government of the people, by the people, and for the people." An organization that has no rules or governing documents to establish a course of action eventually finds itself in a state of anarchy. In the words of Henry M. Robert, who wrote what we know today as *Robert's Rules of Order,* "Where there is no law, but every man does what is right in his own eyes, there is the least of real liberty."

APPLYING DEMOCRATIC PRINCIPLES TO ORGANIZATIONS

For an organization to survive and grow, the democratic model has proved to be the best form of government because it makes use of the talents and abilities of all the members. Organizations are democratic to the extent that they conform in the following ways:

- **The members rule through a decision-making process that they've established by a vote.** The organization's governing documents — its constitution, bylaws, rules of order, standing rules, policy statements, and parliamentary authority (such as *Robert's Rules of Order*) — embody this process. This is government by the consent of the governed.

- **Ideas come from the members and are presented to the assembly to decide upon.** Everyone gets the right to present, speak to, and vote on ideas.

- **Leaders come from the people through an election process.** When a leader's term of office ends, he or she returns to the people. A hierarchy of power doesn't exist; it is shared equally. All members have the right to be considered for office.

- **Checks and balances between the leadership and the members are established in the governing documents.** As an example of checks and balances, officers and boards of directors have only the power that the governing documents assign to them. Those powers not specifically given to officers and boards in the bylaws enable members to reverse decisions made by boards and officers. For example, if the bylaws do not say that the board or officers can set dues, and the board votes do this, then the members can rescind the action. Another check and balance that the bylaws give is the right of the membership to remove ineffective or tyrannical leaders from office.

- **All members are equal — they have equal rights and responsibilities.**

- **The organization is run with impartiality and fairness.** Law and enactment rule the organization, not the whims of the leadership. The rules are applied equally, impartially, and fairly to all and not just a select few.

- **There is equal justice under the law; members and officers have a right to a fair trial if accused.** Written procedures exist for removing and replacing an officer when the officer doesn't fulfill his or her duties.

- **The majority rules, but the rights of the minority and absent members are protected.**

- **Everything is accomplished in the spirit of openness, not secrecy.** Members have the right to know what is going on within the organization by attending meetings, inspecting the official records, and receiving notices and reports from committees, officers, and boards.

- **Members have the right to resign from office or from the organization.**

Governing documents should clearly state the rights and obligations of members and officers. These documents consist of the *corporate charter* (if there is one), which is issued by the state for incorporation, *bylaws* (or the organization's constitution), and any rules of order (parliamentary rules) or standing rules (administrative rules). Each organization should adopt a *parliamentary authority,* which is a book of common parliamentary law that details the rules for conducting meetings, electing officers, and making and adopting motions. All members are entitled to have a copy of their governing rules.

For a democracy to succeed, the members must work harmoniously together. To accomplish this, each member must know the purpose and goals of the organization, its rules, the rights of each individual member, and what each member is expected to do. One of the greatest threats to a democratic organization is for the members to become apathetic and let a small group of the membership do all the work. This creates divisions and promotes authoritarianism. Another threat is for a small group to work secretly behind the scenes to accomplish its own goals or its own agenda and then push it through without the rest of the membership having an input either through discussion or through the investigative process. Such actions cause mistrust and hostility.

If the principles of democracy are not upheld in the organization, knowing and following the rules of parliamentary procedure is valueless.

DEFINING PARLIAMENTARY PROCEDURE

Parliamentary procedure enables members to take care of business in an efficient manner and to maintain order while business is conducted. It ensures that everyone gets the right to speak and vote. Parliamentary procedure takes up business one item at a time and promotes courtesy, justice, and impartiality. It ensures the rule of the majority while protecting the rights of the minority and absent members. Adhering to parliamentary procedure is democracy in action.

The procedures, or rules, are found in the organization's bylaws, in its standing rules, and in its adopted parliamentary authority. A *parliamentary authority* is a reference book that helps the members decide what to do when the group has no written rules concerning how certain things are done. You could adopt this book as a parliamentary authority.

IMPORTANCE OF PARLIAMENTARY PROCEDURES

Parliamentary procedures provide proven, time-tested ways of determining action and carrying on an organization's business. One frequently asked question is, "Why do I need to know these parliamentary rules — what difference do they make?" You might compare knowing parliamentary procedures with knowing the rules of the road. Because you've learned the rules of driving, you know which side of the road to drive on, who has the right of way at street corners, who goes first at a four-way stop, and the rules of turning left in front of oncoming traffic. Obeying the rules of the road keeps traffic flowing smoothly and prevents accidents from happening. When everyone knows the parliamentary rules, meetings run smoothly, and the head-on collisions that can happen during the discussion of controversial motions can be prevented. If everyone in your group learns the basics of parliamentary procedure, you'll have more productive meetings: More members will make and discuss motions, and more members will be willing to serve as officers and committee chairmen.

BASIC PRINCIPLES OF PARLIAMENTARY PROCEDURE

Before learning the specific rules, everyone needs to know three fundamental principles of democracy and parliamentary procedure. If you can remember these principles, you'll be able to solve problems that come up in your organization and meetings, even if you can't remember the specific rules:

- **Take up business one item at a time.** Doing so maintains order, expedites business, and accomplishes the purpose of the organization.

- **Promote courtesy, justice, impartiality, and equality.** This ensures that everyone is heard, that members treat each other with courtesy, that everyone has the same rights, and that no individual or special group is singled out for special favors.

- **The majority rules, but the rights of individual, minority, and absent members are protected.** This principle ensures that, even though the majority rules, the minority has a right to be heard and its ideas are taken seriously. Similarly, the minority doesn't leave the organization because it didn't win; it knows that it may win another day. Following this principle preserves the unity and harmony of the organization.

The following sections explain the individual rules that support these three basic principles.

Taking Up Business One Item at a Time

Like most people, members in a business meeting can do only one thing at a time. Therefore, the first principle of parliamentary procedure is that business is taken up one item at a time. The following rules support this principle:

- **Each meeting follows an order of business called an *agenda*.** Everything on the agenda is reviewed in its proper order and disposed of before members go on to the next item on the agenda.

- **Only one main motion can be pending at a time.**

- **When a main motion is pending, members can make motions from a class of motions called *secondary motions*.** When secondary motions are taken up, they take precedence over the main motion. Discussion must focus on the secondary motion until it is resolved or temporarily disposed of. Some examples of secondary motions are to *amend, refer to a committee,* and *postpone* a main motion (see Chapter 6).

- **Only one member can be assigned the floor at a time.**

- **Members take turns speaking.**

- **No member speaks twice about a motion until all members have had the opportunity to speak.**

Promoting Courtesy, Justice, Impartiality, and Equality

As children, we're taught how to be courteous toward others. In our daily dealings and meetings with other people, courtesies are the necessities of life that promote harmony and unity. Here are ways to apply courtesy during meetings:

- **The chair or presiding officer calls the meeting to order on time.** This shows courtesy to the members present. They shouldn't have to wait for the latecomers to arrive.

- **Members take their seats promptly when the chair calls the meeting to order, and conversation stops.**

- **Those members giving reports during the meeting take seats in front.** Doing so saves time.

- **Members rise to be recognized by the presiding officer and don't speak out of turn.**

- **Members always refer to other members and officers in the third person.** Refer to officers by their title; for example, *Mr. President* or *Madam President, Mr. Chairman* or *Madam Chairman.* Members refer to each other by saying, for example, "the previous speaker" or "the delegate from District 2." This prevents personalizing the debate and, in a worst case scenario, name-calling or personal attacks.

- **In debate, members do not *cross talk,* or talk directly to each other, when another member is speaking.** All remarks are made through and to the chair.

- **Members keep discussion to the issues, not to personalities or other members' motives.**

- **When correcting a member, the presiding officer doesn't use the member's name.** Instead, he or she states, "Will the speaker keep his (or her) remarks to the issue at hand?" Or, if a motion is out of order, the chair states, "The motion is out of order," not "The member is out of order." (To tell a member that he or she is out of order is technically charging the member with an offense.)

- **Members speak clearly and loudly so all can hear.** Members can use a microphone if one is provided.

- **Members listen when others are speaking.**

Here is how justice, impartiality, and equality operate in meetings:

- **The presiding officer doesn't take sides but allows all to be heard equally in debate.** If the presiding officer wants to voice an opinion about the issue under discussion, the presiding officer relinquishes the chair to another officer so that he or she can speak and vote.

- **The presiding officer and members should know the rules and apply them judiciously.** Correct only major infractions. If members' rights aren't being taken away and an infraction is minor, raising a point of order to correct the infraction isn't necessary.

- **The presiding officer ensures that all sides of an issue are heard and that the rules of debate are carefully followed.** These measures prevent a small group from railroading a motion through.

- **Members have the right to make a motion to take a vote by ballot during a controversial issue.** A ballot vote preserves members' privacy and prevents possible retaliation for the way they voted.

- **Members have the right to a trial when they're accused of wrongdoing.**

The Rule of the Majority and Protection of the Minority

One of the most important rights that members have is the right to vote, knowing that the majority rules. At the same time, the majority never has the right to silence or take away rights from the minority, absent members, or individual members. Here's how this principle translates into action:

- **Members have the right to have notice of all meetings.** The organization can give notice by mail, phone, electronic communication, or an announcement at a previous meeting.

- **Members have the right to know by previous notice when there is a proposal to rescind or amend something previously adopted.**

- **In any situation where rights may be taken away from members, two-thirds of the membership must approve the motion (rather than a majority).** Examples include amending the governing documents or removing someone from office or membership.

- **No one has the right to require a higher vote than a majority vote on issues unless the bylaws or the parliamentary authority specifically states that more than a majority is required.**

- **Members have a right to be informed of the work of the organization.** Reading the minutes of the prior meeting allows members to correct inaccurate information and informs the absent members of any action taken. Members have the right to hear reports of board action, committee work, and officers.

2

The Order of a Business Meeting

A business meeting provides members with the opportunity to propose ideas and to participate in forming the plans and actions of the organization. To do this in an orderly and efficient fashion, the business of the meeting is conducted according to the first principle of parliamentary procedure, which states that business is taken up one item at a time. The plan or the established order in which the items of business are taken up is called an *agenda*. This is a Latin word meaning "things to be done." Common parliamentary law over the years has arrived at an accepted order for a business meeting. Sometimes, however, an organization may wish to follow a different order of business. In that case, the organization must write the order of business in its own rules of order, which should be with, but not part of, the bylaws.

This chapter introduces the accepted order of business and explains how to plan and adopt an agenda, as well as determine when special kinds of agendas are needed. It gives an overview of each aspect of the agenda, from determining a quorum and receiving reports from officers and committees to hearing new business and adjourning the meeting.

PLANNING AND USING AGENDAS

In any kind of meeting, the person leading the meeting should preside from an agenda — an outline of items, listed in order of importance, that are to be accomplished at the meeting. Having an agenda keeps the meeting on track and saves time.

The basic structure of an agenda comes from the order of business as established either by the parliamentary authority or by the rules of the organization.

Accepted Order of Business

This section outlines the commonly used order of the agenda. Before any business can be transacted at a meeting, the president must determine that a *quorum* (the required minimum number of members needed to have a meeting) is present. The president then calls the meeting to order. He or she proceeds with the organization's established order of business. If an organization has no established order of business, the following is the customary order of business for organizations that have regular meetings within a quarterly time period.

1. **The minutes of the previous meeting are read and approved.** Often members want to dispense with the reading of the minutes because they do not feel that the minutes are important to hear. However, keep in mind that the minutes are a legal document for the organization. By approving the minutes, the members agree that this is what happened at the meeting. When a legal action has been brought against the organization, courts use minutes for evidence. Therefore, it is important that the assembly (or a committee named for the purpose of approving the minutes) approves the minutes. There is no time limit on minute corrections.

    The minutes also serve to inform members who were absent from the previous meeting of what happened at the meeting. The minutes provide an opportunity to correct oversights. For example, there may be motions that carry over business to the present meeting that are in the minutes but not on the agenda. Members who are alert while the minutes are being read can ask that these motions be added to the agenda of the present meeting. Another important point is that the motion *lay on the table,* which allows members to temporarily set aside a motion in order to take up more urgent business, is recorded in the minutes but not put on the agenda. It is a parliamentary rule that, because the members vote to lay the motion on the table, only the members can make a motion to take it from the table. By listening carefully when the minutes are read, members take note of this and know the right course of action to take.

2. **The reports of officers, boards, and standing committees (those listed in the bylaws) are read and discussed.** The officers and standing committees do not need to give a report at every meeting. Place a report on the agenda only when there is something to report to the membership.

3. **The reports of special committees (if there are any) are heard.** Special committees are created for a particular purpose and are not listed in the bylaws. They cease to exist when they have completed their work and made their final report.

4. **Any special orders are presented.** These are motions postponed to the meeting and by a two-thirds vote made a *special order* so that they come up before unfinished business (see Chapter 6). Or, a special order can be special business that comes up once a year, such as nominations and elections.

5. **Unfinished business and general orders are discussed.** *Unfinished business* is a motion that was under discussion at the time that the previous meeting adjourned. A *general order* is a motion that was postponed to the current meeting but not made a *special order*. (These terms apply only in meetings of groups that meet quarterly or more often.)

6. **The members proceed to new business.** New business proposes an issue that is new to this meeting. It may be something not discussed before or something that was defeated at a past meeting (or even at the last meeting).

7. **When the agenda items are finished and the assembly has no further business to propose, it's time to adjourn.**

Creating a Specific Agenda

After the general outline of an agenda is prepared, the person preparing the agenda fills in the details. Depending on the needs of the organization, this person can add items to the agenda, and he or she can use special types of agendas. The following discussion explains how to prepare an agenda in a logical manner as well as how to add optional agenda items and adopt, mail, and streamline an agenda.

When preparing the agenda, review the minutes and agenda of the previous meeting, looking for things that weren't accomplished; consult the bylaws or other rules of the organization for business that is to be done at specific meetings, like nominations and elections; and check with the officers, committee chairmen, and members to see if they have business to add to the agenda.

Consulting previous meeting minutes

The most important resource for filling in agenda details is the minutes of the previous meeting. From these minutes, the agenda planner should glean any unfinished agenda items.

In agenda planning, look first for any special orders. These may be special orders that were made for the previous meeting but not disposed of before adjournment. They may be motions that were postponed and made special orders for the current meeting. Special orders are of some priority or importance. The category of special orders was created so that members can complete more important tasks before they take up any other business. Items considered special orders, and therefore of high priority, include nominations, elections of officers, and the voting of new members into membership.

After special orders comes unfinished business and general orders. (The term *old business* can be confusing and should not be used.) The first topic taken up under this category is *unfinished business,* which is any motion that was pending at the last meeting when the meeting adjourned. *Pending* means that the motion wasn't voted on but was being discussed when the meeting was adjourned.

Next is any item that was on the agenda of the previous meeting under unfinished business that the members did not have time to take up before adjournment.

Third are motions that were postponed to the previous meeting but the members didn't have time to discuss.

Fourth are *general orders,* which are motions that were postponed to the present meeting. The members take these up in the order in which they were made at the previous meeting.

Asking members for agenda items

In addition to the minutes, the person preparing the agenda has a number of resources to consult, namely the members themselves. Consulting the board members or other officers ahead of time about the agenda items can save time. For example, when filling in the specifics under "reports of officers, boards, and committees," the president or whoever prepares the agenda should ask the appropriate people whether they have anything to report. Only those who have reports to give are put on the agenda. Doing this saves time during the meeting because the president calls on only those who have a report to give.

Under "new business," the person preparing the agenda should ask the board members or other officers if they have something that they want to put on the agenda before the meeting. Some organizations have a rule requiring that members submit any new business items to the secretary in writing before the items are included in the agenda. However, in most organizations, when there is no new business on the agenda, the chair asks the members, "Is there any new business?" Members always have the right to present ideas to the assembly, and "new business" is the place to do it.

Other possibilities for agenda topics

Most organizations incorporate some optional agenda items into their meetings. Examples of optional items are opening ceremonies, roll call, programs, announcements, and "for the good of the order."

Opening ceremonies may be a pledge to the flag, a prayer or invocation, or any ritual that is unique to the organization and has nothing to do with business. This always comes immediately after the meeting is called to order. If there is a roll call of members to record attendance or establish a quorum, it follows the opening ceremonies. The minutes are then read. Programs may include a special speaker or entertainment, and they usually follow new business. Announcements come right before adjournment.

Some organizations take time right before adjournment for the "good of the order." This segment allows members to give suggestions for improvement or to give compliments concerning the work of the organization. Usually business is not brought up during this portion of the meeting. Any ideas for new business that come from this segment are brought up at another meeting. However, if something urgent is brought to the attention of the members, a member can present it as a main motion during this segment. Until someone moves to adjourn the meeting, members can bring forward business.

Adopting the Agenda

Although members may adopt the agenda at the beginning of the meeting, the agenda shouldn't tie the hands of the assembly, prevent members from bringing up business, or enable a small group to railroad through their pet projects. Agendas should have flexibility to provide for unseen things that may come up in a meeting. Some organizations want to adopt an agenda believing that they can add no further items as the meeting progresses, which is not true. If an agenda is adopted, changing it takes a two-thirds vote.

An organization can adopt an agenda only if its governing documents don't include rules of order dictating the order of a business meeting. (Rules of order unique to a particular organization are usually included with, but not part of, the bylaws.)

In some types of meetings — those that occur less than quarterly, conventions, or other sessions that may last for several days — adopting the agenda is most important. Because these meetings take place infrequently, adopting an agenda ensures that participants will accomplish the tasks on the agenda without getting sidetracked by other issues. A majority vote adopts an agenda. After it's adopted, only a two-thirds vote or general consent may change the agenda.

Mailing an Agenda to the Members

Some organizations mail the agenda to their members before the meeting. The purpose is to provide members with information so that they can prepare for the meeting. However, the agenda can still be changed before the meeting. In other words, the agenda is not binding on anyone. Items can be added before the meeting, as well as during the meeting by a motion, a second, and a two-thirds vote. Remember that an agenda is just a suggested outline or structure for the meeting. Things can change between the time the agenda is mailed to the membership and the time that the meeting takes place.

Consent and Priority Agendas

The *consent agenda* (or in some cases, the consent calendar) allows members to vote on a group of items *en bloc* (as a group) without discussion. This is a good way to dispose of business that is noncontroversial. Approving the minutes, paying the bills, and approving customary donations are examples of noncontroversial business. For an organization to use a consent agenda, it needs to adopt a special rule of order.

The presentation of the consent agenda is established by a special rule of order and should be taken up before committee reports. If the consent agenda includes the approval of the minutes, then it should be taken up before any business is transacted. Every member should have a printed copy of the consent agenda when the presiding officer presents it. When presenting it, the chair asks if any member wants to extract an item from the consent agenda.

To extract an item, a member need only rise and request, for example, that item 3 be removed from the consent agenda. This means that the member wants to discuss and vote on this issue separately. The request does not need a second and is not discussed, and no vote is taken to remove it from the consent agenda.

After the members finish extracting items from the consent agenda, the presiding officer presents the modified consent agenda to the assembly once again and takes the vote by general consent. (See Chapter 5 on voting.)

The president could say it this way:

> **President:** Are there items that the members want to remove from the consent agenda? *[Pause; if no one rises, continue.]* If there is no objection, the consent agenda will be adopted. *[Pause; wait to see if anyone objects.]* Hearing no objection, the following items, as published on your consent agenda, are adopted.

The extracted items are added to the regular agenda under the proper categories for bringing up such items.

The consent agenda is useful for streamlining action on a group of items. Also useful, though in a different way, is the *priority agenda*. This type of agenda is a list of tasks to be accomplished, discussed, and voted on in the order of importance. In committee meetings and in groups or work teams that have informal meetings, a priority agenda is a good way to organize the meeting. This concept is also helpful in listing items under new business. The most important or timely topics are placed at the top of the agenda to ensure that they're done before the meeting ends.

QUORUM

As discussed earlier in the chapter, before an organization can legally transact any business at a meeting, a quorum must be present. *Quorum* is a Latin word meaning "of them," as in "do we have enough of them — the members?"

A quorum is the minimum number of members who must be present in order to conduct business. The organization's bylaws should contain this number. If the bylaws don't contain a quorum number, then, according to parliamentary law, the quorum is a majority of the entire membership. The presiding officer should know what that number is and make sure that a quorum is present before calling the meeting to order. To establish that a quorum is present, the president can take a head count of those present, the secretary can call the roll, or members can sign in. However, the officer does not have to state that a quorum is present when he or she calls the meeting to order. If, as a member, you're unsure whether a quorum is present, you may ask the presiding officer after he or she calls the meeting to order. To do this, stand and say the following:

> ***Member:*** Mr. President, I rise to a parliamentary inquiry.
>
> ***President:*** Please state your inquiry.
>
> ***Member:*** Is there a quorum present?

If the president says yes, then say "Thank you" and sit down. If the president says no, remind him or her:

> ***Member:*** Mr. President, we cannot conduct business without a quorum. *[sit down]*

Never conduct a business meeting without a quorum present. If business is transacted without a quorum, it is null and void. It is also important that a quorum be present throughout the entire time that business transactions take place. If you notice that people have left the meeting and a quorum is no longer present, it is your duty to raise a point of order (which points out a breach of the rules) by informing the presiding officer that a quorum is no longer present and any business transacted now will be null and void.

> ***Member:*** *[rises]* Point of order.
>
> ***President:*** Please state your point.
>
> ***Member:*** Members have left and there is no longer a quorum. Any further business transacted is now null and void.
>
> ***President:*** Thank you. Your point is well taken. Since there is no longer a quorum present, this meeting is adjourned. *[raps the gavel once]*

How to Keep a Record of the Quorum

In today's litigious society, having a written record of who attends a meeting is wise. Do this for all meetings, including committee meetings, because a quorum needs to be present at any meeting where business is transacted.

Larger organizations should appoint someone responsible for having members sign in at the meeting. That person should then attach the sign-in sheet to the minutes. If the organization had to prove that a quorum was present at the meeting, it could easily find that information with the minutes of the meeting.

In small groups, a roll call vote is an effective way of establishing that a quorum is present, because the roll call is written into the minutes. It is sufficient for the secretary to write: "The following members were present" and "The following members were absent."

In boards under 12 members, the beginning paragraph of the minutes should include which board members were present and which board members were absent.

What to Do When No Quorum Is Present

If no quorum is present and there is no hope of getting one soon, the president can call the meeting to order to satisfy the bylaw requirement that the meeting is held and then announce that there is no quorum and adjourn the meeting. Or, the president can call the meeting to order, announce to the membership that there is no quorum, and entertain a motion to recess (which enables members to try to obtain a quorum), to establish the time to adjourn (which allows the membership to set another date and time to meet and is considered a legal continuation of the current meeting), to adjourn (which means that the meeting immediately ends), or to take measures to obtain a quorum.

These are the only motions allowed when no quorum is present.

A BUSINESS MEETING IN ACTION

The following section illustrates how a business meeting is conducted from calling the meeting to order to adjournment. Each order of business on the agenda is briefly explained, and then we show how the presiding officer states the agenda item, introduces those giving reports, and recognizes those making motions.

Calling the Meeting to Order

Every meeting must begin somewhere and have someone to lead it. The meeting begins when the president or chairperson calls the meeting to order. To call the meeting to order, the president stands at the front of the room, where everyone can see him or her, and says:

> ***President:*** The meeting will come to order. *[one rap of the gavel]*

If the president doesn't have a gavel, he or she can get the members' attention by asking them to sit down because the meeting is going to begin. Or, the organization can assign a member of the organization to encourage members to sit down. The president then calls the meeting to order.

> ***President:*** *[no gavel]* Will the members please be seated? *[Pause and wait for members to sit, and then say]* This meeting will come to order.

Members should immediately sit down and come to order by the request of the president.

Reading and Approving the Minutes

After the opening ceremonies, the first order of business is reading the minutes. The president asks the secretary to read the minutes of the previous meeting.

> ***President:*** Will the secretary read the minutes of the previous meeting?

The president steps aside or sits down, and the secretary stands to read the minutes.

> **Secretary:** The Santa Rosa Community Action League was called to order at 7:30 p.m., Tuesday, September 12, by the president. The secretary was present.
>
> The minutes were approved as read. The treasurer reported a balance of $500 in the bank account.
>
> John moved that we sponsor a public cleanup day on Saturday, October 2, at the park at noon. The motion was adopted. The president appointed John, Mary, and Mark to plan the event.
>
> The motion to sponsor a community breakfast was postponed to the next meeting.
>
> The meeting adjourned at 8 p.m.
>
> Julie Hayes
>
> Secretary

The secretary sits down, and the president asks the following:

> **President:** Are there any corrections?

The president then pauses and waits to see if there are corrections. If there are no corrections, the president says:

> **President:** The minutes are approved as read.

If a member has a correction, the member rises, addresses the chair, and states:

> **Member:** Mr. President, I believe that Margaret was also appointed to plan the cleanup day at the park.

The president then says:

> **President:** If there is no objection, the minutes will be corrected by adding Margaret's name to the minutes. Are there further corrections? *[pause]* Hearing none, the minutes are approved as corrected.

If someone makes a motion to dispense with the reading of the minutes, it means that the minutes are not read at this time but that they will be read at a later time — at the next meeting or later in the present meeting. This motion is not debatable and takes a majority vote to adopt. If the members vote to dispense with the reading of the minutes, the president can order the minutes read at any time later in the meeting when no business is pending. Someone must make a motion to have the minutes read. This motion needs a second, is not debatable, and takes a majority vote to adopt.

Reports of Officers

After the secretary reads the minutes, the next order of business is to hear the reports of the officers. Officers give reports in the order that the bylaws list. The most common officer's report is that of the treasurer.

The president announces the next business in order and calls on the first officer to give his or her report.

> **President:** The next business in order is reports of officers. May we have the treasurer's report?

The treasurer stands to give the report, and the president stands to the side or sits down during the report.

> **Treasurer:** The report of the treasurer as of September 30:

Balance on hand	$500.00
Dues paid	$125.00
Expenditures	None
Balance on hand	$625.00
Jody Parker	
Treasurer	

The treasurer steps aside, and the president assumes his or her place. The president then asks:

> **President:** Are there any questions?

If there are no questions, the treasurer gives the report to the secretary, and the President says:

> *President:* The treasurer's report is filed.

If a member has a question to ask the treasurer, that person can rise, address the president, and ask:

> *Member:* Mr. President, will the treasurer please tell us whether we are going to receive any funds from the school activity fund this year?

The president turns to the treasurer and says:

> *President:* Will the treasurer please answer the member's question.

The president steps aside while the treasurer answers the question.

> *Treasurer:* We will receive $100.

> *President:* Are there further questions? *[pause]* If not, the treasurer's report is filed.

The treasurer's report is always filed with the secretary, and it's never approved or adopted by the assembly. However, when the treasurer's books are audited, the assembly adopts the auditor's report.

Remember, keeping order in the meeting is important, so, as a member, address all questions to the president. The president then can answer your question or ask another member to answer the question.

After all the reports of officers are given, the next business in order is the reports of the committees.

Reports of Committees

Two kinds of committee reports exist. The first gives information about what the committee has been doing. The second asks members to decide a question and includes a motion at the end of the report.

President: The next business in order is to hear reports of the committees. Will the program committee report?

The president steps aside, and the committee chairman takes his or her place at the lectern.

Program Committee Chairman: The programs for this year are a field trip to the area recycling plant, the Festival of Lights party in December, and the International Festival in April.

John Hamilton

Chairman

The committee chairman stands aside while the president asks:

President: Are there any questions?

Members can now ask questions. After questions, the committee files its report with the secretary.

President: The program committee's report is filed.

If a committee report includes a recommendation of action that it wants the organization to take, its report should include a motion at the end. For example, say that the program committee wants to bring in a speaker and charge admission to the general public as a way to raise money for the organization. The committee can give its report this way:

President: May we have the program committee's report.

Program Committee Chairman: The program committee would like to sponsor a workshop on parliamentary procedure to help us and other members of the community have more orderly meetings. We have found a parliamentarian who will give an all-day workshop for $200. We can charge an admission fee of $25 per person, pay for the parliamentarian, and make a profit of $500.

Gloria Smith

Chairman

> By direction of the committee, I move that we sponsor a
> parliamentary workshop on April 10 at the Community
> Center and charge $25 per person. *[The chairman sits
> down.]*

The president then repeats the motion and asks for discussion. A motion from a committee of more than one does not need a second because the committee has already voted to present the motion.

> **President:** The question is on the adoption of the motion
> to sponsor a parliamentary workshop on April 10 at the
> Community Center and charge $25 per person. Is there any
> discussion?

The members discuss the motion and take a vote. If members adopt the motion, the action is carried out.

Unfinished Business and General Orders

If there are no special orders, then after the committee reports, the next business in order is the unfinished business and general orders. This is business that was left undecided at the last meeting, or it is business that was delayed to the current meeting by making the motion to postpone to the next meeting.

If there is unfinished business, it is placed on the agenda and the president states it. The president does not ask for unfinished business.

> **President:** The next business in order is unfinished business. At the last meeting, a motion to sponsor a community
> breakfast was postponed to this meeting. Is there any
> discussion?

Members then discuss and vote on the motion.

New Business

If there is no unfinished business or general orders, the president goes on to the next business in order, which is new business. If there is no new business listed on the agenda, the president can ask:

> **President:** Is there any new business?

If there is new business on the agenda, the president states what it is. For example, say the high school drama club asked the president whether the Community Action League would make a $100 donation for stage sets. The president can say:

> **President:** The next business in order is new business. The first item of new business is a request by the drama club that we donate $100 for stage-set materials. What are the members wishes?

If the members want to do this, someone must make a motion to do so. If no one wants to donate $100, the members remain silent. The president then asks:

> **President:** Is there any further business?

Members always have a right to bring forward ideas or business for the entire membership to discuss, which they do by making a main motion. Ideas are not discussed first and then a motion made, but rather a motion is made and then discussed. The principle of taking up one item of business at a time especially applies to main motions. Members can present only one main motion at a time.

Members can continue bringing up new business by making motions, discussing them, and voting on them. After each motion is voted on, the president asks the members:

> **President:** Is there any further business?

When no one has anything further to bring before the members, the chair doesn't have to ask for a motion to adjourn, but can say:

> **President:** Is there any further business?

The president pauses to look around the room to give any member the opportunity to rise and make a motion. If no one rises, the president says:

> ***President:*** If there is no objection, the meeting will now adjourn. *[Pause to look around the room.]*

There are still five things that members can do before the meeting adjourns, which are explained in Chapter 8 under "Adjourn."

> ***President:*** Since there is no objection, the meeting is adjourned. *[one rap of the gavel]*

Adjourning the Meeting

Members can make a motion to *adjourn* — to end the meeting — at any time during the meeting unless members have set a fixed time to adjourn. (See Chapter 8, "Fix the Time at Which to Adjourn.") To move to adjourn, a member must rise, address the president, be recognized by the presiding officer, and say:

> ***Member:*** Mr. President,
>
> ***President:*** *[recognizes member by either nodding at the person or by stating his or her name]*
>
> ***Member:*** I move that the meeting adjourn.
>
> ***Member 2:*** Second.

This motion needs a second; it is not debatable. The president takes a vote immediately:

> ***President:*** It is moved and seconded that the meeting adjourn. All those in favor say "Aye." Those opposed say "No." The ayes have it, and the meeting is adjourned. *[one rap of the gavel]*

3

Presenting Business to the Assembly

The most common way to present business to the members at a meeting is to make a main motion. An idea is not discussed first and then a motion made; instead, a motion is made and then the idea is discussed. This chapter explains the basic steps in presenting a motion: how to make a main motion, how to discuss it, and how to take a vote on the motion. It also explains when a motion is out of order. For example, motions are out of order when they conflict with the rules of the organization or the laws of the land, or when they propose action outside the scope of the organization's objectives.

BASIC STEPS IN PRESENTING A MOTION

Before you present a motion, make sure that it contains all the pertinent information, including who, what, where, and when. Word the motion in the positive, not in the negative. Here is an example of a main motion:

> ***Member:*** Madam President, I move that we have a picnic on Saturday, June 15, at 3 p.m. in the park.

This motion includes all the necessary information and states it in a positive manner. It is ready to present.

1. A member stands and addresses the chair, saying:

> ***Member:*** Mr. President [or Madam President]

or

Member: Mr. Chairman [or Madam Chairman]

2. The chair assigns the member the floor by stating the member's name or nodding at the member.

    The member states the motion:

    Member: I move that . . .

    or

    Member: I move to . . .

    Member: I move to have a picnic on Saturday, June 15, at 3 p.m. in the park.

3. Another member seconds the motion by calling out:

    Member: I second the motion.

    or simply

    Member: Second.

4. The chair restates the motion and places it before the assembly by saying:

    President: It is moved and seconded that . . . . Is there any discussion?

    President: It is moved and seconded to have a picnic on Saturday, June 15, at 3 p.m. in the park. Is there any discussion?

5. The members now have the right to debate or discuss the motion.

6. When the discussion is finished, the chair puts the motion to a vote by saying:

    President: All those in favor say "Aye." Those opposed say "No."

7. The chair announces the vote and who will carry out the action if it is adopted.

President: The ayes have it, and the motion is carried. We will have a picnic on Saturday, June 15, at 3 p.m. in the park. The Social Committee will take care of the details.

or

President: The noes have it, and the motion is lost. We will not have a picnic on Saturday, June 15, at 3 p.m. in the park. Is there further business?

Now let's look at the steps for making a motion in detail.

MAKING A MAIN MOTION

To make a main motion, a member must obtain the floor. To do so, stand and address the president, saying:

Member: Mr. President [or Madam President]

or

Member: Madam Chairman [or Mr. Chairman]

This is the correct parliamentary terminology. Many people want to say *chairwoman* or *chairperson,* but these terms are incorrect. The English language does not have feminine or masculine words, as do the Latin-based languages. The word *chair* in English is the neuter gender, neither masculine nor feminine. It refers either to the person or the place (chair) occupied by the person. The word *man* at the end does not mean a masculine person but stands for the neuter gender *all mankind,* including both men and women. So in English, to acknowledge the gender of the person presiding in the chair, use the honorifics *Mr.* or *Madam,* as follows: *Mr. Chairman* or *Madam Chairman.*

After the chair is addressed, the presiding officer recognizes the member by saying his or her name or nodding at the member. This means that the member is assigned the floor and can speak.

The correct way to state a motion is:

> **Member:** I move that . . .

It helps to memorize and practice this phrase. Here's an example:

> **Member:** Madam President, I move that we have a picnic on Saturday, June 15, at 3 p.m. in the park.

State motions in the positive, not the negative. Write the motion on a piece of paper and give it to the president after you state it. This helps the chairman (or chair) repeat the motion to the assembly exactly the way it was moved. The way in which the presiding officer states the motion to the assembly is the official wording of the motion, and it's recorded in the minutes. Many times, presiding officers do not repeat the motion exactly as the member has stated it. If you put the motion in writing and give it to the presiding officer, the officer can repeat it exactly as you presented it, and the secretary can record it correctly in the minutes.

After you make the motion, sit down. Another member must second the motion. A *second* simply means that another member thinks the motion should be discussed. It does not mean that the member is necessarily in favor of it.

The person who seconds the motion does not need to rise and address the president but can call out the second from where he or she sits. The member can say:

> **Member:** Second.

or

> **Member:** I second the motion.

If no one seconds it, the president can ask:

> **President:** Is there a second?

Member: I second it.

If the motion does not get a second, members can't discuss it and the president goes on to the next business in order. The president can say:

President: Without a second, the motion will not be considered.

Avoid using the phrase "dies for lack of a second."

If the motion is seconded, the president restates the motion to the members. This is called *placing the motion before the assembly.* The president must do this so that members can discuss the motion. The president says:

President: It is moved and seconded that we have a picnic on Saturday, June 15, at 3 p.m. in the park. Is there any discussion?

The president needs to memorize the following phrase in restating the motion:

President: It is moved and seconded that . . . . Is there any discussion?

DISCUSSING A MOTION

Members always have the right to debate or discuss a main motion. After the president asks for discussion, members can give reasons why they think having a picnic is a good idea or a bad idea.

The person who makes the motion has the first right to speak to the motion. To do that, the member rises, addresses the president, obtains the floor, and then speaks to the motion. After the member is done, he or she sits down so that someone else can speak to the motion — either for or against it. In discussing the motion, everyone gets to have a turn to talk, but everyone must wait his or her turn. A member can speak to a motion only when no one else is assigned the floor. If two people stand to speak at the same time, the president designates who should speak. The member not recognized sits down. When the other member finishes speaking, the member who did not speak can then stand to speak.

In debate, members address all remarks through the chair. Cross talk between members is not allowed, and mentioning other members' names is avoided as much as possible. All remarks are made in a courteous tone.

In most meetings, each member may speak two times on a debatable motion, but the member does not get the second turn as long as another member wants to speak for the first time. A member is not permitted to speak against his or her own motion. However, if the member changes his or her mind after hearing the motion discussed, the member may vote against it. (For more specific rules of debate, see Chapter 4.)

When speaking to a motion that you haven't made, a common courtesy before you begin your remarks is to say:

> **Member:** I speak for the motion.

or

> **Member:** I speak against the motion.

This way, the assembly knows which side of the issue you are supporting. It also helps the president keep a balance in the debate. If there are more people speaking against the motion, the president may ask if anyone wants to speak for the motion.

In debate, everyone has the right to speak, and the president must be just and impartial in assigning the floor, allowing all sides of the issue to be heard.

Discussion continues until the president realizes that the membership is ready to vote.

TAKING THE VOTE

When no one rises to speak to the motion, the president calls for the vote. Most voting takes place via a voice vote. A majority vote adopts main motions, which means that more than half of the members voting favor the motion.

> **President:** Is there any further discussion? [*Pause and look around the room to see if anyone wants to speak.*] Hearing none, the question is on the adoption of the motion to have a picnic on Saturday, June 15, at 3 p.m. in the park. All those in favor say "Aye." Those opposed say "No."

The president always announces the result of the vote. If the affirmative wins, he or she announces the vote this way:

> **President:** The ayes have it, and the motion is carried. We will have a picnic on Saturday, June 15, at 3 p.m. in the park.

If the negative wins, the president announces the vote this way:

> **President:** The noes have it, and the motion is lost. We won't be having a picnic on Saturday, June 15, at 3 p.m. in the park.

The president asks only for the yes and no votes and does not ask for those who want to abstain. The president always takes the no vote, even if the yes vote sounds unanimous.

The members must feel that any vote taken is a fair vote. If any member doubts the results of a voice vote, the member can call out:

> **Member:** Division.

or

> **Member:** I call for a division.

or

Member: I doubt the result of the vote.

In this one instance, a member does not have to rise to obtain the floor but can call out "Division" from wherever he or she is sitting. It does not need a second.

The president immediately retakes the vote as a rising vote by asking the members to stand. The chair makes a visual judgment and does not count the vote. The president says:

President: All those in favor please rise. Be seated. Those opposed please rise. Be seated. The affirmative has it, and the motion is carried.

Or, if the majority of members were opposed, the president states:

President: The negative has it, and the motion is lost.

If the president is in doubt as to which side wins, he or she can retake the vote and have it counted. If a member wants the vote counted, the member makes a motion to have a counted vote. The motion requires a second, is not debatable, and must pass by a majority vote.

In addition to a voice vote, the organization can take a vote by general consent, a show of hands, a rising vote, or ballot. The chair can choose to take the vote by voice, show of hands, or rising. To take a ballot vote, a member must make a motion to do so. A ballot vote ensures the secrecy of each member's vote. If you do not want others to know how you voted, or if you want an accurate count of the vote, a ballot vote is the way to accomplish your goal. (For a more thorough explanation of these voting procedures, see Chapter 5.)

To ask for a ballot vote, a member must rise, address the chair, and move to take the vote by ballot. This motion needs a second, is not debatable, and must pass by a majority vote.

> **Member:** Mr. President, I move that this vote be taken by ballot.
>
> **Member 2:** Second.
>
> **President:** It is moved and seconded to take this vote by ballot. All those in favor say "Aye." Those opposed say "No." The ayes have it, and we will take the vote by ballot.

If the members vote against the motion, the chair says:

> **President:** The noes have it, and the vote will not be taken by ballot.

COMPLETING THE ACTION ON THE MOTION

The action on the motion is completed when the president announces the result of the vote as well as how the action will be carried out. Members can expect that the approved action is carried out as authorized unless they decide to *reconsider the vote, rescind the action,* or *amend the adopted motion* (see Chapter 10).

IMPORTANT POINTS TO REMEMBER BEFORE MAKING A MOTION

Not every main motion is in order, and both the members and the presiding officer need to know when a presented motion violates the following rules. If a main motion violates the following rules, it is the presiding officer's duty to rule the motion out of order. If the chair does not do this, a member should call this to the assembly's attention by raising a point of order.

1. **No motion is in order that conflicts with federal, state, or local law; with the rules of a parent organization; or with the organization's constitution or bylaws or other rules of the organization. Even if a unanimous vote adopts the motion, it is null and void if it conflicts with the previously mentioned rules.**

For example, if someone makes a motion to expand the clubhouse and city or state zoning laws prohibit doing so, the motion is out of order; or, if the school district has rules against having a student dance on a week night, a motion by a student group to have a dance on Tuesday evening is out of order.

2. **A motion that proposes action outside the scope of the organization's object (which should be written in the corporate charter or bylaws) is not in order unless the members vote to allow it to be considered. Doing so takes a two-thirds vote.**

For example, suppose an organization's object is to take care of stray animals and build a shelter for them. A member also wants to create a soup kitchen for homeless people. Unfortunately, doing so is outside the scope of the organization's object.

If the member makes a motion that is outside of the organization's object, the presiding officer states:

President: The motion to have a soup kitchen for homeless people is outside the object of the organization. According to our parliamentary authority, a two-thirds vote is required for this motion to be considered. Members can now discuss whether they want to consider the motion. Is there any discussion about whether we should consider the motion?

Discussion can focus only on whether the members should consider the motion. Any discussion about whether to have a soup kitchen is out of order. After discussion, the president should first explain the effect of a yes or no vote on the consideration of this motion, and then put it to a vote:

President: If you think this motion is within the scope of the object of the organization and should be considered, vote yes. If you think this motion is outside the scope of the organization and should not be considered, vote no. You are only voting on considering the question. The vote taken does not adopt the motion. Are there any questions? All those in favor, please rise. *[Members rise.]*

Be seated. *[Members sit down.]*

Those opposed please rise. *[Members rise.]*

Be seated. *[Members sit down.]*

There is a two-thirds vote in the affirmative, and we will consider the question. It is moved and seconded that we have a soup kitchen for homeless people. Is there any discussion?

If the noes have it, the chair states:

President: There is less than a two-thirds vote in the affirmative. The negative has it, and we will not consider the motion to have a soup kitchen for homeless people.

Even though a parliamentary rule states that members, by a two-thirds vote, can consider something outside the object of the organization, remember that the object is part of the bylaws. When members consider something outside the object of the organization, they are, in essence, suspending part of the bylaws. The best approach in handling the situation is to amend the object of the organization. Give members previous notice of the proposed change and time to think about what the real purpose of the organization should be.

3. **A main motion is not in order if it conflicts with a motion that was previously adopted by the assembly and that is still in force. However, the assembly can decide to rescind the action or amend something previously adopted.**

For example, say that the club adopted a motion to give $100 yearly to the local humane society. If a member makes a motion to give $200 yearly to the humane society, the motion conflicts with what was already adopted and is therefore not in order. However, if the member phrases it as the motion to amend something previously adopted, it is in order and requires a two-thirds vote or a majority vote of the entire membership to adopt if no previous notice has been given. If previous notice has been given, it requires a majority vote to adopt. This rule protects the rights of the absent members.

4. **A main motion is not in order when it presents substantially the same question as a motion that was rejected during the same session. However, members can bring up the motion at another meeting, and this is known as *renewing the motion.***

    For example, suppose that the members vote down a motion to have a car wash to raise money for the dance fund. During discussion, members make it clear that they do not want to have a car wash to raise money for anything. If later in the meeting a member makes a motion to have a car wash to raise money for the leadership training series, it is out of order. The motion can, however, be brought up at another meeting.

    There is one way this motion can be brought up again at the same meeting, and that is if a member who voted on the prevailing side (in this case the negative side) makes the motion to reconsider the vote on the motion to have a car wash (see Chapter 10).

5. **A main motion is not in order if it conflicts with or presents substantially the same question as one that has been temporarily disposed of and is still within control of the assembly. Here are examples:**

    If a motion has been referred to a committee and the committee has not reported, the committee can be discharged and the assembly can take up the motion (see Chapter 10).

    If a motion has been postponed to later in the meeting or to another meeting, a member can move to suspend the rules and take up the motion at that time. (See Chapter 9, "Suspend the Rules.")

    If a motion is laid on the table, members can take it from the table.

Members need to be alert to meeting tactics that refer a motion to a committee to *bury it* (don't investigate it) or lay it on the table to kill it. Or, while a motion is in the committee or laid on the table, someone presents another version of the motion. Members must realize that even though a motion is in committee or on the table, it is still under the control of the assembly and must be decided first.

RESOLUTIONS

A *resolution* is a formal way of presenting a motion. It is a main motion, needs a second, and is handled like any other main motion except that it is always presented in writing. The name of the organization is mentioned in the resolution, and the word "resolved" is always italicized. A resolution can be as simple as:

> *Resolved,* That the Glee Club sponsor a "Day of Singing" on April 25 to honor Glee Clubs in our state.

If a resolution is proposed at a mass meeting, word it in the following way:

> *Resolved,* That in the sense of this meeting, we form a Neighborhood Watch program and send letters to all the homes between Martin and Smith streets inviting home-owners to participate.

Sometimes a resolution includes a preamble. A *preamble* enables members to give background information and to state the reasons why the motion should be adopted. However, a preamble to a resolution is usually not necessary. In fact, a preamble should be used only when the maker of the resolution wants to give little-known information or wants to present important points regarding the adoption of the motion if there is some doubt about whether it will pass. A preamble contains *whereas* clauses that communicate the important background information to the assembly; the actual resolution then follows. A resolution with a preamble should contain only as many whereas clauses as necessary. For example,

> *Whereas,* A study done by the city commission reveals that there are 100 stray dogs and 250 stray cats in Center City;
>
> *Resolved,* That the Morningside City Improvement Corporation form a committee of five to be appointed by the board to investigate the cost of establishing a feeding program, as well as establishing a shelter for these animals, and report its findings at the next meeting.

If the resolution has more than one whereas clause, write it this way:

> *Whereas,* A study done by the city commission reveals that there are 100 stray dogs and 250 stray cats in Center City;
>
> *Whereas,* These hungry animals are wreaking havoc with garbage; and
>
> *Whereas,* They are having kittens and puppies every two to three months; now, therefore, be it
>
> *Resolved,* That the Morningside City Improvement Corporation form a committee of five to be appointed by the board to investigate the cost of establishing a feeding program, as well as establishing a shelter for these animals, and report its findings at the next meeting.

4

Debating the Motion

Every member has the right to debate or to discuss business that is introduced to the assembly in the form of a main motion. Only a motion to limit debate or to close debate (which is accomplished through a motion called *previous question*) can take away or limit this right, and either motion must have a two-thirds vote. (See Chapter 7, "Limit or Extend the Limits of Debate" and "Previous Question.")

The assembly can make an informed decision from the facts and persuasive arguments that members present only through discussion. Members should never be tempted to *gavel through* an issue (rush through a motion without any discussion) in an effort to save time or silence the opposition.

In his book *Parliamentary Law,* Henry Robert gives a word to the wise when he states,

> Where there is radical difference of opinion in an organization, one side must yield. The great lesson for democracies to learn is for the majority to give the minority a full, free opportunity to present their side of the case, and then for the minority, having failed to win a majority to their views, gracefully to submit and to recognize the action as that of the entire organization, and cheerfully to assist in carrying it out, until they can secure its repeal.

This chapter explains the rules of debate and the circumstances under which debate can be limited. It also lists those motions that are debatable and those that are not.

RULES OF DEBATE

Even though members have the right to debate, established parliamentary rules concerning the privileges of debate exist:

- A member must obtain the floor and be recognized by the presiding officer before beginning to speak. A member can't begin talking while seated. However, in small board meetings where rules of debate are less formal, talking while seated is allowed. (See Chapter 11, "Board Meetings.")

- The member who made the motion has the first right to speak to the motion. He or she does so by rising and obtaining the floor after the chair places the motion before the assembly for discussion.

- A member can speak twice to the motion on the same day, but he or she can take the second turn only after everyone who wishes to speak the first time has spoken. If debate on the motion is continued at the next meeting, which is held on another day, the member's right to debate is renewed.

- Each member can speak for ten minutes on each turn unless the assembly has adopted rules that state another amount of time.

- Debate must be *germane* (relevant) to the motion.

- Speakers must address all remarks to the chair; cross talk between members is not allowed.

- Speakers must be courteous and never attack other members or question the motives of the members. In controversial issues, the discussion is focused on ideas, not on personalities. Members must not use inflammatory statements such as "it's a lie," "it is a fraud," or "he's a liar." However, a member may say,

    Member: I believe there is strong evidence that the member is mistaken.

    Profane language is also prohibited.

- In debate, speakers refer to officers by title and avoid mentioning other members' names. Instead, they should refer to the members by identifiers such as "the member who just spoke" or "the delegate from Hawaii."

- When speaking to a motion, it is important for the member to first let the assembly know which side of the issue he or she is on. If in favor of the motion, the member states

  Member: I speak for the motion.

  and gives the reasons why. If opposed, the member states

  Member: I speak against the motion.

  and gives the reasons why. Doing so helps the chair alternate the debate.

  In controversial issues, the presiding officer should alternate the debate between those speaking for and those speaking against the motion. After someone speaks for the motion, the chair asks:

  President: Would anyone like to speak against the motion?

  After someone speaks against the motion, the chair asks:

  President: Would someone like to speak in favor of the motion?

  This practice ensures that all sides are represented, keeps tempers down, and prevents one side from dominating the discussion.

- The member who makes the motion can't speak against his or her own motion, although he or she can vote against it. The person who seconds the motion, however, can speak against the motion because a second means "Let's discuss it," not "I agree." Sometimes a member seconds a motion so he or she can speak against it.

- A member can't read (or have the secretary read) from part of a manuscript or book as part of his or her debate without the permission of the assembly. However, the member can read short, relevant printed extracts in debate to make a point.

- During debate, a member can't talk against a previous action that is not pending, unless one of the motions to *rescind, reconsider,* or *amend something previously adopted* is pending; or unless the member concludes his or her remarks with one of these motions.

- During debate, members should take care not to disturb the assembly by whispering, talking, walking across the floor, or causing other distractions.

- During debate, the presiding officer sits down when a member is assigned the floor to speak. Or if, when seated, members can't see the presiding officer, the officer stands back from the lectern while the member is speaking. (Like the rule of one item of business at a time, this rule allows only one person at a time to have the floor.)

- If at any time during debate the presiding officer needs to interrupt the speaker for a ruling (for example, if the chair is correcting something that the speaker is doing) or needs to give information (facts related to the discussion, for example), the member should sit down until the presiding officer finishes. The member can then resume speaking.

- In deliberative assemblies (bodies that meet to consider proposals made to them), members do not have the right to give some of their time to another member. If a member has not used his or her ten minutes, the member forfeits the unused portion.

- As the chairman, the presiding officer must remain impartial. As a member, the presiding officer has a right to debate. Thus, if the presiding officer wishes to speak to an issue, he or she relinquishes the chair to another officer (the vice president, for example) who has not spoken and does not wish to speak. If no officer wishes to take the chair, a member who has not spoken and has received the assembly's approval can preside. The presiding officer resumes the chair when the motion has been either voted on by the assembly or temporarily put aside by a motion to *refer to a committee, postpone to another time,* or *lay on the table.*

■ In debating an issue, members also have the right to conclude their debate with a higher-ranking motion than the one pending. (See Chapter 6 for a chart on ranking motions.) This action upholds the parliamentary principle that when the chair recognizes a member for any legitimate purpose, the member has the floor for all legitimate purposes.

LIMITATIONS ON DEBATE

Members can put limits on debate and even stop the debate altogether. To do so, members must make a motion. The presiding officer cannot cut off the debate as long as one member wishes to rise and speak. Neither can one member stop the debate by yelling out "Question" or "It's time to take a vote."

Only the motion to *limit debate* can limit debate; and debate can be closed only by the motion *previous question* or *close debate.* These motions need a second, are not debatable, and require a two-thirds vote to adopt. A rising (but not counted) vote is required. (For more details about these motions, see Chapter 7.)

DEBATABLE MOTIONS AND UNDEBATABLE MOTIONS

Not all motions are debatable. Some motions are debatable in some situations and not in others. It is important to study the chapters on motions (Chapters 6 through 10) to understand what each motion is and the reasons why some motions are debatable and some aren't. The following is a list of debatable and nondebatable motions.

DEBATABLE MOTIONS

Main motion

Postpone indefinitely

Amend

Refer to a committee

Postpone to a certain time

Appeal from the decision of the chair

Rescind

Amend something previously adopted

Reconsider

Recess (as an incidental main motion)

Fix the time to which to adjourn (as an incidental main motion)

UNDEBATABLE MOTIONS

Limit or extend the limits of debate

Previous question (close debate)

Lay on the table

Take from the table

Call for the orders of the day

Raise a question of privilege

Recess (as a privileged motion)

Adjourn

Fix the time to which to adjourn (as a privileged motion)

Point of order

Withdraw a motion

Suspend the rules

Object to consideration of the motion

Division of the assembly

Division of the question

Incidental motions relating to voting, when the subject is pending

Dispense with the reading of the minutes

5

Voting

In democratic societies, citizens have the right to assemble, the right to speak, and the right to vote. The *right to assemble* allows people of common interests to join together to accomplish a goal or common purpose. The *right to speak* allows members of that assembly to voice their opinions and concerns and to persuade others that their opinions and concerns are valid and to take action. The *right to vote* is the assembly's way of allowing all members to decide an issue, in a democratic manner, after they have assembled and heard their fellow members' opinions and concerns.

The right to vote is essential in preserving democracy in organizations and elected bodies. There are three principles that require consideration when a vote is taken:

- Is the vote taken in a fair and impartial manner?

- Does everyone who wants to vote get to vote?

- Does the announced result represent the way the members voted?

These principles underlie the parliamentary procedures for voting; indeed, the specific rules of voting are designed to uphold them. This chapter explains these voting rules and the situations in which they are violated. The chapter begins with the procedure for taking a vote and then discusses the idea of majority rule and defines majority vote. It also explains the numerous ways a vote can be taken and the appropriate actions to take when the result of a vote is doubted. Finally, it answers frequently asked questions about voting.

PROCEDURE FOR TAKING A VOTE

In taking a vote, the presiding officer or chair must follow an established general procedure:

1. The chair always asks for the affirmative vote first.

2. The chair always asks for the negative vote, even if the affirmative vote seems unanimous.

3. The chair does not ask for abstentions.

4. The chair always announces the result of the vote and states what has just happened. If the affirmative won, the chair also states who is responsible for carrying out the action. If the chair is in doubt about who should carry out the action, the members need to make a motion to determine who should carry it out.

5. The chair must stay neutral in asking for the vote so as not to sway the membership. The chair does not say, for example:

    President: All those in favor say "Aye." Contrary say "No."

6. The chair does *not* phrase the vote this way:

    President: All those in favor say "Aye." Those opposed "same sign."

    If the vote were taken this way, it would mean that both those in favor and those opposed would say "Aye." So then who wins?

    However, phrasing the vote this way is acceptable:

    President: As many as are in favor say "Aye." Those opposed say "No."

    Another accepted way is to say:

    President: All those in favor say "Aye." All those opposed say "No."

7. It is understood that during all methods of voting a quorum must be present.

8. If the chair is in doubt about the result of the vote, the chair can request a rising vote or a rising and counted vote to retake the vote.

9. If a member doubts the result of the vote, the member should call out "division." For an explanation of this action, see "Doubting the Result of the Vote," later in this chapter.

THE MAJORITY RULES

A fundamental principle in democratic societies is that the majority rules, but the rights of the minority and individual members are also protected. Most business is adopted by a majority vote of members who are voting at a meeting where a quorum is present. However, to protect the rights of the minority and absent members, some motions require a two-thirds vote. The principle used to determine when to take a two-thirds vote is based on the rights of the members or the assembly. When a proposed action takes away members' rights, a two-thirds vote is necessary. Motions to limit or extend debate, to close debate, to make a motion a special order, to rescind an action when no previous notice is given, and to suspend the rules are some of the motions that require a two-thirds vote. Some actions are so important (for example, amending the bylaws and other governing documents, or removing a member from office or membership) that they require both previous notice and a two-thirds vote.

If an organization wants the vote on certain issues to be greater than a majority or two-thirds vote, or it wants to require that previous notice of a vote be given, the bylaws should clearly state and define these qualifications. However, requiring a vote higher than a majority or two-thirds vote can allow a minority to rule instead of the majority, and a unanimous vote may end up allowing one person to rule. A vote requiring more than a majority should not be stated in terms of a "super majority" (because that term is not specific) but should specify, for example, 80% of the members, three-fourths of the members, or a majority of the entire membership.

Majority Vote Defined

A *majority vote* simply means that more than half of those voting approve a motion. More specifically, it means that more than half of the votes cast by persons legally entitled to vote at a properly called meeting with a quorum present approve a motion. Blank ballots or abstentions do not count. By this definition, those voting — not necessarily those present — determine the majority. Here is an example:

> If 20 people are present at the meeting and 15 members vote, the majority is 8, because the majority is determined by the number voting, not by the number present.

Modifications in Majority Vote

Organizations can qualify a majority vote by adding these phrases to the word "voting" in their bylaws:

- "a majority of those present"
- "a majority of the entire membership"

These phrases change how the organization figures the majority. The more qualified the bylaws make a majority vote, the more difficult it is to adopt motions. Except for important issues and amending the bylaws, a simple, unqualified majority vote should adopt all actions.

A majority of those present

If an organization's bylaws state that a majority of those present must adopt a motion, the majority is figured by the number of members present, not by the number of those voting. Here is an example:

> A meeting has 20 members present.
>
> A majority of those present is 11 votes. This number does not change, no matter how many members present vote. If 15 people vote, and the following occurs,

10 members vote in the affirmative

5 members vote in the negative

5 members do not vote (abstain),

the motion fails because 11 people must vote in favor of the motion to sustain a majority of those present and adopt the motion.

In this example, those not voting are said to support the negative rather than remain neutral. For that reason, this qualification is not recommended.

A majority of the entire membership

If the bylaws state that a majority of the entire membership must adopt a motion, the number of the entire membership determines the majority, not the number of members who are present or the number of members who vote. Here are some examples:

The membership of the organization is 40.

The majority is always 21 votes in the affirmative.

At a meeting, 21 members attend. All would have to vote in favor of a motion in order for it to be adopted.

If only 20 attend the meeting, no motions can be adopted because it takes 21 votes to adopt.

If 30 members attend the meeting, and the votes are

20 votes in the affirmative

7 in the negative

3 abstentions,

the motion is lost because it takes 21 votes to adopt.

Requiring a majority of the entire membership is a helpful and useful qualification in one case: when the board is very small. Suppose an organization has an executive board of five members and the quorum is three members. If the bylaws state that a majority vote must adopt all action, and if only three members come to a meeting, two members are the majority and can make a decision. In this case, it is appropriate for the bylaws to require a majority vote of the entire membership of the board. Doing so ensures that if only three members attend a meeting, all three have to agree before any action is adopted.

Note: When the bylaws state "a majority of the entire membership," this means a majority of the members who are qualified to vote. Some organizations have a provision in the bylaws that states, "Members who have not paid their dues or are on probation cannot vote." Members who are not eligible to vote are not counted when figuring the number of votes required to get a "majority of the entire membership."

A majority of the fixed membership

If the governing documents state "a majority of the fixed membership," a majority is based on the total number of members, whether they are eligible to vote or not. For example, in condominium or homeowner associations, the majority is often based upon the number of lots or units in the association. This is considered a majority of the fixed membership. In this case, if the owner of a lot or unit does not pay the assessment, it does not affect the number of votes required to achieve the majority of the fixed membership. The number of votes required for a majority doesn't change unless more units are built or more lots are made available for sale.

The requirement to have a majority of the fixed membership can affect boards of directors if there are unfilled vacancies on the board. A majority of the *fixed* membership is based on the total number of the board positions, not the total number of persons serving in them. In contrast, if the majority is of the *entire* membership of the board, vacancies don't count. Only those positions in which there are directors serving are considered in the total number of board members. For example, if a board has 12 positions and three positions are vacant, and the basis is a majority of the *entire* membership, the count is based on the nine positions that are filled. The majority of the *entire* membership is five. However, a majority vote of the *fixed* membership is seven because it is based upon all 12 directors' positions, whether or not they are filled. When establishing the vote in the bylaws, take special care with how qualifications for the majority are worded. The more stringent you make the majority, the more difficult it is to obtain the majority and get things done.

To set the majority of the entire membership, the bylaws can state: "All motions shall be adopted by a majority of the entire board (not counting vacancies)."

To set the majority of the fixed membership, the bylaws may state: "All motions shall be adopted by a majority of the entire 12 directors of the board."

A TWO-THIRDS VOTE

In keeping with accepted parliamentary procedure, there are times when a two-thirds vote is required. This means that at a meeting where a quorum is present, it takes two-thirds of those voting in the affirmative to adopt a motion. Those who abstain are not counted.

To balance the rights of the individual member with the rights of the assembly, the following procedures require a two-thirds vote:

- Limiting or closing debate
- Suspending or modifying a rule or order previously adopted
- Taking away membership or office
- Motions that close nominations or the polls
- Preventing the introduction of a motion

The two-thirds vote is taken by a rising vote. If the chair is uncertain whether there is a two-thirds vote in the affirmative, he or she should count those voting.

A THREE-FOURTHS VOTE

Some organizations require a three-fourths vote instead of a two-thirds vote in adopting certain types of business, electing officers, or electing applicants into membership. These organizations want to know that most of the members agree with what is proposed. They believe that the more members that are in favor of any proposal, the better the cooperation they will get in carrying out what is adopted. An easy way to figure this vote is to remember that every no vote needs three yes votes.

THE TIE VOTE

A tie vote occurs when 50% vote in favor and 50% vote against. No one receives a majority vote. If there is no way to break the tie vote, the motion is lost.

If the presiding officer has not voted and is a member of the assembly, he or she can vote to make or break the tie. He or she can also vote to make a two-thirds vote or to reject a two-thirds vote. If 50 members vote for the motion and 49 members vote against the motion, the presiding officer can state that he or she votes no, meaning that the vote is a tie and the motion is therefore lost. The presiding officer cannot vote twice, however — once as a member and once as the presiding officer. For example, if the presiding officer votes in a ballot vote with the other members and the result is a tie, the officer can't break the tie as the presiding officer. In this case, the motion is lost because the vote is a tie vote.

WAYS THE VOTE CAN BE TAKEN

There are numerous ways a vote can be taken: by voice, by show of hands, by standing, by ballot, by roll call, and by general consent. The chair or presiding officer decides whether to take the vote by voice, by show of hands, by standing, or by general consent. However, the assembly must order a vote by ballot or roll call. (See Chapter 18 for a discussion of the roll call vote.)

After members have discussed a motion, the chair puts it to a vote. The chair may ask,

    Chairman: Are you ready for the question?

or

    Chairman: Is there further discussion?

If no one rises to speak, the chair takes the vote, asking for the affirmative first and then the negative. The chair does not ask for abstentions.

Taking a Vote by Voice

In taking a vote by voice, the chair states:

    Chairman: The question is on the adoption of the motion to buy a computer and a laser printer for the office. All those in favor say "Aye." Those opposed say "No."

The chair then repeats the outcome. If the ayes have it, the chair states:

    Chairman: The ayes have it. The motion is carried, and we will buy a computer and a laser printer for the office. The secretary will purchase it.

If the noes have it, the chair states:

    Chairman: The noes have it. The motion is lost, and we will not buy a computer and a laser printer for the office. Is there further business?

Taking a Vote by Show of Hands

In taking a vote by show of hands, the chair says:

    Chairman: All those in favor, please raise your right hand. *[raise hand]* Please lower them. Those opposed raise their right hand. *[raise hand]* Please lower them.

The chair then announces the vote. If the affirmative has it, the chair states:

Chairman: The affirmative has it. The motion is carried, and we will buy a computer and a laser printer for the office. The secretary will purchase it.

If the negative has it, the chair states:

Chairman: The negative has it. The motion is lost, and we will not buy a computer and a laser printer for the office. Is there further business?

Taking a Vote by Rising (Standing)

Use the rising (or standing) method when taking a two-thirds vote as well as when retaking a voice vote when a member calls for a division.

In taking a rising vote, the chair says:

Chairman: All those in favor, please rise. *[Members rise.]* Be seated. *[Members sit down.]* Those opposed please rise. *[Members rise.]* Be seated. *[Members sit down.]*

The chair then announces the vote. If the affirmative has it, the chair states:

Chairman: The affirmative has it. The motion is carried, and we will buy a computer and a laser printer for the office. The secretary will purchase it.

If the negative has it, the chair states:

Chairman: The negative has it. The motion is lost, and we will not buy a computer and a laser printer for the office. Is there further business?

Taking a Vote by Ballot

When taking a ballot vote, everyone gets to vote, including the presiding officer (if he or she is a member), unless the organization has a rule that states differently. In this case, the chair explains the procedure to the membership as it happens:

Chairman: This vote will be taken by ballot. Will the tellers please give a ballot to each member. *[Pause while this happens.]*

Does everyone have a ballot? *[Wait for a response. If someone doesn't have a ballot, direct a teller to give one to that member.]*

If you are in favor of buying a computer and a laser printer for the office, write "yes" on the ballot. If you are opposed, write "no." Fold the paper in half, and give it to the tellers' committee when they collect the ballots.

If there is a ballot box, the chair instructs the members to rise and put the ballots in the box.

After it looks like everyone has voted, the chair can ask:

Chairman: Has everyone voted who wants to vote?

If there is a motion to close the polls at this time, it needs a second, and it requires a two-thirds vote to adopt. If someone has not voted and wants to, this is the time to speak up. After the polls are closed, a majority can reopen them for voting. The chair waits for a response, and if no one rises to hand in a ballot, the chair states:

Chairman: The polls are closed, and the tellers will count the votes.

The tellers' committee (see Chapter 12) then counts the ballots and puts the result on a teller's sheet.

The chairman of the tellers' committee reads the report to the membership but does not announce the result of the vote. He or she then hands the report to the presiding officer, who states:

Chairman: The teller's report reads:

22 ballots are cast.

A majority to adopt is 12.

15 voted in the affirmative.

7 voted in the negative.

The affirmative has it, and the motion is adopted. We will buy a computer and a laser printer. The secretary is responsible for purchasing it.

In taking a ballot vote:

- The president (if a member) votes with the other members.

- The chairman of the tellers' committee reads the report but does not announce the vote.

- The president repeats the tellers' report and announces the vote. The tellers' report is included in the minutes in its entirety.

- Tellers should be appointed for their fairness and accuracy in counting the vote. If the issue is controversial, appoint members from both sides to count the ballots.

Taking a Vote by Mail

In large international organizations, some homeowners and condo associations, or organizations whose members are not centrally located, a mail ballot is a common practice to elect officers and amend the bylaws. An organization's bylaws must state that it can use a mail ballot. Likewise, the organization should adopt procedures on how to handle the mail ballot. If the secretary is not responsible for sending out the mail ballots, an accurate up-to-date membership list should be given to those responsible for mailing the ballot.

If the ballot is not secret, the organization may follow these procedures:

- On the ballot, include a place for the member's signature and instructions on how to mark the ballot, how to send it back, and the date the ballot is due to be considered valid. You may also include other materials. For example, if members are voting for officers, you may include information about each officer.

- Include a return envelope printed with the name and address of the secretary or officials collecting the ballots.

This envelope may be an unusual color or size so the organization knows that it is a ballot instead of regular mail.

If the mail ballot is secret, follow other procedures:

- Send the ballot with two envelopes. Provide an inner envelope for the member to insert his or her ballot. The member needs to sign the outside of the inner envelope. The member then places this envelope in a mailing envelope with the name and address of the person responsible for collecting the ballots.

- Don't open the ballots until it is time for the tellers to count the vote. The first thing the tellers do is open each envelope and take out the inner envelope. The signature on the envelope is checked against the membership list to see that only one vote is cast per member. After this is done, the inner envelopes are opened and the folded ballots put into a receptacle. After all the envelopes are opened and the folded ballots are placed in the receptacle, the ballots are counted. See Chapter 12 under "Elections" to find out how the tellers count the vote.

Record the vote in the minutes of the next meeting. If the association meets yearly but has quarterly or monthly board meetings, record the vote in the minutes of the next board meeting, and send an announcement of the election results to all members.

Taking a Vote by E-mail

The procedure for voting by mail can be adapted to e-mail voting in the following manner. The person who collects the ballots sends out the e-mail ballot to all eligible voters. The sender should use an e-mail program that requests a *return receipt* from the recipient. Doing so shows that members received the ballot and that the return ballot comes from the member to whom the e-mail was sent. Balloting instructions should tell how to fill out the ballot and how to return it to the organization. The first instruction on the ballot should say "hit 'reply'; this enables you to fill out the ballot." The instructions should also tell how to send the ballot back once it is filled out. (This is the instruction to click "send.") The person who originally sends it out receives the ballot.

The person collecting the ballots should have a "ballot box" folder in his or her e-mail program. When ballots come in, put them in the ballot box folder. After all the ballots come in, save them on a disk as a back-up. Then print out the ballots so a tellers' committee can count them. As additional back-up, you can also print out and put in a file each ballot as it comes in.

The drawback to e-mail voting is that members give up their right to have a secret vote. The tellers' committee will know how each member voted. It is also possible for hackers to break into e-mail systems.

Taking a Vote by General or Unanimous Consent

General consent is a very effective way to take care of non-controversial issues or motions for which it looks like there will be no objection. *General consent* does not mean that everyone is in favor of the motion; it means that the opposition feels that discussing or voting on the issue is useless and therefore decides to keep silent, accepting the results. Do not confuse general consent with a unanimous vote in which all the votes are the same, whether in favor of or in opposition to some issue.

In taking the vote by general consent, the chair states:

Chairman: Is there any objection to . . .

Is there any objection to paying the bills?

Hearing none, the bills will be paid by the treasurer.

Is there any objection to taking a five-minute recess?

Hearing none, the meeting stands in recess for five minutes.

Is there any objection to withdrawing the motion?

Hearing none, the motion is withdrawn.

Is there any objection to adjourning the meeting?

Hearing none, the meeting is adjourned.

If a member calls out "I object!" the president puts the motion to a formal vote:

> **Chairman:** All those in favor of paying the bills say "Aye." Those opposed say "No." The ayes have it. The motion is carried, and the treasurer will pay the bills.

Another aspect of general consent is that the chair can assume a motion; he or she does not have to wait for someone else to make the motion. For example, after the treasurer or the secretary submits the amount of the bills to be paid, the chair assumes the motion to pay the bills and then asks if there is any objection to paying them.

> **Chairman:** Is there any objection to paying the bills for a total of $100? Hearing no objection, the bills will be paid.

If a member makes a motion to recess as a privileged motion, the chair can ask:

> **Chairman:** Is there any objection to taking a five-minute recess? Hearing none, the meeting stands in recess for five minutes.

If a member objects, it does not necessarily mean that the member is against the action but that the member thinks that taking a formal vote is wise.

If a member objects, and no formal motion has been presented, the chair must then either ask for a motion or assume a motion, ask for discussion, and then take a formal vote.

> **Chairman:** The question is on the adoption of paying the bills for $100. Is there any discussion? *[Pause and wait for discussion. If none, take the vote.]* Hearing none, all those in

favor of paying the bills say "Aye." Those opposed say
"No." The ayes have it, and the motion is carried. The
treasurer will pay the bills.

If a member is not sure about the effect of taking a vote by
general consent, the member can call out, "I reserve the right
to object." After a brief consultation, the member must either
object or relinquish the right to object.

DOUBTING THE RESULT OF THE VOTE

It is the presiding officer's duty to announce the result of the
vote, and the way he or she announces it determines the
action taken. If the members do not immediately doubt the
result of the vote, the chair's declaration stands as the decision of the assembly. The members have the right to doubt
the result of the vote until the chair states the question on
another motion.

Calling for a Division

If a member thinks that the vote is too close to call or that
the noes have it, and the chair announces the ayes have it,
the member can call out

>   ***Member:*** Division.

or

>   ***Member:*** I doubt the result of the vote.

This should not be used as a dilatory tactic to delay the
proceedings when it is apparent which side has won.

A division is an *incidental motion:* It deals with a procedural
question relating to a pending motion or business. It does not
need a second and is not debatable. One member can ask to
retake the vote, and the vote is never retaken in the same
way. Thus, a doubted voice vote must be retaken visually, by
a rising vote. This way, all the members can see how people
are voting. The chair states:

Chairman: A division has been called for. All those in favor please rise. *[Members rise.]* Be seated. *[Members sit down.]* Those opposed please rise. *[Members rise.]* Be seated. *[Members sit down.]*

The chair then announces the vote.

If the vote still looks too close to call, the chair can retake it by having it counted. If a member wants the vote to be counted, he or she makes a motion to take a counted vote. The motion to take a counted vote needs a second, is not debatable, and takes a majority to adopt.

The chair retakes the vote by first asking those in favor of the motion to stand and count off. The chair then asks those opposed to a motion to stand and count off. (The member sits down as he counts off.) After all have voted, the chair announces the vote. The vote should be recorded in the minutes by saying how many have voted in the affirmative and how many have voted in the negative.

Doubting the Result of a Ballot Vote or Roll Call Vote

If the members doubt the result of a ballot vote or roll call vote, a member must make a motion to recount the teller's tabulation. This motion takes a majority to adopt unless the organization has a rule that states differently. After a ballot vote, if there is no possibility that the assembly may order a recount, a motion should be made to destroy the ballots; or they can be filed for a specified time with the secretary and then destroyed.

Record the result of every ballot and roll call vote in the minutes.

OTHER VOTING PROCEDURES

There are other voting methods, such as proxy voting, absentee voting, and preferential voting. If an organization wishes to use any of these methods, the bylaws should state this fact as well as include the written procedures for carrying out the voting.

FREQUENTLY ASKED QUESTIONS ABOUT VOTING

Q. Does a member have to vote?

A. *No. Choosing not to vote is* abstaining. *Even though having each member vote is in the best interest of the member and the organization, no one can compel a member to vote.*

Q. Is an abstention counted as a yes vote or a no vote?

A. *To abstain means "not to vote." You can't count a nonvote. Therefore, an abstention counts as a zero.*

Q. Can an abstention affect the result of a vote?

A. *Yes, when the vote is qualified in some way, such as when a majority of those present or a majority of the entire membership is required. If the majority is determined by "those present," and 20 people are present, a majority is 11. If 10 vote in the affirmative, 9 vote in the negative, and 1 person abstains, the motion is lost because it takes 11 voting in the affirmative to adopt the motion. In this case, the abstention helps those voting no.*

Q. Is there a time when a member is not allowed to vote?

A. *Yes, when a motion is of direct personal or monetary interest to the member and to no one else, the member should not vote.*

Q. Is there a time when a member can vote on a motion that directly affects him or her?

A. *Yes, when the member is named with other members in a motion. For example, when the member is a delegate to a convention or when the member is nominated for an office.*

Q. Can a member vote if his or her dues are not paid?

A. *If a member has not been dropped from the rolls and is not under disciplinary action, the member still has the full rights of membership, including the right to vote, unless the bylaws specifically address this situation.*

Q. Can a member change his or her vote?

A. *Yes, a member has the right to change his or her vote until the result is announced. After the result is announced, however, the member can change his or her vote only by permission of the assembly. Permission can be granted by general consent or by a motion to grant permission which needs a second, is undebatable, and takes a majority vote to adopt.*

Q. Who makes the final decision on judging voting procedures?

A. *The assembly makes the final decision on judging voting procedures unless the bylaws state differently. For example, if the tellers are unsure about how a ballot is marked, they can bring it to the assembly to decide.*

Q. What is an illegal vote and how is it counted?

A. *An illegal vote refers only to a vote taken by ballot. An illegal vote is a ballot:*

- *That is unreadable.*

- *In which someone who is not a member of the organization has been voted for (for example, in an election if someone writes in "Robin Hood").*

- *In which a person who is a member but does not meet the eligiblility requirements to run for office has been voted for.*

- *In which two or more written ballots are folded together. However, if a blank ballot is folded inside a written ballot, it is not considered an illegal vote because blank ballots are not counted.*

- *In which someone votes for too many candidates for a given office (this part of the ballot is considered illegal but not necessarily the entire ballot).*

- *That has been cast by someone who is not eligible to vote.*

Q. What happens to an illegal ballot?

A. *An illegal ballot is not counted, but it is considered in the number for establishing the majority. It is listed on the teller's report as an illegal ballot. For example, if 20 people vote, a majority is 11. If 10 people vote for candidate X, 8 people vote for candidate Y, and 2 votes are illegal (one is unreadable; the other voted for Robin Hood), no one wins because no one received a majority vote. Another vote is required.*

Q. How should the tellers collect a ballot vote?

A. *There are three possible ways:*

- *Members can come to the front and drop their ballots in a ballot box under the charge of two tellers.*

- *Tellers can pass a receptacle to collect the ballots, with one teller collecting the ballots and the other following to make sure that each member casts one ballot.*

- *Members can hand their ballots to a teller, who feels to see that only one ballot is cast; the teller then deposits the ballots in a container.*

Part II

MOTIONS SIMPLIFIED

6

Motions

Motions are tools that enable an organization to accomplish business efficiently and smoothly. They are the means of bringing business before the assembly, disposing of it quickly, and resolving matters of procedure and urgency. This chapter explains the five classes of motions and how each is used.

CLASSES OF MOTIONS

Motions help the members accomplish what they have come to the meeting to do. There are five classes of motions:

FIVE CLASSES OF MOTIONS		
I. Main	II. Subsidiary III. Privileged IV. Incidental (Secondary)	V. Motions that bring a question again before the assembly

The first class of motions — *main motions* — is used to present new business. The secondary motions — *subsidiary, privileged,* and *incidental motions* — can either help adopt the main motion or help business move forward according to the members' wishes. The last class of motions returns a motion to the assembly for reconsideration. Each class of motions has a certain purpose and is assigned an order in which it can be brought up in a meeting. This assigned order is called *ranking motions* and follows the principle of taking up business one item at a time.

The better the members understand how to use motions correctly to expedite the organization's business, the shorter the meetings and the happier the members because they have accomplished their business in a minimum amount of time.

Main Motions

There are two forms of a main motion. The first form introduces new business to the assembly. The other form is the *incidental main motion,* which deals with procedural questions arising out of pending motions or business; it does not introduce a new topic.

Motions that introduce new business

A main motion that brings new business before the assembly is made while no business is pending. It needs a second, is debatable and amendable, and takes a majority vote to adopt. A main motion is phrased in the positive. Usually when the members don't want to do something, making a motion is not necessary. For example, if an organization received a request to donate money to the parade fund, and the members don't want to do this, they don't make a motion. It's not necessary for a member to make a motion stating "we will not give money to the parade committee." However, there is an exception to this rule. If a *subsidiary body* (for example, a board of directors) has the ability to give the donation without membership approval, it is then appropriate to make a motion to refrain from giving money to the parade committee. Therefore, the board cannot give money, because the membership specifically voted not to do that. A board cannot rescind what the members have voted to do, or not to do in this case.

Only one main motion can be pending at a time. (*Pending* refers to a motion placed before the assembly for discussion by the chair.) A main motion is the lowest ranking of all the motions. This means that any secondary motion is discussed and voted on before a pending main motion.

An important point to remember in presenting business and making a main motion is that of ownership — who owns the main motion. When a member makes a main motion, it belongs to the maker of the motion until it is repeated by the chairman and placed before the assembly. Before the chair repeats the main motion, the person making the main motion can withdraw it or modify it without asking permission of the assembly.

After the chair places the main motion before the assembly, it belongs to the entire assembly, not to the maker of the motion. The assembly now decides what happens to the motion. It can be killed, delayed, or altered to suit the assembly's wishes. The assembly may make changes of which the maker of the motion disapproves. This is part of the democratic process: the right of the assembly to decide what affects it as a whole body. Therefore, after the motion is placed before the assembly, no one has to ask the maker of the motion for permission to make any changes.

Incidental main motions

An incidental main motion is also made while no business is pending, but it does not introduce new business. Instead, it deals with procedure. An example of a main motion is: "I move to buy a new computer and a laser printer." After this motion is adopted, an incidental main motion is: "I move that the finance committee be in charge of purchasing the computer and the laser printer." This incidental main motion is debatable and amendable. It is related to the main motion because it deals with who is going to carry out the adopted action of the main motion. Therefore, the motion is *incidental* to the motion from which it arises. Key words to use to identify incidental main motions include *ratify, adopt, limit,* and *recess.* For example, a member may make an incidental main motion to adopt proposals made in a committee report, ratify action taken in the absence of a quorum, or recess when no business is pending.

The motion to *ratify* is a useful motion when the assembly has to confirm action taken when there was no quorum present; when the assembly has to take emergency action without a quorum present; when officers, committee members, or delegates have acted in excess of their instructions; or when a local unit needs the approval of the state or national organization before something can be done. A motion to ratify needs a second, is debatable, and needs a majority vote to adopt. The assembly can only ratify what it would have had the right to do in advance. It can't ratify something that goes against the bylaws or other governing documents.

The motion to ratify can be amended by substituting the motion to censure. *Censure* is a way for the members to show displeasure with a member's or officer's conduct. Instead of ratifying an action, members can censure officers or committee members for taking action without getting prior approval. Censure shows the assembly's indignation without going so far as expulsion or removal from office. The motion to censure is debatable. The person being censured can debate the motion but cannot vote on the motion. The vote should be taken by a secret ballot. See Chapter 15 for more information on discipline.

Secondary Motions

In the five classes of motions, three are considered secondary motions: subsidiary, privileged, and incidental. *Secondary motions* help the assembly decide what to do with the main motion or how to get things done in the meeting. Secondary motions enable more than one motion to be pending at a time but still follow the principle of taking up business one item at a time. In parliamentary terminology, *pending* means "a motion that is stated by the chair and placed before the assembly for discussion and has not yet been disposed of by the assembly." While a main motion is pending, a member can propose a secondary motion. Secondary motions are taken up in the order that they are made. As each secondary motion is proposed, it is considered the immediately pending motion. The assembly discusses the most recently proposed secondary motion instead of the main motion or a previously pending secondary motion.

Secondary motions are assigned an order, called a *ranking of motions* (see "The Ladder of Motions" later in this chapter), in which they are proposed, discussed, and voted on.

Members can make motions of higher rank while a motion of lower rank is pending; but members can't make a lower-ranking motion while a motion of higher rank is pending. As each higher-ranking motion is proposed, members stop discussing the lower-ranking motion and immediately discuss the higher-ranking motion, which now becomes the pending motion. The following explains how the subsidiary, privileged, and incidental motions fit into this hierarchy of motions.

Subsidiary motions

Subsidiary motions help the assembly dispose of the main motion. Adopting a subsidiary motion always does something to the main motion. Subsidiary motions are assigned an order of precedence or rank so that the organization can take up business one item at a time. The following list shows subsidiary motions ranked from top to bottom. The highest-ranking subsidiary motion is *lay on the table* and the lowest is *postpone indefinitely.*

LAY ON THE TABLE
(set aside temporarily)
PREVIOUS QUESTION
(stop debate)
LIMIT OR EXTEND LIMITS OF DEBATE
(shorten or lengthen debate)
POSTPONE TO A CERTAIN TIME
(put off to another time)
REFER TO A COMMITTEE
(let a committee investigate)
AMEND
(change a motion)
POSTPONE INDEFINITELY
(kill a motion)

LOWEST TO HIGHEST

Privileged motions

Privileged motions do not relate to the pending main motion. Instead, they relate to special matters of immediate importance that may come up in the business meeting. Because these are usually urgent matters, the organization must take them up immediately. Thus, privileged motions are of higher rank and take precedence over subsidiary motions. They are undebatable, but some are amendable. After they have been made and seconded, the chair takes a vote without discussion. Like subsidiary motions, privileged motions are assigned an order in which they can be made and voted on. When a motion of lower rank is pending, only a higher-ranking motion can be made. As the following list shows, the highest-ranking privileged motion is *fix the time to which to adjourn*. (This is the highest ranking of both privileged and subsidiary motions.) If this motion is made while any other subsidiary or privileged motion is pending, the members must vote on it first.

LOWEST TO HIGHEST

FIX THE TIME TO WHICH TO ADJOURN
(set another time
to continue the meeting)
ADJOURN
(end meeting now)
RECESS
(take a break)
RAISE A QUESTION OF PRIVILEGE
(welfare of individual/assembly)
CALL FOR THE ORDERS OF THE DAY
(stick to the agenda)

Incidental motions

Incidental motions deal with questions of procedure arising from the pending business, but they do not affect the pending business. Examples are raising a question about parliamentary procedure in the meeting, asking a question about the motion under discussion, or pointing out that a very important rule was broken or ignored. Incidental motions are usually not debatable and must be decided upon immediately. They have no rank because they are taken up immediately when made. Here are some of the incidental motions:

POINT OF ORDER
(that's against the rules)
APPEAL
(disagree with chair's ruling)
DIVISION OF THE ASSEMBLY
(doubt the result of the vote)
REQUESTS AND INQUIRIES
(I have a question)
SUSPEND THE RULES
(temporarily put aside a rule)
DIVISION OF THE QUESTION
(divide a motion into two
or more questions)

Motions That Bring a Question Again Before the Assembly

The purpose of the last class of motions is to bring a motion back before the assembly for its consideration. For example, a motion that was *laid on the table* (temporarily set aside) is brought back by the motion *take from the table*. When members want to change their minds about a motion that was just voted on, they can *reconsider the vote*. If members are unhappy with action taken at a previous meeting, they can *rescind the action* or *amend something previously adopted*. One other motion in this category is to *discharge a committee*. Discharging a committee takes a motion out of committee before the committee has made its final report and puts it back into the hands of the assembly. All these motions are made when no other business is pending. They need a second and are debatable except for *take from the table,* which is not debatable. If no previous notice has been given, *rescinding* or *amending something previously adopted* requires a two-thirds vote. This protects the rights of the members who are not at the meeting to vote against the change.

PREVIOUS NOTICE OF MOTIONS

Some motions are so important that the membership has the right to know beforehand that they are going to be presented at the meeting. Doing so is called *giving previous notice*. Examples of motions that need previous notice are amending the bylaws and rules of order. Organizations may state in their bylaws that previous notice must be given for selling and buying property or for spending large amounts of money. Giving previous notice when a member wants to rescind or change an adopted motion allows a majority vote to adopt it. Previous notice protects the rights of members by alerting them that such action will be taken. Those who voted in favor of the action are sure to attend the meeting to support the decision they have already made.

Members can give previous notice in several ways. If a member submits a written notice to the secretary, the secretary is obligated to put it into the call letter to the meeting. Or, members can give notice orally at the previous meeting. The person giving previous notice may simply state the intent instead of giving the entire motion, unless the organization has rules stating differently. For example, a member can say, "I will be making a motion at the next meeting to rescind the charity ball."

THE RANKING OF MOTIONS

The principle of taking up one item of business at a time requires that main motions, subsidiary motions, and privileged motions are assigned a rank.

If you think of this rank of motions as a ladder, the main motion is the bottom rung. The following chart, "Ladder of Motions in Order of Rank," illustrates this idea. When the main motion is pending (being discussed), someone can make a motion of higher rank. For example, someone can make the motion to amend. If you look at the chart, notice that you are two steps up the ladder. *Amend* becomes the pending question because it is a higher-ranking motion than the main motion. Discussion is now on the motion to amend and not on the main motion. A member can now make a higher-ranking motion than *amend,* but no one can make the motion to *postpone indefinitely* because it is a lower-ranking motion than *amend.*

When making the motions, you go up the ladder, and when voting on the pending motions, you go backward down the ladder. For example, say the following motions have been made and are pending:

Recess

Postpone to a certain time

Amend

Main motion

In taking the vote, the president starts with the motion to *recess.* If adopted, the members take a recess and begin discussing *postpone to a certain time* when they return. They then vote on it. If adopted, the proposed amendment and main motion are put off until a later time. When the time arrives to take up this main motion and amendment, the members begin the meeting with discussing the amendment. After the amendment is voted on, the members vote on the main motion.

LADDER OF MOTIONS IN ORDER OF RANK

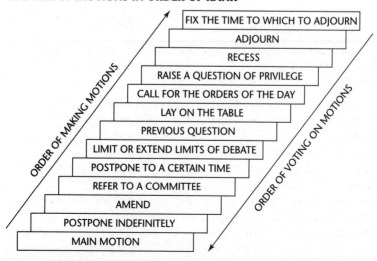

7

Using Subsidiary Motions to Help Adopt a Main Motion

This chapter looks at each subsidiary motion and how it can help move the main motion forward until the assembly arrives at its final decision. The discussion begins with the lowest-ranking subsidiary motion, which is *postpone indefinitely,* and explains each motion in turn, through *lay on the table,* which is the highest-ranking motion. The purpose of each motion, its restrictions (whether it needs a second, is amendable, is debatable, and so on), and the result of that subsidiary motion on the main motion are outlined at the beginning of each section. Likewise, examples show you how to use the motion correctly. (See also Appendix A.)

Postpone Indefinitely

✦ **Purpose:** To kill the main motion for the duration of the meeting without taking a direct vote on it.

✦ Needs a second.

✦ Not amendable, but while this motion is pending, members can amend the main motion.

✦ Debatable, and debate can go to the merits of the main motion.

✦ Majority vote required to adopt.

✦ Members can reconsider only an affirmative vote.

✦ **Result:** Kills the main motion for the duration of the session.

The motion *postpone indefinitely* is the lowest-ranking of the subsidiary motions, which means that members can make a higher ranking motion while this motion is pending. In addition, the main motion can be amended, referred to a committee, postponed to a certain time, or laid on the table. If the main motion is referred to a committee while *postpone indefinitely* is pending, *postpone indefinitely* does not go to committee with the main motion. By referring the motion to a committee, it means that the members don't want to kill it; they want to consider it further.

Members can close debate or limit or extend debate on *postpone indefinitely* without affecting the main motion.

To make the motion, phrase it this way:

Member: I move to postpone the motion indefinitely.

or

Member: I move that the motion be postponed indefinitely.

Member 2: Second.

The president states it this way to the assembly:

President: It is moved and seconded to postpone the motion indefinitely. Is there any discussion on postponing indefinitely?

After any discussion, the chair takes the vote.

President: All those in favor say "Aye." Those opposed say "No."

If the ayes have it, the chair states:

President: The ayes have it. The motion is carried and is postponed indefinitely. Is there further business?

If the noes have it, the chair states:

President: The noes have it, and the motion is lost. Is there further discussion on . . . *[main motion]*?

Amend

- ✦ **Purpose:** To change the pending motion before it is acted upon; proposed amendments must be germane to the main motion.

- ✦ Needs a second.

- ✦ Amendable, but the secondary amendment must be germane or related to the primary amendment.

- ✦ Debatable. Debate goes only to the amendment.

- ✦ Majority vote required to adopt. If amending a motion or document that takes a two-thirds vote to adopt, the proposed amendment takes only a majority vote.

- ✦ Can be reconsidered.

- ✦ **Result:** If adopted, the proposed change becomes part of the pending motion.

The purpose of this motion is to change the main motion. There are four ways to amend:

- Insert words within a motion.
- Add words at the end of a motion.
- Strike out words.
- Strike out and insert words.

Anyone can make the motion to amend. The amendment must be germane, or related, to the motion it is amending. In the House of Representatives, members are allowed to attach anything to a bill, but this is not the case in deliberative assemblies, which follow adopted parliamentary authorities. For example, in a deliberative assembly, if the members are discussing a motion to paint the clubhouse, a member can't propose to add an amendment to sponsor a dance on July 4. Sponsoring a dance on July 4 is not germane to painting the clubhouse; it is really a new main motion. Anytime there is a question about whether an amendment is germane, the president can let the members decide by a vote.

An amendment can be hostile to the main motion and still be germane. For example, say a member makes a motion to increase the secretary's salary by $20 a week. Another member can propose an amendment to strike out "increase" and insert "decrease." So, if adopted, the motion would be "to decrease the secretary's salary by $20 a week."

An amendment can be amended. The first amendment is a *primary amendment,* and it applies to the main motion. Its amendment is called a *secondary amendment* and applies only to the primary amendment. The secondary amendment must be germane to the primary amendment. It needs a second and is debatable. Debate is on the merits of the secondary amendment. An amendment to the third degree is not allowed. Only one set of primary and secondary amendments can be pending at the same time.

Members can apply the motion *amend* to any motion that has a variable. This includes some subsidiary motions as well as some privileged motions.

Here's an example of each of the ways to amend a main motion. A member makes the main motion to buy a computer and laser printer.

> **Member:** I move to buy a computer and laser printer.

The following illustrations show examples of how to word the various forms of amending.

- To amend by inserting words within the motion:

> **Member:** I move to amend the motion by inserting "brand X" before the word "computer."

> **Member 2:** Second.

The presiding officer repeats it this way:

> **President:** It is moved and seconded to amend the motion by inserting "brand X" before the word "computer." If adopted, the motion would read, "to buy a brand X computer and laser printer." Is there any discussion on the

proposed amendment? *[Discussion is only on whether to buy "brand X," not on whether to buy a computer and laser printer.]*

■ To amend by adding words at the end of the motion:

Member: I move to amend the motion by adding at the end "not to exceed the cost of $1,000."

Member 2: Second.

President: It is moved and seconded to amend the motion by adding at the end "not to exceed the cost of $1,000." If adopted, the motion would read, "to buy a computer and laser printer not to exceed the cost of $1,000." Is there any discussion on the proposed amendment? *[Discussion is only on "the cost of $1,000," not on buying the computer and laser printer.]*

■ To amend by striking out (deleting) words:

Member: I move to amend the motion by striking out "and laser printer."

Member 2: Second.

President: It is moved and seconded to amend the motion by striking out "and laser printer." If adopted, the motion would read, "to buy a computer." Is there any discussion on the proposed amendment?

■ To amend by striking out and inserting words (deleting something in the motion and replacing it with something else):

Member: I move to amend the motion by striking out "and laser printer" and inserting "and ink jet printer."

Member 2: Second.

President: It is moved and seconded to amend the motion by striking out "and laser printer" and inserting "and ink jet printer." If adopted, the motion would read, "to buy a computer and ink jet printer." Is there any discussion on the proposed amendment?

VOTING ON AMENDMENTS
TO THE MAIN MOTION

Many people get lost in the amendment process. If you are presiding, write down the amendments as they are proposed so you don't get lost. It is also helpful for the secretary to follow the procedure carefully and write down the amendments as well, so that if the president asks "Where are we?" the secretary can provide that information.

The following section takes you through the entire process of voting on amendments and how they are incorporated into the motion, if adopted.

Begin with the following as the main motion:

> To buy a computer and laser printer not to exceed the cost of $ 1,000.

After some discussion, the following primary amendment is proposed:

> ***Member 2:*** I move to amend the motion by striking out $1,000 and inserting $2,000.
>
> ***Member 3:*** Second.
>
> ***President:*** It is moved and seconded to amend the motion by striking out $1,000 and inserting $2,000. If adopted, the motion would read, "to buy a computer and laser printer not to exceed the cost of $2,000." Is there any discussion on the proposed amendment?

There is now a main motion and primary amendment pending. After some discussion, a member proposes another amendment. This is called a *secondary amendment.*

> ***Member 4:*** I move to amend the amendment by striking out $2,000 and inserting $2,500.
>
> ***Member 5:*** Second.
>
> ***President:*** It is moved and seconded to amend the amendment by striking out $2,000 and inserting $2,500. If adopted, the motion would read, "to buy a computer and laser

printer not to exceed the cost of $2,500." Is there any discussion on the proposed amendment?

At this point, discussion goes only to the secondary amendment. There are now three motions pending:

Secondary Amendment

Primary Amendment

Main Motion

In voting, the chair begins by taking a vote on the secondary amendment, then the primary amendment, and then the main motion. This is an example of ranking of motions. The secondary amendment is the highest-ranking motion in this series of motions.

President: The question is on the adoption of the proposed amendment to strike out $2,000 and insert $2,500. If adopted, the motion would read, "to buy a computer and laser printer not to exceed the cost of $2,500." All those in favor of striking out $2,000 and inserting $2,500 say "Aye." Those opposed say "No." The ayes have it and $2,500 replaces $2,000.

The effect of this vote now makes the secondary amendment the primary amendment. So, the members still need to vote on whether "$2,500" should replace the "$1,000" that was stated in the original main motion. The president continues:

President: The question is on the adoption of the proposed amendment to strike out $1,000 and insert $2,500. If adopted, the motion would read, "to buy a computer and laser printer not to exceed $2,500." Is there further discussion?

Members now have the opportunity to discuss whether they want to pay $2,500 for a computer and laser printer or pay $1,000.

President: All those in favor of striking out $1,000 and inserting $2,500 say "Aye." Those opposed say "No." The ayes have it, and $2,500 replaces $1,000. The question is now on the adoption of the main motion as amended, "to buy a computer and laser printer not to exceed the cost of $2,500." Is there any discussion?

Adopting the amendment does not adopt the main motion. It only indicates that a majority of the membership thinks $2,500 is enough money to buy a computer and laser printer. Members must now vote on adopting the main motion as amended.

> **President:** The question is on the adoption of the motion as amended, "to buy a computer and laser printer not to exceed the cost of $2,500." All those in favor say "Aye." Those opposed say "No." The ayes have it, and the motion is carried. We will buy a computer and laser printer not to exceed the cost of $2,500. The secretary and treasurer will be in charge of buying it.

The key point to remember when voting on amendments is to follow the correct order of amendments back to the original main motion. The presiding officer always begins voting with the secondary amendment, moves to the primary amendment, and finally takes the vote on the main motion.

This is what happens if the secondary amendment is defeated.

> **President:** The question is on adopting the proposed amendment by striking out $2,000 and inserting $2,500. If adopted, the motion would read "to buy a computer and laser printer not to exceed the cost of $2,500." All those in favor of striking $2,000 and inserting $2,500 say "Aye." Those opposed say "No." The noes have it and the proposed amendment is lost.

Because the secondary amendment was defeated, the president now asks for the vote on the primary amendment.

> **President:** The question is on the adoption of the proposed amendment to strike out $1,000 and insert $2,000. If

adopted, the motion would read "to buy a computer and laser printer not to exceed the cost of $2,000." Is there any discussion on the proposed amendment? Hearing none, all those in favor say "Aye." Those opposed say "No." The ayes have it, and $2,000 replaces $1,000.

Now the vote is taken on the main motion as amended.

President: The question is on the adoption of the main motion as amended, "to buy a computer and laser printer not to exceed the cost of $2,000." Is there further discussion? Hearing none, all those in favor say "Aye." Those opposed say "No." The ayes have it and the motion is carried. We will buy a computer and laser printer not to exceed the cost of $2,000.

If the proposed amendment to strike out $1,000 and insert $2,000 had been defeated, the members would have voted on the main motion as originally presented, "to buy a computer and laser printer not to exceed the cost of $1,000."

After the members finish voting on the secondary amendment and the primary amendment, but before they vote on the main motion as amended, members can still amend the motion further. They can strike out "laser" and insert "ink jet" or "dot matrix." They can also insert a brand name before "computer," if they so desire.

The most important rule to remember in amending motions is that the secondary motion must be germane to the primary motion or it is not in order. For example, with the primary amendment to strike out "$1,000" and insert "$2,000" pending, proposing an amendment to strike out "laser" and insert "ink jet" would be out of order, because the type of printer is not germane to the cost. Replacing "ink jet" with "laser" is considered the beginning of another group of amendments. Once the members begin with amending the cost, they must follow all the steps of the amending process in order until the assembly decides the cost issue. After this is done, members can amend another part of the motion.

Refer to a Committee

+ **Purpose:** Have a small group investigate a proposal.

+ Needs a second.

+ Any variable in the motion is amendable.

+ Debatable. Debate goes only to the merits of referring the motion to a committee.

+ Majority vote required to adopt.

+ Can be reconsidered if the committee hasn't started considering the motion.

+ **Result:** If adopted, the motion goes to the committee to investigate and does not return to the membership until the committee is ready to report or until the membership has adopted a time for the committee to report back to the assembly.

The purpose of the motion *refer to a committee* is to obtain information by referring the pending motion to a small, selected group of members for investigation. When making the motion *refer to a committee,* state which committee, what it is to do, and when it is to report back to the membership. If you do not set a date when the committee is to report, the motion may die in committee. To make the motion *refer to a committee,* state it this way:

Member: I move to refer the motion to the finance committee to investigate which is the best kind of computer and laser printer and what the cost is, and to report back to us at the next meeting.

Member 2: Second.

President: It is moved and seconded that we refer the motion to the finance committee to investigate which is the best kind of computer and laser printer and what the cost is, and to report back to us at the next meeting. Is there any discussion about referring the motion?

Another form of this motion is to move that the assembly act as a *committee of the whole*. In small assemblies (those under 50 members), the motion is *consider informally*.

Committee (or Quasi-Committee) of the Whole

✦ **Purpose:** Have the members of a large (or medium-size) assembly act as a committee.

✦ Needs a second.

✦ Amendable.

✦ Debatable.

✦ Majority vote required to adopt.

✦ The negative can be reconsidered. The affirmative can be reconsidered only until the assembly goes into committee of the whole.

✦ **Result:** If adopted, the assembly becomes the committee, and the motion referred to it is handled the same way a regular committee takes up its work.

This variation of *refer to a committee* allows the membership of a large assembly to act as a committee. The advantage of functioning as a committee of the whole is that members may speak an unlimited number of times to an issue. Any actions by a committee of the whole are not decisions of the assembly but are recommendations of the committee of the whole to the assembly.

The presiding officer of the assembly (who steps down while the committee of the whole is in session) appoints the chair of the committee of the whole. The secretary keeps minutes of the committee's proceedings. In very large assemblies, the secretary too may leave the chair, and an assistant secretary may be appointed to serve for the committee of the whole. When a committee of the whole votes, members cannot reconsider the issue voted on because the vote is not binding — it is only a recommendation on which the assembly will later vote. The chair of the committee of the whole reports to the assembly, which then may consider, discuss, and vote on the recommendations (if any) from the committee.

Another form of the motion to act as a committee of the whole is the motion to act as a *quasi-committee of the whole,* which is designed for medium-size assemblies. In this form of the motion, the presiding officer of the assembly remains in the chair and presides, and the secretary of the assembly keeps the minutes of the committee's votes and recommendations. If a member does not make a motion be discharged from further consideration of the subject, the chair reports decisions to the regular assembly for consideration.

Consider Informally

+ **Purpose:** Have the assembly conduct an informal discussion.

+ Needs a second.

+ Debatable.

+ Majority vote required to adopt.

+ Only the negative vote can be reconsidered.

+ **Result:** If adopted, this motion enables the assembly to act as the committee. Its effect is to take away the restriction on debating the main motion and any proposed amendments. Any other motions made are under the regular rules of debate. By a two-thirds vote, members can limit the length or number of speeches or can close debate.

The motion *consider informally* is another form of the motion *refer to a committee.* This motion is used only in assemblies having fewer than 50 members. (In large assemblies, use the motion to go into a *committee of the whole.*)

To make the motion, state:

> *Member:* I move that the motion be considered informally.
>
> *Member 2:* Second.

> **President:** It is moved and seconded to consider the motion informally. Is there any discussion?

Informal consideration removes the limit on the number of times members can speak in debate. The regular presiding officer remains in the chair and presides. No separate committee is created, and the actions and votes of the assembly are recorded in the minutes. The results of votes taken while in informal consideration are decisions of the assembly and are not voted on again in the assembly.

Anytime the members want to end informal consideration, someone can move that the question be considered formally. Adopting the motion to consider the question formally takes a majority vote.

As soon as the motion is disposed of temporarily or finally, informal consideration ends. Business conducted while under informal consideration is recorded in the minutes of the meeting.

Postpone to a Certain Time

+ **Purpose:** To put off or delay a decision.
+ Needs a second.
+ The time element is amendable.
+ Debatable. Debate goes only to the merits of postponing.
+ Majority vote required to adopt.
+ Can be reconsidered.
+ **Result:** Discussion and decision are put off until later in the meeting. If postponed to the next meeting, the motion comes up under general orders and unfinished business.

Don't confuse the motion *postpone to a certain time* with *lay on the table.*

In many groups, it's common to hear "let's table the motion to the next meeting." However, this is an incorrect usage of *lay on the table* and does not accomplish what the member actually intends. If such a motion is made, the chair should restate the motion as *postpone to the next meeting* and ask for a discussion.

The motion to postpone has certain time limits. A motion can't be postponed beyond a quarterly time interval or the next regular business meeting (whichever comes first). Likewise, members can't use the motion *postpone* as a motion to kill. If the motion *postpone to the next meeting* is adopted, the motion in question appears on the agenda under unfinished business and general orders. To make the motion *postpone to a certain time,* say:

> **Member:** I move to postpone the motion to the next meeting.
>
> **Member 2:** Second.
>
> **President:** It is moved and seconded to postpone the motion to the next meeting. Is there any discussion on postponing the motion?

If a motion is made to "postpone to the next meeting at 8 p.m.," the motion is taken up at approximately that time. If other business is being discussed at 8 p.m., the members finish with that business and then take up the motion that was postponed until 8 p.m. When members want a motion to come up at an exact time in the meeting, even if it interrupts business under discussion, it needs to be made a special order for that time.

Postpone to a Certain Time Made into a Special Order

✦ **Purpose:** To ensure that a motion is taken up at a specified time.

✦ Needs a second.

✦ Debatable.

✦ Time is amendable.

✦ A two-thirds vote is required to adopt.

✦ Can be reconsidered.

+ **Result:** If adopted, this motion must be taken up at the specified time, even if business is pending. (If the members don't want to take it up at that time, the members can set aside the special order. See "Call for the Orders of the Day" in Chapter 8.)

To postpone the motion and make it a special order, say:

Member: I move to postpone the motion to the next meeting and make it a special order for 8 p.m.

Member 2: Second.

President: It is moved and seconded to postpone the motion to the next meeting and make it a special order for 8 p.m. This motion is amendable and takes a two-thirds vote to adopt because it requires a suspension of a rule. Is there any discussion on postponing the motion?

The chair takes the vote as a rising vote.

Limit or Extend the Limits of Debate

+ **Purpose:** To limit or extend the length of debate or the number of times a person can speak in debate; or, to put a time limit on a particular motion. For example, to limit the entire debate to 30 minutes.

+ Requires a second.

+ Time element is amendable.

+ Not debatable.

+ Takes a two-thirds vote to adopt.

+ Can reconsider an affirmative vote without debate before the time limit expires. If partially carried out, can reconsider only the time remaining.

+ If the motion has been voted down, members can make it again after there is some progress in the debate.

+ **Result:** This motion changes the standard rules of debate.

If an assembly has no special rule of order about how long or how many times a member can speak in debate, a member may speak twice to a motion and up to ten minutes each time. If a member wishes to extend or limit the debate, he or she makes this motion. Conventions have standing rules that regulate how long each motion or topic can be considered. If this is the case, when the time has arrived to go on to the next business in order, a member can make the motion to extend the limits of debate. A two-thirds vote is needed to adopt because the motion alters the rights of the individual members.

There are several ways members can use this motion. One way is to reduce the number of speeches or the time allowed for members to speak to an issue:

Member: I move to limit debate to five minutes per person.

Member 2: Second.

President: It is moved and seconded to limit debate to five minutes per person. This motion is not debatable but is amendable. Are you ready for the question? All those in favor please rise. Be seated. Those opposed please rise. Be seated. The affirmative has it, and debate will be limited to five minutes per person.

or

President: The negative has it, and debate will not be limited. Each person can speak ten minutes to the question. Is there any discussion?

Another way to use this motion is to extend debate that is set for a certain time. For example, a convention may have a rule that debate stops at a certain time; if so, members can then make a motion to extend this time.

Member: I move to extend the debate five more minutes.

Member 2: Second.

President: It is moved and seconded to extend the debate five more minutes. This motion is not debatable but is amendable. Are you ready for the question? All in favor please rise. Be seated. Those opposed please rise. Be seated. The affirmative has it, and debate will be extended five more minutes.

or

The negative has it, and the debate will not be extended. It is time to take a vote on the motion to . . . . All those in favor say "Aye." Those opposed say "No." *[Announce the vote.]*

Members can also use the motion *limit or extend the limits of debate* to fix the hour for closing debate and taking the vote.

Member: I move that at 3 p.m., debate is closed and the vote taken.

Member 2: Second.

President: It is moved and seconded that at 3 p.m., debate is closed and the vote taken. This motion is not debatable but is amendable. Are you ready for the question? All those in favor please rise. Be seated. Those opposed please rise. Be seated. The affirmative has it, and debate will close at 3 p.m. and the vote taken.

or

President: The negative has it, and debate will not end at 3 p.m. Is there further discussion?

Previous Question (Close Debate)

✦ **Purpose:** To stop debate and immediately take the vote.

✦ Needs a second.

✦ Not amendable.

✦ Not debatable.

✦ Requires a two-thirds vote to adopt.

✦   Can reconsider without debate before the vote has been taken on the motion in which debate has been closed. If the members vote against this motion, it can be made again after progress in the debate.

✦   **Result:** If adopted, the members vote on the immediate pending question. If the *previous question* is called on all pending questions, the vote is taken on all pending questions.

The motion *previous question* is the most misunderstood and misused motion in meetings. There is only one way to stop debate: A member must move the *previous question*. Because it takes members' rights away, this motion requires a two-thirds vote to close debate.

Many people do not understand *previous question*. They think that they can just yell out "Question!" and the chair should stop debate and take a vote on the motion. The chairman never has the authority to close debate as long as one person wants to discuss the motion. The chair can close debate when members adopt the previous question.

The time to make a motion for the *previous question* is when a member thinks the debate on the motion has become tedious. The member wants to close debate and take a vote so that the membership can proceed to other business. The member must rise, address the chair, and move the previous question:

> **Member:** I move the previous question.

or

> **Member:** I move to close debate and take the vote immediately.
>
> **Member 2:** Second.

The president handles the motion this way:

President: The question is on adopting the previous question on the pending motion. If adopted, this will stop debate and we will vote immediately. All those in favor please rise. Be seated. Those opposed please rise. Be seated. *[Announce the vote.]*

If the affirmative has it:

President: There are two-thirds in the affirmative, and the previous question is adopted. Debate is stopped. All those in favor of buying a computer and laser printer say "Aye." Those opposed say "No." *[Announce the result of the vote.]*

If the negative has it:

President: There are less than two-thirds in the affirmative. The previous question is lost. Is there further discussion?

In its unqualified form, this motion applies only to the immediate pending motion. If adopted, debate ceases and the vote is taken immediately on the pending question. The previous question may be made on all pending questions or on consecutive pending questions.

Note: Even though this is one of the highest-ranking subsidiary motions, it is not proper to make this motion before everyone has had the right to debate. If a controversial issue is presented to the membership, it is unfair to close debate before someone in the opposition has the right to speak. Henry Robert, in his book *Parliamentary Law,* says:

Where there is radical difference of opinion in an organization, one side must yield. The great lesson for democracies to learn is for the majority to give to the minority a full, free opportunity to present their side of the case, and then for the minority, having failed to win a majority to their views, gracefully to submit and to recognize the action as that of the entire organization, and cheerfully to assist in carrying it out, until they can secure its repeal.

Lay on the Table

+ **Purpose:** To set the main motion aside temporarily in order to take up something of immediate urgency. The intent is not to kill the motion or to put it off to the next meeting.

+ Needs a second.

+ Not amendable.

+ Not debatable.

+ Requires a majority to adopt.

+ Can't be reconsidered. If adopted, members can take from the table the main motion and any of its adhering motions. If it is defeated, members can make the motion *lay on the table* again after debate has progressed and something more urgent comes up again.

+ **Result:** If adopted, this motion places the main motion and any of its adhering motions on the table or in the hands of the secretary. It stays on the table until someone moves to take it from the table.

The motion *lay on the table* is the second most misused motion in meetings. Members either "table it" to kill a motion or "table it" to postpone a motion. In essence, the motion *lay on the table* takes away the members' right to debate with a majority vote, instead of a two-thirds vote.

When *lay on the table* is adopted, it allows the members to immediately halt consideration of the motion without debate. When a motion is laid on the table, and if the meeting adjourns before the motion is taken from the table, it is not put on the agenda for the next meeting. A member must take it from the table at the next meeting before discussing it again. Because the members moved to lay it on the table, only the members can take it from the table. Therefore, this motion is reserved for an immediate urgency only. When a member makes this motion and does not state the reason for making the motion, the chair should ask the member to state his or her reason for making the motion. If it is apparent that the member wants to kill the motion, the chair should rule the motion out of order and explain to the member that the proper motion is *postpone the motion indefinitely,* if it is in order at that time; or, the chair can take the liberty to place the motion before the assembly as *postpone it indefinitely* and ask for discussion.

A member should state the reasons he or she makes this motion. A member cannot lay a motion on the table and then make another motion that conflicts with the motion laid on the table. If the motion is not used correctly, the chair should rule it out of order and then state the proper procedure. If the chair does not do this, a member should rise to a point of order and explain the correct procedure.

When a main motion is laid on the table, all adhering subsidiary motions go with it. For example, if a main motion and its subsidiary motions *amend* and *refer to a committee* are pending, these go to the table with the main motion.

The motion *lay on the table* is recorded in the minutes, but it is not put on the agenda. A member must remember to make the motion *take from the table*. If a motion is laid on the table and is not taken from the table by the end of the next meeting, it dies. After it dies, a member has to present it as a new main motion.

To make this motion a member states:

> **Member:** I move to lay the motion on the table.
>
> **Member 2:** Second.
>
> **President:** It is moved and seconded to lay the motion on the table. All those in favor say "Aye." Those opposed say "No." [Announce the vote.]

LEGITIMATE USES OF THE MOTION
LAY ON THE TABLE

Members cannot use the motion *lay on the table* to kill a motion or to put it off to a later time. The motion *lay on the table* is reserved for circumstances when an urgent matter that can't wait must be introduced.

The chair is allowed to rule whether the matter is urgent and whether the motion will be entertained.

Examples of urgent situations are:

- The speaker for the program has arrived and needs to leave early, so a member can move to lay the pending business aside as a courtesy to the speaker.

- Something on the agenda needs to be resolved during the current meeting. It is getting late, and the member is concerned that the meeting will adjourn without resolving the important business. If the important business is the next agenda item, a member can move to lay the pending business on the table to take up this important matter. If the important agenda item is several agenda items away, the members can lay each item on the table until they get to the item they want to discuss. If no business is pending and members want to take an agenda item out of order, instead of using the motion *lay on the table,* they should use the motion *suspend the rules* (see Chapter 9).

Use the motion *lay on the table* sparingly in meetings, if at all. This motion cannot be used during a special meeting that has been called to address a specific issue.

8

Using Privileged Motions

This chapter addresses *privileged motions,* those motions that do not relate to the pending motion but that are special matters of immediate importance arising in the meeting. The chapter begins with the lowest-ranking privileged motion — *call for the orders of the day* — and proceeds to the highest-ranking one — *fix the time to which to adjourn.* The purpose of each motion, its restrictions (whether it needs a second, is amendable, and so on), and the result of that privileged motion are outlined at the beginning of each section. Examples show you how to use the motion correctly.

Call for the Orders of the Day

✦ **Purpose:** To make the assembly conform to the agenda or order of business, or to make the assembly take up a general or special order.

✦ One member can call for the orders of the day.

✦ Does not require a second.

✦ Not amendable.

✦ Not debatable.

✦ No vote is taken unless the members want to set aside the orders of the day, which takes a two-thirds vote.

✦ Cannot be reconsidered.

✦ **Result:** Stops whatever the assembly is doing and the meeting proceeds to the orders of the day.

When the agenda isn't being followed or a motion that was made a special order is not being taken up at the right time, one member can call for the orders of the day. This motion does not require a second. It is not debatable. The chair must immediately go to the orders of the day or take a vote to set aside the orders of the day. If the chair assumes a motion to set aside the orders of the day, a two-thirds vote in the negative must adopt it. If a member moves to set aside the orders of the day, it requires a two-thirds vote in the affirmative to adopt.

Say, for example, the members are debating the motion to buy a computer. The chair either has forgotten that it's time to take up a special order or has decided to ignore it. A member calls for the orders of the day. The chair can do one of two things. The chair can stop the discussion and go to the orders of the day. Or, if the chair feels that the members are almost ready to vote on the computer and would like to set aside the orders of the day to finish the business at hand, the chair can take a vote on the motion to call for the orders of the day.

> **Member:** I call for the orders of the day.
>
> **Chairman:** The orders of the day are called for. The order of the day is the motion to give $1,000 to the Environmental Club. The question is: Will the members proceed to the orders of the day? As many as are in favor please rise. *[A few members rise.]* Be seated. Those opposed please rise. *[Many members rise.]* Be seated. There is a two-thirds vote in the negative, and we will not proceed to the orders of the day. Is there any further discussion about buying a computer and laser printer?

If the vote is less than two-thirds in the negative, the chair states:

> **Chairman:** There is less than a two-thirds vote in the negative, and we will now proceed to the orders of the day. The question is on the motion to give $1,000 to the Environmental Club. Is there any discussion?

When this motion has been disposed, the members return to the motion to buy a computer and laser printer.

If a member wants to set aside the orders of the day, he or she can state, "I move that the time for considering the pending question be extended." This motion takes a two-thirds vote in the affirmative to adopt.

Raise a Question of Privilege

✦ **Purpose:** Permits a member to make a request or a main motion relating to the rights and privileges of the assembly or an individual member and to consider it immediately, because of its urgency, while other business is pending.

✦ Does not require a second.

✦ Not debatable.

✦ Chair rules on the request.

✦ **Result:** The chair's ruling determines the outcome.

A common question of privilege deals with noise or temperature in the assembly room. There are questions of privilege concerning the assembly and questions of privilege concerning the individual. Of the two, privilege of the assembly has a higher priority. To raise a question of privilege, a member usually makes his or her statement this way:

Member: Madam President, I rise to a question of privilege concerning the assembly.

President: Please state the question.

Member: It is too hot in here. Can we have the heat turned down?

The chair then makes a ruling.

President: Is there any objection to turning down the heat? Hearing none, will Member X turn down the thermostat?

An example of a question of personal privilege is when a member can't hear the speaker.

> **Member:** Madam President, I rise to a question of personal privilege.
>
> **President:** Please state the question.
>
> **Member:** I can't hear the speaker.

The chair then makes a ruling. The chair may say, "Will the speaker talk louder?" or "Will the speaker go to the microphone so all can hear?"

Another example of a motion that is considered a question of privilege is the motion to go into executive session, during which time the proceedings are kept secret.

To make a motion to go into executive session, a member states:

> **Member:** Madam President, I rise to a question of privilege to make a motion.
>
> **President:** Please state your motion.
>
> **Member:** I move that we go into executive session to discuss this issue.
>
> **President:** The chair rules that the question is one of privilege to be entertained immediately. Is there a second?
>
> **Member 2:** Second.
>
> **President:** It is moved and seconded to go into executive session. Is there any discussion?

Debate follows on whether to go into executive session; this motion is amendable. A vote is then taken. If the motion is adopted, those who are not members must leave and the meeting goes into a secret session. The minutes of this portion of the meeting can be approved only at an executive session.

Recess

✦ **Purpose:** To take a short intermission and then resume business where the members left off. As a privileged motion, members make a motion to recess when other business is pending.

✦ Needs a second.

✦ Length of recess is amendable.

✦ Not debatable.

✦ Requires a majority vote to adopt.

✦ Can't be reconsidered, but it can be made again after some progress in the meeting.

✦ **Result:** Members take a short break.

To make this motion, a member says:

Member: I move to take a ____ minute recess.

Member 2: Second.

President: It is moved and seconded to take a ____ minute recess. All those in favor say "Aye." Those opposed say "No." The ayes have it, and we will take a ____ minute recess. This meeting stands in recess for ____ minutes. *[one rap of the gavel]*

When the recess is finished, the president calls the meeting to order with one rap of the gavel.

A recess is generally short in duration. Although it may last several hours, it is never longer than a day. Organizations do not take long recesses like the U.S. Congress. If members want to take a longer recess, they should set an adjourned meeting. (See the motion *fix the time to which to adjourn,* later in this chapter. Also see "Adjourned Meetings" in Chapter 16.)

Note that it is also possible to recess when no business is pending. The motion to recess when no business is pending is an incidental main motion. The difference between this motion and recess as a privileged motion is that recess as an incidental main motion is debatable and the previous use of recess is not debatable.

Adjourn

✦ **Purpose:** To end the meeting immediately.

✦ Needs a second.

✦ Not amendable.

✦ Not debatable.

✦ Requires a majority vote to adopt.

✦ Can't be reconsidered, but if the motion is not approved, members can make it again after some progress in the meeting.

✦ **Result:** It ends the meeting, and the business halts at the point where the members adjourned. If the members are in the middle of discussing a motion, this motion will come up at the next meeting under unfinished business and general orders.

As a privileged motion (one made when other motions are pending), *adjourn* takes precedence over all other motions, except the motion *fix the time to which to adjourn.* If adopted, and before the chair announces the adjournment, members can rise to make announcements, give previous notice about a motion to be made at the next meeting, and make a motion to *reconsider,* to *reconsider and enter on the minutes,* or to *fix the time to which to adjourn.* If the meeting adjourns while business is pending, this business carries over to the next meeting and appears on the agenda under unfinished business and general orders. For example:

Member: I move to adjourn.

Member 2: Second.

President: It is moved and seconded that we adjourn. All those in favor say "Aye." Those opposed say "No." The ayes have it, the motion is carried, and the meeting is adjourned.

or

President: The noes have it, the motion is lost, and the meeting will not adjourn. Is there further business?

The motion to adjourn is not in order when the assembly is engaged in voting or verifying a vote, or before the chair announces the result of a vote. However, if the assembly is taking a vote by ballot, the motion to adjourn is in order after the tellers have collected all the ballots and before the results are announced.

While the motion to adjourn is pending, the following procedures are in order:

- To inform the assembly of important business that needs to be done before adjournment

- To make important announcements

- To make a motion to reconsider the vote on a previous motion

- To make a motion to reconsider the vote and enter on the minutes

- To give previous notice on a motion to be made at the next meeting

- To make the motion to fix the time to which to adjourn.

Members can also make the above motions and announcements after the vote on *adjourn* is adopted but before the chair adjourns the meeting.

Fix the Time to Which to Adjourn

✦ **Purpose:** To set a later time to continue this meeting before the next regular meeting. In parliamentary terminology, it sets the time for an *adjourned meeting.*

✦ Needs a second.

✦ The time and date of the adjourned meeting are amendable.

✦ Not debatable.

✦ Requires a majority vote to adopt.

✦ Can be reconsidered.

✦ **Result:** Sets the date, place, and time for the meeting to continue.

As a privileged motion, *fix the time to which to adjourn* is the highest-ranking motion. An adjourned meeting is a legal continuation of the present meeting. This motion never adjourns the present meeting; it sets the time and date for another meeting. (See Chapter 16 for information about an adjourned meeting.)

When no business is pending, the motion *fix the time to which to adjourn* is an incidental main motion. The difference between the motion as an incidental main motion and as a privileged motion is that, as an incidental main motion, it has all the characteristics of a main motion, which includes the right to debate. To make the privileged motion, a member states:

> *Member:* I move that when this meeting adjourns, it adjourn to meet tomorrow at 8 p.m.
>
> *Member 2:* Second.
>
> *President:* It is moved and seconded that when this meeting adjourns, it adjourn to meet tomorrow at 8 p.m. All those in favor say "Aye." Those opposed say "No." The ayes have it, and when this meeting adjourns, it will meet tomorrow at 8 p.m.

The chair goes back to whatever business was pending.

If the noes have it, the chair states:

> **President:** The noes have it, and the motion is lost. We won't have an adjourned meeting.

Sometimes members want to set the time for the meeting to adjourn at the beginning of the meeting. To do so, members can use the motion *fix the time at which to adjourn.* Students of parliamentary procedure must study carefully the difference between the following motion and the privileged motion *fix the time to which to adjourn.*

Fix the Time at Which to Adjourn

+ **Purpose:** To set the time to adjourn the meeting.

+ Needs a second.

+ The time for adjournment is amendable.

+ Debatable because it is an incidental main motion.

+ Requires a majority to adopt.

+ Can't be reconsidered.

+ **Result:** The members must adjourn at the time that they have set for adjournment. When that time comes, the presiding officer must announce that the time for adjournment has arrived and then adjourn the meeting. If members want to continue the meeting at this point, they must move to suspend the rules in order to continue the meeting.

Because this is an incidental main motion, members make it when no other business is pending. To fix the time at which to adjourn, a member states:

> **Member:** I move that the meeting adjourn at 9 p.m.
> **Member 2:** Second.

President: It is moved and seconded that the meeting adjourn at 9 p.m. Is there any discussion?

After the vote is taken, the chair announces the result this way if the affirmative wins:

President: The ayes have it, the motion is carried, and the meeting will adjourn at 9 p.m.

If the negative has it, the chair announces it this way:

President: The noes have it, and the motion is lost.

Even though this motion sets the time for adjournment, members can still make the motion to adjourn at any time during the meeting. If adopted, the meeting will adjourn. The purpose of the motion *fix the time at which to adjourn* is to avoid letting a meeting run longer than the assembly desires. For example, this motion is helpful if someone has to leave the meeting at a certain time and does not want to miss any important business. If this motion is adopted, it ensures that no further business is considered after the set adjournment time.

9

Using Incidental Motions

This chapter looks at *incidental motions,* those motions that concern questions of procedure related to the pending business. Incidental motions are not ranked because they are taken up immediately when made. The purpose of each motion, its restrictions (whether it needs a second, is amendable, is debatable, and so on), and the result of that incidental motion are outlined at the beginning of each section. Examples show you how to use the motion correctly.

Point of Order

✦ **Purpose:** To correct a breach in the rules.

✦ No second.

✦ Not debatable.

✦ Presiding officer rules on the point.

✦ Cannot be reconsidered.

✦ **Result:** The chair's ruling stands unless someone appeals it.

The purpose of a *point of order* is to correct a breach in the rules when the presiding officer does not correct it, or when the presiding officer makes a breach of the rules. Point of order should not be used for minor infractions. It does not need a second, can interrupt a speaker, and is ruled upon by the chair. A point of order is made at the time of the infraction. If the infraction is of a continuing nature, members can make a point of order at any time. An infraction of a continuing nature is:

- An adopted main motion that conflicts with the bylaws; corporate charter; governing documents of a parent organization; or federal, state, or local laws.

- An adopted main motion that conflicts with a main motion previously adopted and still in force. For the motion to be valid, members have to rescind or amend something previously adopted.

- Any action that is in violation of basic parliamentary principles.

- Any action that is in violation of rules that protect either the absent member or individual member.

To make a point of order, the member says:

Member: I rise to a point of order.

or

Member: Point of order.

President: Please state your point.

Member: There is no longer a quorum present, and any business transacted will be null and void.

President: Your point is well taken. Since there is no longer a quorum present, this meeting is adjourned. *[one rap of the gavel]*

The president can rule against the point of order by stating:

President: Your point is not well taken, and the meeting will continue.

If a member does not agree with the chair's ruling, the member can appeal from the decision of the chair.

Appeal from the Decision of the Chair (Appeal)

- ✦ **Purpose:** To disagree with the chair's ruling and let the members decide the disagreement by taking a vote.

- ✦ Needs a second.

✦ Motion must be made at the time the ruling was made.

✦ Debatable. However, it is not debatable if it relates to rules of speaking, the priority of business (order of business), or a ruling on an undebatable motion.

✦ Not amendable.

✦ A majority or tie vote sustains the decision of the chair.

✦ Can be reconsidered.

✦ **Result:** If adopted, it upholds the chair's ruling.

Members make an appeal immediately after the ruling of the chair. This motion needs a second and is debatable unless it is made while an undebatable motion is pending or relates to the priority of business. The chair has the first opportunity to speak to the appeal. After members of the assembly have spoken to the appeal, the chair has the last right to speak before taking the vote. A majority vote is needed to sustain the decision of the chair.

For example, say the members are discussing a motion to send delegates to the state convention. A member makes the motion to amend by adding at the end "and to build tennis courts." The presiding officer rules the proposed amendment out of order because it is not related to the motion. The member proposing the amendment then makes the motion to appeal from the decision of the chair. He states:

> *Member:* I appeal from the decision of the chair.
>
> *Member 2:* Second.
>
> *President:* It is moved and seconded to appeal from the decision of the chair. The question before the assembly is, "Shall the decision of the chair be sustained?" Is there any discussion?

If the chair wants to speak first — which he or she can do — the chair states:

> *President:* The chair ruled that the amendment was not germane because building the tennis courts is not related

to sending delegates to the convention. Is there further discussion?

Each member has the right to speak once to the appeal. After everyone who wishes to speak has spoken, the chair can again give his or her reason for the ruling. The chair then takes the vote. The correct phrasing for the vote is:

> ***President:*** The question is, "Shall the decision of the chair be sustained?" All those in favor say "Aye." Those opposed say "No."

The chair announces the vote and whether the decision is sustained or not sustained.

If the members vote for the decision of the chair, business continues in accordance with the chair's ruling. In this case, the proposed amendment to add "and to build tennis courts" to the motion is not in order. The members will only consider sending delegates to the convention.

If the members vote against the decision of the chair, the proposed amendment "and to build tennis courts" is considered a valid amendment and the members will discuss and vote on the proposed amendment.

REQUESTS AND INQUIRIES

Requests and inquiries, which do not require motions, help members obtain information. One way to obtain information is to ask for parliamentary information. This request is called a *parliamentary inquiry*. The chair answers the inquiry. Another way to obtain information is to ask for information about the subject being discussed, which is called a *point of information*. Requests and inquires are always directed to, or through, the chair. For example:

> ***Member:*** I rise to parliamentary inquiry.
>
> ***President:*** Please state your inquiry.

Member: Is it appropriate to lay this business on the table so that we can take up the item on the agenda to send delegates to the state convention?

President: *[gives an opinion]*

The president's remark is only an opinion, not a ruling, and is not subject to an appeal. The member can follow the chair's advice or ignore it. To make a point of information, a member states:

Member: I rise to a point of information.

President: Please state your point.

Member: Do we have enough money in the treasury to send four delegates to the convention?

If the chair does not know the answer, he or she can ask someone who does.

President: Will the treasurer please answer the member's question?

Treasurer: We have allotted $1,000 to send delegates.

President: Does that answer the member's question?

Member: *[answers either yes or no]*

Members can make other requests besides those listed previously. For example, if a member wants to read extracts from a paper to support his or her arguments, he or she must ask permission of the assembly to do so. If no one objects, he or she can proceed to read from the written materials. However, if someone objects, the presiding officer places the request as a motion before the assembly. It takes a majority vote to grant permission to read from a paper or book. To make the request a member rises, addresses the chair, and asks:

Member: Mr. President, I request permission to read a statement. *[Explain briefly what it is.]*

President: Is there any objection to the member reading the statement? Hearing none, the member has the assembly's permission to proceed.

If there is an objection, the chair takes a vote:

> **President:** All those in favor of letting the member read a statement say "Aye." Those opposed say "No". The ayes have it, and the member can proceed.

If the noes have it, the chair states:

> **President:** The noes have it, and the member will not read from the statement.

Request for Permission to Withdraw or Modify a Motion

+ **Purpose:** Withdraw or modify a motion without taking a vote.

+ Does not need a second if asking permission to withdraw. Needs a second if modifying the motion.

+ Not debatable.

+ Vote by general consent when asking permission to withdraw.

+ The vote to modify can be reconsidered. Only the negative vote in withdrawing the motion can be reconsidered.

+ **Result:** When withdrawn, it is as if the motion had never been made. If modified, it is presented to the assembly in the modified form.

Before the chair states the motion, it belongs to the maker of the motion and he or she can withdraw it or modify it without the permission of the assembly. After the chair states the motion, it belongs to the assembly and the maker must ask permission to modify or withdraw it.

Note: This procedure is often misunderstood. If the chair has not stated the motion, the member can withdraw it without permission of the person who seconded it. If the member modifies the motion and the person who seconds it withdraws his or her second, someone else must second the motion.

Remember: After the chair states the motion, the motion belongs to the assembly and not to the maker of the motion. The assembly, not the person who seconded the motion, must give permission to withdraw the motion or modify it.

After a motion is seconded but not repeated by the presiding officer, the maker of the motion can quickly rise and say:

> **Member:** Madam President, I wish to modify my motion by adding at the end "not to exceed the cost of $1,000."

or

> **Member:** Madam President, I wish to withdraw the motion.

The president either repeats the motion in the modified version or states that the motion is withdrawn. If the person who seconds the motion withdraws his or her second from the modified form, the president can ask for a second.

Before the chair states the motion, another member can rise and ask the president if the maker of the motion will accept a change in the motion. The maker can either accept or reject the proposed change. If the maker rejects the proposed change, the member suggesting the change can propose an amendment after the motion has been placed before the assembly. If the maker accepts the change, the changed motion becomes pending. Some authorities refer to this type of change as a *friendly amendment*.

If the motion is under discussion and the maker of the motion wants to withdraw it, he or she must ask permission of the assembly. The member states:

> **Member:** Mr. President, I ask permission to withdraw the motion.

This request should be handled by general consent:

> **President:** Is there any objection to withdrawing the motion? Hearing none, the motion is withdrawn.

If there is an objection, the presiding officer puts it to a vote.

A withdrawn motion is not recorded in the minutes unless the motion has carried over from another meeting.

Request To be Excused from a Duty

+ **Purpose:** Allows a member with the consent of the assembly to be excused from duties assigned in the bylaws.

+ Needs a second when moved formally by the person asking to be excused. If another member makes the motion, it does not need a second.

+ Amendable.

+ Debatable.

+ Requires a majority vote. Usually settled by general consent.

+ **Result:** After a member learns that he or she has been excused, only the negative vote can be reconsidered.

When the bylaws assign certain duties to the members and a member can't fulfill the duty, he or she must make a formal request to the assembly to be excused from a duty.

If a duty is not compulsory, a member can decline the duty. For example, if the member is elected to an office or appointed to a committee, he or she can decline without having to ask the assembly.

If a member finds that she can't continue the work during her term of office or while serving on a committee, she should submit her resignation to the secretary. The chair then puts the resignation to a vote. A member can't abandon her duties until her resignation is accepted.

If a member wishes to withdraw from the organization, he should submit a letter to the secretary. If the member has paid his dues, his resignation should be accepted immediately. If a member has not paid his dues, the organization does not have to accept the withdrawal and the member may have to pay more dues. If the member refuses to pay dues, the society may expel him. If a member submits a resignation to escape charges against him, the society can refuse to accept the resignation and proceed with the trial.

Object to Consideration of a Question

+ **Purpose:** To prevent the main motion from being considered.

+ No second.

+ Not debatable.

+ Requires a two-thirds vote in the negative not to consider.

+ Only a negative vote, not an affirmative vote, can be reconsidered.

+ **Result:** If two-thirds of the members vote in the negative, the motion cannot be considered for the duration of the meeting. However, members can propose it again at another meeting.

The purpose of *object to consideration of a question* is to prevent a motion from being considered. This motion should not be used as a dilatory tactic. Only when a member feels that it would be divisive for the motion to come before the assembly should he or she make this objection. Anyone can object to consideration, including the presiding officer. This motion does not need a second and is not debatable or amendable. The chair takes a vote immediately on whether the motion should be considered. The objection must be made before any discussion begins on the motion. Sustaining the objection takes a two-thirds vote against consideration.

To make this motion, a member must rise immediately after the chair states the motion and say:

> *Member:* Mr. President (or Madam President), I object to consideration of the question.

The chair immediately takes a vote. In taking a vote, the chair phrases his or her request this way:

President: The consideration of the question is objected to. Shall the question be considered? Those in favor of considering the question rise. *[pause]* Be seated. *[pause]* Those opposed to considering the question rise. *[pause]* Be seated.

If more than a third of the membership is in favor of considering the question, the chair announces the vote this way:

President: There are less than two-thirds opposed, and the objection is not sustained. The question is on the motion . . . .

If two-thirds of the membership votes against considering the question, the chair announces the vote this way:

President: There are two-thirds opposed, and the question will not be considered. Is there further business?

In putting the question to the membership, the chair states:

President: Shall the question be considered?

Those who want to prevent consideration must vote in the negative. If the members vote against considering the question, the question can be brought up again at another meeting.

Division of the Assembly

+ **Purpose:** To doubt the result of the vote.
+ No second.
+ Not debatable.
+ **Result:** The vote is immediately retaken in a different way than it was originally taken.

For examples of using this motion, see "Taking the Vote" in Chapter 3 and "Doubting the Result of the Vote" in Chapter 5.

Division of the Question

✦ **Purpose:** To divide a motion that has several topics that can stand as separate motions. Members can apply this motion to main motions and their amendments.

✦ Needs a second.

✦ Amendable.

✦ Not debatable.

✦ Majority vote.

✦ Can't be reconsidered.

✦ **Result:** The motion is divided into its separate parts and the assembly considers each part individually without affecting the other parts.

Sometimes a member gets carried away with what he or she proposes, and the main motion includes several things that he or she wants to do. Here's an example of such a motion:

> ***Member:*** Madam President, I move that we paint the clubhouse blue, buy a new stove for the kitchen, and give the janitor a $100 bonus for spring clean-up.

This motion has three distinct parts that can stand alone:

1. Paint the clubhouse blue.
2. Buy a new stove for the kitchen.
3. Give the janitor a $100 bonus for spring clean-up.

In this case, dividing the question into its three parts is in order. To do this, a member states:

> ***Member:*** Madam President, I move to divide the motion into three parts. The first motion is to paint the clubhouse blue. The second motion is to buy a new stove for the kitchen. The third motion is to give the janitor a $100 bonus for spring clean-up.

This motion needs a second and is not debatable; the presiding officer immediately takes a vote. The motion can also be adopted by unanimous consent.

> **President:** Is there any objection to dividing the motion into three parts? Hearing none, the motion is divided. The question before you is to paint the clubhouse blue. Is there any discussion?

Or, the chair can take a formal vote.

> **President:** All those in favor say "Aye." Those opposed say "No."

The chair then announces the vote. If the noes have it, the motion is considered in its original form. If the motions are considered separately, the chair presents each one for discussion and vote.

Another way members can divide this motion is if someone only wants to consider giving the janitor a bonus as a separate question. In this case, the member phrases the division of the question this way:

> **Member:** Madam President, I move to divide the question so that we consider giving the janitor a $100 bonus separately.

Members can divide only motions that can stand by themselves. If a series of resolutions are presented that can stand alone, one member can ask the assembly to consider a certain resolution separately, without taking a vote. This is similar to the procedure of working with a consent agenda (see Chapter 2).

Suspend the Rules

+ **Purpose:** To set aside a rule of the assembly (except bylaws, the corporate charter, fundamental principles of parliamentary law, or rules that protect the absent members or basic rights of the individual).

✦ Needs a second.

✦ Not debatable.

✦ Not amendable.

✦ Requires a two-thirds vote to suspend a parliamentary order or order of business; needs a majority vote to suspend a standing rule.

✦ Cannot be reconsidered.

✦ **Result:** Rules are set aside so that members can do something contrary to the rules.

The motion *suspend the rules* is used primarily to take up a particular item of business out of its regular agenda order or to set aside a procedural rule or an ordinary standing rule. Here are examples of how to apply this motion:

■ To enable the assembly to take up something out of its proper order in the agenda; for example, to take up something under new business before taking up unfinished business. To move to suspend the rules, a member says:

Member: I move to suspend the rules and take up the topic "to repair the clubhouse."

Member 2: Second.

■ To suspend the rules of debate and amendment and vote immediately, a member says:

Member: I move to suspend the rules and agree to the resolution . . . .

Member 2: Second.

Any rule that suspends a parliamentary rule or order of business requires a two-thirds vote. If the motion is not controversial, the vote can be taken by general (unanimous) consent ("Without objection . . . ").

The presiding officer takes the vote this way:

President: It is moved and seconded to suspend the rules and take up the repairs to the clubhouse. All those in favor please rise. Be seated. Those opposed please rise. Be seated. The affirmative has it, and the rules are suspended. We will proceed to the item about repairing the clubhouse.

At this point the member who suspended the rules should rise and make a motion about repairing the clubhouse.

To take the vote by general (unanimous) consent, the chair states the motion this way:

President: Is there any objection to suspending the rules and taking up the item to repair the clubhouse? *[pause]* Hearing none, the rules are suspended, and the next item of business is repairing the clubhouse.

When the members dispose of the motion to repair the clubhouse, they return to the place in the agenda where they left off.

■ To suspend an ordinary standing rule of the society. Standing rules of the society are rules that do not have to do with parliamentary procedure but with the policies of the society, time of the meetings, or something of an administrative nature. A majority vote can suspend these rules because they do not involve the protection of a minority. The rules are suspended only for the duration of the meeting. Suspending the rules does not bind any future meetings. The rules that can't be suspended are bylaws (unless their suspension is provided for in the bylaws themselves) and rules protecting absent members or the basic rights of individual members. A member also can't make a motion to dispense with an entire established order of business.

Rules that pertain to fundamental principles of parliamentary law can't be suspended. For example, it is out of order to suspend the rule that allows the assembly to consider only one question at a time, and it is out of order to allow a non-member to vote. Rights that pertain to the absent members can't be suspended — the rule for a quorum or the requirement of previous notice if a proposal is made to amend a bylaw, for example. No one can suspend the rights of another member, such as the right to make motions, debate, and vote. This can only be done through disciplinary proceedings.

10

Using Motions That Bring a Question Again Before the Assembly

There are two ways to bring a motion back before the assembly. One way is called *renewing a motion:* If a motion is defeated, a member can reintroduce it as new business at the next meeting. The second way is by using a group of motions that are described in this chapter. It is a parliamentary rule that any main motion that is defeated can't be brought before the assembly at the same meeting unless it is substantially a new question, its wording has changed significantly, the time or conditions in the motion have changed, or the special procedures explained in this chapter are used.

The motions discussed in this chapter show the correct way to return a question to the assembly for reconsideration. Members make these motions when no other business is pending. The purpose of each motion, its restrictions (whether it needs a second, is debatable, can be reconsidered, and so on), and the result of the motion are outlined at the beginning of each section. Examples show you how to use the motion correctly.

Take from the Table

+ **Purpose:** To take a motion from the table.
+ Needs a second.
+ Not debatable.
+ Requires a majority to adopt.

◆   Cannot be reconsidered.

◆   **Result:** Takes a motion from the table, which becomes the immediate pending business.

When a motion is laid on the table (set aside temporarily), members must take it from the table by the end of the next meeting or it dies. Members must make this motion when no other business is pending. Anyone can make this motion. It needs a second and is not debatable. The vote is taken immediately, and it requires a majority vote to adopt. If adopted, the motion that was tabled is now before the assembly. For example, if several motions were pending when it was laid on the table @md a main motion, an amendment, and *refer to a committee* @md the chair begins discussion with the last motion made, which was *refer to a committee*.

To make the motion, a member says:

Member: I move to take from the table the motion relating to the computer.

Member 2: Second.

President: It is moved and seconded to take from the table the motion relating to the computer. All those in favor say "Aye." Those opposed say "No." The ayes have it, and the motion to buy a computer and laser printer is taken from the table. The last pending motion was *refer to a committee.* Is there any further discussion on referring to a committee?

Reconsider

◆   **Purpose:** To reconsider the vote on a motion.

◆   Only a member who voted on the prevailing side can make the motion.

◆   Needs a second.

◆   Debatable if the type of motion it reconsiders is debatable.

◆   Requires a majority vote to adopt.

◆   Cannot be reconsidered.

✦ This motion can be made but not considered when other business is pending.

✦ **Result:** If adopted, the original motion is placed before the assembly as if it had not been previously voted on.

The motion *reconsider* allows the assembly to change its mind about how the membership voted on a motion. In a group whose meetings last one day, members must make this motion at the same meeting in which the vote was taken. In conventions or sessions of more than one day, members can reconsider a motion voted on at one meeting the next day. If time has run out on the motion to reconsider, members can offer the motion to rescind the action or amend something previously adopted (explained later in this chapter). If the motion was defeated at the previous meeting, a member can renew the motion by reintroducing it as new business.

Reconsider is an unusual motion; making the motion to reconsider suspends all action until the motion to reconsider is taken up or terminates. Therefore, to prevent its dilatory use by the losing side, only a member that voted on the prevailing side can make the motion, although anyone can second it. It is debatable if the type of motion to be reconsidered is debatable, and debate can go to the merits of the main motion. The motion to reconsider is not amendable and requires a majority vote for adoption.

A member who makes this motion should state that he or she voted on the prevailing side. If the member doesn't state this, it is the chair's duty to ask the member whether he or she voted on the prevailing side. If there is no business pending, the motion is taken up immediately. If business is pending, the chair tells the secretary to make a note that the motion to reconsider has been made; it isn't taken up until a member calls the motion to reconsider the vote when no other business is pending, which can be at another meeting. If the motion to reconsider the vote is carried, the motion being reconsidered is placed before the assembly as if it had never been voted on. And, if a member has exhausted his or her right to debate the motion, the member can't debate it again unless it is taken up at another meeting.

Members cannot reconsider a motion in the following cases:

- When the provisions of the motion have been partially carried out
- When a vote has caused something to be done that can't be undone
- When a contract has been made and the other party has been notified of the vote
- When some other parliamentary motion can obtain the same result

To make the motion to reconsider, a member states:

> **Member:** I move to reconsider the vote on the motion to buy a computer and laser printer. I voted on the prevailing side.
>
> **Member 2:** Second.
>
> **President:** It is moved and seconded to reconsider the vote on the motion to buy a computer and laser printer. Is there any discussion on reconsidering the vote?

Members can discuss the merits of the main motion. The members must remember that this is a two-step process. They first vote on whether to reconsider the vote. If this motion is adopted, the motion to be reconsidered is again under discussion and they take another vote on it.

Because the motion to reconsider suspends action on the issue at hand until it is taken up, it has a time requirement. If the assembly can't take up the motion to reconsider at the meeting in which the motion was made, and if the assembly's next meeting is within a quarterly time interval, the assembly must take up the motion to reconsider before the end of the next meeting. If it isn't taken up, the members can proceed with the action. If the next meeting is more than a quarterly time interval, members must take up the motion to reconsider at the current meeting. If it isn't taken up, the members proceed with the action.

If business is pending when the motion to reconsider is made, it must be *called up* when no business is pending. To call up the motion to reconsider, a member rises, addresses the chair, and states:

Member: I call up the motion to reconsider.

Because the motion to reconsider was seconded when it was originally proposed, the chair immediately states it this way:

President: It is moved and seconded to reconsider the vote on the motion to buy a computer and laser printer. Is there any discussion on the motion to reconsider the vote?

Rescind and Amend Something Previously Adopted

♦ **Purpose:** To change something previously adopted either by striking out the entire action or by changing part of it.

♦ Needs a second.

♦ Amendable.

♦ Debatable.

♦ If no previous notice is given, either a two-thirds vote or a majority of the entire membership is needed, whichever is more practical to obtain. If previous notice is given, the motion requires a majority vote to adopt.

♦ Can reconsider only a negative vote.

♦ **Result:** If this motion is adopted, the previously adopted motion is reversed or changed.

The rules concerning the two motions to *rescind* and *amend something previously adopted* by the assembly are very similar. These are considered incidental main motions. They need a second and are debatable. They are not in order if the action has already been carried out and is impossible to undo.

Debate can go to the merits of the original motion.

A motion can't be rescinded or amended:

- If someone makes the motion to reconsider the vote and it can be called up.

- If action on the motion has been carried out, and it is impossible to undo.

- When a resignation is acted upon and the person notified.

- When a person is elected to membership or expelled from membership and notified. (If expelled from membership, this person has to reapply according to the bylaws.)

- When an officer is elected to or removed from office and notified. (If a person is elected to office and the members want to rescind the action, they can do so if the bylaws permit this action.)

The vote requirements for rescinding or amending a motion previously adopted are as follows:

- With previous notice, it takes a majority vote.

- Without previous notice, it takes a two-thirds vote or a majority vote of the entire membership. The reason for such a high vote is to protect the rights of the absent members.

Giving previous notice is best, especially when the issue is controversial. To give previous notice, a member can request that the notice is included in the letter sent to the membership notifying them of the meeting; or, a member can give notice orally at the previous meeting.

To give previous notice at a meeting, a member states:

Member: Mr. President, I rise to give previous notice that at the next meeting I will make a motion to rescind the action that we give a donation to the Fourth Annual President's Night banquet.

Previous notice is never seconded. However, when the member makes the motion at the next meeting, it requires a second. The secretary records the previous notice in the minutes.

At the next meeting, the member rises and states the motion.

> **Member:** I move to rescind the action that we give a donation to the Fourth Annual President's Night banquet.
>
> **Members 2:** Second.
>
> **President:** It is moved and seconded to rescind the action that we give a donation to the Fourth Annual President's Night banquet. Because previous notice has been given, it takes a majority to adopt. Is there any discussion?

If the member did not give previous notice, the chair states:

> **President:** Because no previous notice has been given, this motion requires a two-thirds vote to adopt (or a majority of the entire membership, whichever is the easiest to obtain).

To phrase a motion to amend something previously adopted, a member says:

> **Member:** I move to amend the motion that was adopted to give $100 to Habitat for Humanity, by striking out $100 and inserting $200.
>
> **Member 2:** Second.
>
> **President:** It is moved and seconded to amend the motion that was adopted to give $100 to Habitat for Humanity, by striking out $100 and inserting $200. If adopted, we will give $200 to Habitat for Humanity. Is there any discussion on the proposed amendment?

Discharge a Committee

+ **Purpose:** For the assembly to take a matter out of the hands of a committee or subcommittee before its report is given so that the assembly can decide.

+ Needs a second.

+ Amendable.

+ Debatable. Debate can go to the merits of the question in the committee.

+ If no previous notice is given, either a two-thirds vote or a majority of the entire membership is needed, whichever is more practical to obtain. If previous notice is given, the motion requires a majority vote to adopt.

+ **Result:** If adopted, and if a motion was referred to the committee by a subsidiary motion, the motion is immediately placed before the assembly for discussion.

Note: If the committee fails to report at the time specified in the subsidiary motion, discharging a committee requires only a majority vote. Or, if the committee gives a partial report, members can discharge the committee by a majority vote.

The motion to discharge a committee is an incidental main motion and can be made only when no other business is pending. Use this motion only when a committee fails to report at the specified time or when something urgent comes up and the assembly needs to decide immediately. This motion is useful to prevent a motion or question from dying in committee.

> ***Member:*** Madam President, I move to discharge the committee to select new furniture for the office.
>
> ***Member 2:*** I second it.
>
> ***President:*** It is moved and seconded to discharge the committee to select new furniture for the office. Because no previous notice was given, this takes a two-thirds vote to adopt. Is there any discussion?

Part III

MEMBERSHIP

11

Officers

The bylaws of every organization should include a provision for officers. Each organization has the right to determine the number of officers, their duties, how they are elected, the term of office, and whether they can be removed from office, along with the reason and the stated procedure for removal.

This chapter looks in detail at the two offices that are essential to an efficient organization: those of the president and the secretary. It examines their duties, responsibilities, and limitations. Other topics in this chapter include the purpose and content of the minutes, the roles of the treasurer and the board, and the steps members can take to ensure the vitality and long life of the organization.

ELECTED OFFICERS

Officers are usually selected from an organization's membership. However, in some legislative bodies, the U.S. Senate for example, the president comes from outside the membership. In certain circumstances where a controversial issue is being discussed, members may want the option to hire the services of a nonmember — a professional presiding officer — to conduct the meeting.

When members become officers, they still retain all the rights that they had as regular members: the right to make motions, to debate, and to vote. However, a member serving as president must remain impartial. For this reason, rules exist that govern when the president can make a motion, participate in a debate, and vote.

Those people elected to office or appointed to a committee chairmanship are responsible for keeping records of their assignments and then giving those records to their successors. If an organization has a permanent facility, the permanent records of the society, meeting minutes, treasurer's books, checkbooks, and records of any investments should be kept at the facility — not taken home with the officers. Likewise, the organization's facility should offer the secretary and the treasurer a place to do their work. In a small organization, where the officers frequently keep the records of the society in their homes, the organization should make provisions to have these records returned to someone in the organization if that member is not re-elected to his or her office, resigns membership, or dies. A common problem in small organizations is getting the checkbook back from the treasurer or the minutes book back from the secretary if he or she is not re-elected to office or stops attending meetings.

When electing officers, the membership needs to take into consideration the reliability of the people being considered for office. Those elected to office need to seriously consider the obligations and duties of that office before accepting the position. If, during a term, an officer realizes that he or she cannot keep up with the demands of the office, the officer should either arrange for help with his or her duties or resign. If the officer resigns, all the documents entrusted to him or her should be returned at the same time as the officer's resignation letter. Should the officer be unable to return the documents in person, he should mail them to the secretary by certified mail with a return receipt. Doing so ensures that the records of the organization arrive safely.

Organizations need a minimum of two officers: a president and a secretary. The president presides at the meeting, and the secretary records the transactions of the meeting in the minutes.

THE PRESIDENT

The office of president and its duties vary according to how the organization is structured in the bylaws. Primarily, the office of president includes fulfilling a leadership role by setting goals or a specific tone for the organization during the term of office, performing administrative duties as assigned by the bylaws, and presiding at the meetings.

Whatever the structure of the organization, the president has authority to do only the things that are assigned to that office by the bylaws. Often, those elected to the office of president misunderstand their role in the organization and believe that the members have given them free reign to run the organization any way they please, thus setting up a dictatorship.

Setting Goals for the Organization

In some social or professional organizations, the president is the most important officer for determining the focus and action of the organization. Those running for the office of president may actually run on *platforms,* with members voting for candidates based on the philosophy, goals, or plans for the organization presented in their platforms. In other organizations, the primary responsibility of the president is presiding at meetings, while many of the administrative duties are invested in committees and the legislative power is vested in an executive board.

Performing Administrative Duties

The chief administrative duty of the president is to represent the organization. The president signs all legal documents; supervises the employees and the activities of the organization; represents, or speaks for, the organization; and presides at meetings. These duties vary between organizations and should be stated in the bylaws.

Presiding at Meetings

This section focuses on the president's responsibilities as a presiding officer and the rules that the president must follow when presiding at meetings.

The key duties of the presiding officer are to:

- Keep order.

- Be fair and impartial.
- Protect the rights of all the members.

Keeping order
To keep order in a meeting, the president should be thoroughly familiar with the bylaws, other rules of the organization, parliamentary procedure in general, and the organization's selected parliamentary authority in particular. The president has the following specific responsibilities:

- The president should be familiar with the basic rules of calling a meeting to order; how to establish and follow an agenda or order of business; the proper steps in making, debating, and voting on motions; and the different classes or types of motions and how they are ranked. (Part II of this book covers these basics.)

- The president and the secretary should prepare the agenda together. The president should be familiar with any unfinished business and any new business that must appear on the agenda. If the proposed business is controversial, the president can plan ahead for problems that may arise during the meeting and consult with a parliamentarian beforehand to learn how to handle the situation.

- If standing committees are to give reports, the president should call these committee members prior to the meeting to see if they have a report to give. At the meeting, the president should call on only those people who have indicated in advance that they have reports.

- The president should come to the meeting with paper and pencil to write down motions as the members make them. At the meeting, the president or the secretary should have a copy of the organization's bylaws, standing rules, rules of order, and the parliamentary authority. The president should have a thorough working knowledge of these governing documents.

- The president should call the meeting to order on time and determine that a quorum is present before proceeding with the meeting. (The president does not have to announce that a quorum is present.)

- The president should announce all business in the proper sequence and entertain every motion that is in order. If in doubt about why a member rises, the president can ask:

President: For what purpose does the member rise?

If the member rises to do something that is not in order at that time, asking this question allows the president to stop the incorrect procedure immediately without wasting the assembly's time. If it is in order, the president allows the member to proceed. This phrase keeps business going in the right direction.

- The president must state each legitimate motion for the purpose of discussion and for taking a vote. The president ensures the rights of the members to debate the motion by allowing each side fair representation during controversial issues and by keeping debate to its time limits. The president takes the vote on motions and knows the proper type of vote required for the different classes of motions. He or she announces the result of the vote so that all members know what action is taken and, if adopted, who is responsible for carrying out the action.

- The president should rule on any procedure that does not follow correct procedures (for example, motions that are not in order at a certain time, debate that gets off the subject, and any effort by members to deprive others of their rights to debate and make motions). The president must entertain all appeals to his or her rulings and let members vote on the appeal. The president has an obligation to answer any member's questions about the discussed business or any parliamentary inquiries about procedure.

- The president declares the meeting adjourned by vote of the assembly at the end of the program or in cases where an uncontrollable situation such as a riot takes place or when the health or safety of the members is in danger.

Ensuring fairness and impartiality

The most important principle that all presiding officers must remember is that they represent all the members, not just a select few and not just those with whom they agree. The duty of the presiding officer is to keep control of the meeting, but more than that it is to see that during debate, all the facts — pros and cons — come out in the discussion so that the assembly can make an informed decision. No member should feel that the presiding officer takes sides, but rather that the officer allows the assembly, through the democratic process, to arrive at the will of the majority. To ensure fairness and impartiality, the president adheres to the following rules:

- In a business meeting, the president cannot make motions or enter into debate.

  The president can enter into debate only if he or she leaves the chair and lets the vice president or another officer preside; that is, if the president gives up his or her function of presiding over the meeting. If the presiding officer steps down and enters debate, he or she must stay out of the chair (not return to presiding) until the motion has been disposed of either temporarily or finally.

  The president also steps down from the chair and lets the vice president or another officer preside when a motion has direct personal or monetary interest, or when he or she is censured. However, the presiding officer can stay in the chair during nominations and elections when he or she is a candidate for office or is being considered in a motion with others — for example, if there is a motion to send delegates to a convention and the president is nominated as one of the candidates.

- The president does not vote except in three situations: 1) if the president's vote would break a tie vote; 2) if the president's vote would create a tie vote; or 3) if the vote is taken by ballot (see Chapter 5).

- The president can give information, correct misinformation, and help members with parliamentary procedures. The president is obligated to help members phrase motions, even when he or she is opposed to the motion. When giving information or correcting misinformation, the president states: "The chair has information that . . . ." The chair should never say that a member is lying or wrong, but should simply state the facts and let the members decide what is the truth.

- If possible, the president sits down when a member is assigned the floor. If there is no place to sit, or if members can't see the president when he or she is seated, the president stands back from the lectern.

- The president is responsible for enforcing the rules and decorum of debate and alternating debate between the pros and cons in a controversial situation (see Chapter 4).

- The presiding officer always refers to himself or herself in the third person when talking to the members. For example, the presiding officer may say,

President: The chair rules the discussion is out of order at this time.

Protecting the rights of the members

A truly effective president protects the rights of the members by personally following the laws. The president upholds the bylaws and other rules of the organization and enforces them by informing the members when bylaws are ignored or disobeyed. The president rules out of order all motions that conflict with the bylaws and other governing documents of the organization, as well as any motions that violate local, state, or national government. If members propose a motion that conflicts with the bylaws, the president should rule the motion out of order and explain the procedure for amending the bylaws, if doing so is possible. If members propose a motion that violates parliamentary rules, the president should rule it out of order and then explain the proper procedure that helps the members accomplish their goals. To protect the rights of the members, the president has the following specific responsibilities:

■ The president protects the assembly from frivolous or dilatory motions (undemocratic ways of delaying business) and from any attempt by members to push an action through without following the democratic process. (See "Important Points to Remember Before Making a Motion," in Chapter 3.)

Dilatory practices that a president should look for are:

- A member calling for a division when it is very clear which side has won, or calling for a division after every vote that is taken.

- A member continually making the motion to adjourn for the purpose of obstructing business.

- A member making absurd motions or amendments.

- Several members raising *points of order* for no reason.

■ If members are using dilatory practices to obstruct the meeting, the chair needs to remain calm and courteous, but firm. The chair can do one of two things: not recognize the members or rule the motions out of order. However, the chair must not do either of these two things to speed up a meeting. These are strictly measures to take if a member is clearly being dilatory. The president's duty is to serve the wishes of the entire assembly, and he or she should not allow any personal feelings to affect his or her judgment.

■ The chair should know the procedures for calling to order a member who is unruly and disruptive. To call a member to order, the chair can say:

President: The member is out of order and will be seated.

If the member continues to misbehave, the president can ask the secretary to record in the minutes the objectional behavior or language. If the member does not quiet down or apologize for his or her behavior, the next step is to name the offender, which is called *preferring charges*. The president should use this option only as a last resort. If the president prefers charges, the president should state what the member has done. The assembly must then decide what action to take. If members do not readily come forth with a motion that sets a penalty, the president can ask:

President: What penalty shall be imposed on the member?

The membership must now propose a penalty. The motion is debatable, and the member facing the potential penalty has a right to speak to the motion. This motion takes a majority vote unless the motion takes away rights of membership, in which case a two-thirds vote is needed.

The president should try to resolve difficult situations without resorting to this procedure. If the conduct of a member gets out of hand, the president can always declare a recess and talk with the member during the recess to try to resolve the problem.

Becoming an Effective Presiding Officer

The president should cultivate certain qualities in order to be an effective presiding officer. In fact, every member of an organization should strive to represent these qualities, because at times (for example, when the president is absent) other members need to preside at a meeting. The primary qualities of an effective presiding officer are:

- Good judgment — knowing when to strictly enforce the rules and when strict enforcement impedes the flow of business.

- Teachability — the willingness to learn the correct procedures and to use them fairly and judiciously.

- Active listening skills — what are the members saying and what signals are they giving to the presiding officer to help the officer expedite business?

- Calmness — the ability to keep peace if the meeting becomes turbulent.

- Humility — not taking offense if the members correct what the presiding officer is doing or if they appeal from the decision of the chair.

- Firmness — staying the course and following proper procedures when necessary and not allowing members to take shortcuts when doing so impedes the rights of a member of the assembly.

Legal and Ethical Considerations

Although the president is given the power to sign legal documents and represent the society, he or she should never bind the society to contracts that the members have not agreed to by a vote; nor should the president speak to an issue in public without the permission of the society. By taking such actions without the society's permission, the president invites the members to begin proceedings for removal from office.

THE VICE PRESIDENT

The office of vice president might be called *president in training*. One of the specific parliamentary duties of the vice president is to preside when the president is unable to be at a meeting or when the president has to step down from the chair because he or she wishes to debate an issue. The vice president also presides if the president is being censured or if a motion is being made that concerns only the president.

Normally, the vice president takes over the office of president if that office is vacated for any reason. If an organization has more than one vice president, the vice presidential offices should be numbered in the bylaws. The bylaws should also state the order of succession if the office of president is declared vacant.

When the vice president presides, members address him or her as "Mr. President" or "Madam President." When the vice president and the president are both on the platform, members address the vice president as "Mr. Vice President" or

"Madam Vice President." If in doubt, "Mr." or "Madam Chairman" is also correct.

If the bylaws specifically say that the president is to appoint all committees, and the vice president is presiding when a member makes a motion to form a special committee, the vice president cannot appoint the committee members unless the bylaws provide for this particular rule's suspension. (Note that no other presiding member can make the appointments either.)

THE SECRETARY

Organizations need a minimum of two officers to conduct a meeting and to keep the organization together: the president and the secretary. Many people think that the president is the most important member of the organization. Others argue that the secretary is, because this officer is responsible for keeping all the records of the organization, preparing the agenda, handling correspondence, sending notices of meetings to members, taking and recording the minutes, and performing other administrative duties assigned by the organization.

In general, the secretary is responsible for:

- Keeping all the records of the organization (including committee reports) on file and keeping an up-to-date list of all the members.

- Notifying members of their election to office or appointment to committees, and furnishing them with the proper documents.

- Notifying members of election or of appointment as a delegate at a convention, and furnishing them with credentials.

- Signing all the minutes and other certified acts of the organization, unless the bylaws specify differently.

- Maintaining the official documents of the organization, including the bylaws, rules of order, standing rules, correspondence, and minutes. The secretary keeps the bylaws and other governing documents up-to-date with any changes made through the amendment process.

- Mailing members a notice for each forthcoming meeting.

- Taking minutes at all business and board meetings, handling the correspondence, and preparing the agenda for the meetings (unless the president prefers to do this). The secretary must know how to call a meeting to order if the president and vice president are absent and know how to preside until the assembly elects a temporary chairman.

- Bringing to each meeting the minutes book, bylaws, rules, membership list, a list of committees and their membership, the agenda, records, ballots, and any other necessary supplies.

If the secretary or any of the officers have duties other than those listed in the adopted parliamentary authority, the bylaws or standing rules should contain the additional duties.

Meeting Minutes

The question most frequently asked by someone who has just been elected or appointed to the office of secretary is, "What do I put in the minutes?" If a person asks enough parliamentarians, reads enough books on the subject, and consults various parliamentary authorities, he or she will find many viewpoints on this subject. The answer is to follow the recommendations of the organization's parliamentary authority and the wishes of the organization itself regarding the contents of the minutes. If the secretary is recording minutes for a legislative body, for example a city government, state codes may govern the content of the minutes.

The minutes should contain a record of what is done, not what is said. Minutes do not contain interjected personal comments or someone's opinion about what has happened. The assembly is responsible for approving and correcting the minutes. What the assembly approves is considered the final wording of the minutes. If someone finds a mistake in the minutes at any later time, the secretary can correct it by bringing it to the attention of the assembly. This is done by making the motion *amend something previously adopted,* or the chair can assume the motion and take the vote by general consent. Many times, the presiding officer, together with the secretary, reviews the minutes for accuracy and wording before the secretary puts them into final form. However, the president should not insist on a particular wording merely to make himself or herself look good or to change the outcome of decisions made.

If the minutes are published (for example, when minutes of public meetings of government bodies are sent to all the members), the minutes should contain, in addition to the standard information, a list of speakers on each side of the question, with an abstract text of each address. Also, committee reports and the action taken on them are printed in full. Recording such meetings is wise.

When writing the minutes, a good technique is to write so that anyone else reading the minutes is able to visualize what was done at the meeting. Write the minutes as soon as possible after the meeting while it is fresh in your mind. See Appendix C for an example of good meeting minutes.

The Structure of the Minutes

The secretary may ask, "Why do I need a thorough knowledge of parliamentary procedure simply to take the minutes?" If the secretary does not understand, for example, the ranking of motions or other key procedures, the minutes will not be accurate. For example, all adopted secondary motions — subsidiary, privileged, and incidental — must be recorded in the minutes. (The secretary who has a thorough knowledge of parliamentary procedure can also be of great help to the presiding officer when there is no parliamentarian present.) The following sections explain the contents of each part of the minutes.

The opening paragraph

The opening paragraph includes the following items:

- **Call to order:**
  - The name of the organization, the date and time, the place of meeting if different from the usual, and the kind of meeting — regular, special, or adjourned.
  - The fact that the regular presiding officer and the secretary were present — or the names of their substitutes.
  - The roll call (if required by the rules of order): those who are present and those absent, and whether any member comes late or leaves early. In board minutes, naming those present and those absent is always a good idea.

- **Approval of the minutes of previous meeting(s):** What action was taken on the minutes of the previous meeting (*approved as read* or *corrected*). The secretary should record corrections in the minutes of both meetings, that is in the minutes where the mistake was found, and in the minutes of the meeting where they were read.

  For example, the minutes for a meeting on August 3 read: "The minutes of the meeting on July 3 were corrected to read 'the balance in the treasury is $500.' The minutes were approved as corrected."

  The secretary then corrects the minutes for July 3 by drawing a line through the mistake, writing above the mistake "$500," and initialing it.

The body of the minutes

The following items are included in the body of the minutes, with or without headings:

- **Reports of officers and committees:** The fact that the reports of officers, boards, and standing and special committees were given, and what action was taken, if any. Occassionally, secretaries will include a brief summary of the committee reports, if they give information about the year's work. Some minutes give the entire treasurer's report, and some just give beginning and ending balances. Members should decide how much of the treasurer's report they want in the minutes. If the members receive a copy of the treasurer's report, perhaps only the beginning balance, total income, total expenditures, and the ending balance need to go into the minutes.

- **Special orders — election of officers:** When nominations and elections are being recorded, the names presented by the nominating committee are recorded first, and then the names of those nominated from the floor. In reporting the vote, the secretary includes the tellers' committee report — a record of all the candidates and how many votes each received — in the minutes. The chair's declaration of each member elected is then recorded. (For an example of a teller's report and how the president handles it, see Chapter 12, "Election by Ballot Vote" and "Teller's Sheet and Report.") The number of votes each nominee received is also recorded in the minutes, as well as a statement of the term of office.

Here's an example of problems that arise when details are left out of the minutes. An organization elected board members for a three-year term. It elected two board members in odd years, and three members in even years. Some board members moved and left the organization, which created vacancies that had to be filled. Because the organization didn't record in the minutes which members were elected at which time, the members didn't know if they were electing members to fill a full three-year term or a shorter remaining term. The lesson here is obviously to be specific in recording elections in the minutes.

- **Unfinished business:** The minutes should include unfinished business only if there was unfinished business on the agenda. The minutes should state what action was taken on business that carried over from the previous meeting.

- **New Business:**

  - The name of the maker of a motion but not the person who seconds it — unless doing so is customary or the group desires it.

  - The final wording of all main motions (with amendments incorporated) and all motions that bring a question back before the assembly. Also, what happened to each motion — whether it was adopted, lost, or temporarily disposed of. If a motion was withdrawn, it is not recorded. (However, if a motion has been postponed to another meeting and then withdrawn, note this fact in the minutes so that there is some record of the disposition of the motion.)

    If a motion was laid on the table and not taken from the table at the same meeting, record this fact in the minutes. Also, the motions to *postpone* and *refer to a committee* should be included in the minutes, if they were adopted.

    Note: When an assembly adopts a motion that is of a continuing nature (for example, changing the time of the meeting, buying plaques for outgoing officers, giving money to an organization on a yearly basis, having a yearly dance, or setting a function at a certain time), such motions should also be recorded in a notebook of *standing rules*. These motions are ongoing and can be rescinded or amended only by previous notice and a majority vote, or by a two-thirds vote without notice. They are easier to find if kept in a separate document because the secretary does not have to go through all the minutes to find the original motion. These motions are numbered when put in the standing rules.

  - Secondary motions that are adopted. If the motion to recess is adopted, the minutes should state what time the members recessed and what time the meeting was called back to order.

- **Program and announcements:** The following items are grouped together in separate paragraphs and come at the end of the minutes:

  - Speaker: The name of the guest speaker and the program, if there is one. Make no effort to summarize points given by the speaker.

  - Previous notice: All previous notice of motions and their content. For example, if someone gives previous notice to rescind or amend a previous action, the minutes should record that "Member X gave previous notice that, at the next meeting, she will rescind . . . (include here the approximate wording of what the member proposes to rescind)." See "Rescind and Amend Something Previously Adopted" in Chapter 10.

  - Announcements: Any important announcements, such as the chair announces that the time and the location of the next meeting will differ from the norm.

Other important items to include

These items are included in the minutes as they occur:

- **The results of a counted or a balloted vote.** If a counted vote is ordered or if a ballot vote is taken during the meeting, the votes on each side should be recorded in the minutes. However, the votes are not recorded if the organization has a rule or tradition that they are not. If a roll call vote is taken, record the names of those voting on each side and those answering "present."

- **The fact that the assembly has gone into a committee of the whole or quasi committee of the whole, and its report.** For further information, see "Committee (or Quasi-Committee) of the Whole" in Chapter 7.

- **All points of order and the chair's ruling.** Also recorded are all appeals and whether they were sustained or lost.

Adjournment and signature of the secretary

The last paragraph of the minutes contains the hour of adjournment. The last item on the minutes is the signature and title of the person who took the minutes. The president signs if customary or desired by the assembly. (The person signing can omit the traditional phrase "respectfully submitted.")

Approval of and Corrections to the Minutes

The minutes of the previous meeting are read immediately after the call to order and the opening ceremonies. (If an assembly meets quarterly, the minutes of an annual meeting are approved at the next regular meeting or by a committee appointed to approve the minutes.)

The minutes are usually approved by general consent, and they can be approved as read or as corrected. Minutes may be corrected whenever an error is found, regardless of the time that has elapsed. To correct the minutes after they have been approved requires a two-thirds vote, unless previous notice has been given.

Nothing is ever erased from the minutes. Corrections are made in the margin. (If the minutes are double-spaced, the secretary can write the correction above the incorrect information.) When material is expunged, a line is drawn through the words that are to be expunged. Crossed out material should still be readable.

When minutes are approved, the word "approved" and the secretary's initials and date of the approval are written next to the signature of the secretary. Alternatively, a line can be provided at the bottom of the page that says "approval date." For an example of minutes in finished form, see Appendix C.

Finalized Form of the Minutes

These days, very few secretaries write the minutes by hand in a bound ledger book with numbered pages. The pen has given way to the computer, so organizations need to find ways to keep their minutes on consecutively numbered pages, and have them bound yearly.

When writing the minutes, each subject is a separate paragraph. Some parliamentarians recommend putting headings at the top of each new paragraph. Examples include "Reports of Officers and Committees," "Reports," "Unfinished Business," "New Business," and so on. Some secretaries leave a wide margin and then put a short summary of the paragraph in the margin. Doing this enables those looking at the minutes months or years later to easily find the item for which they are searching. However you choose to construct the minutes, be consistent.

Having the minutes carefully reviewed for accuracy, spelling, and grammar before putting them in their final form is a good idea.

Carrying out the Actions in the Minutes

Often the members of an organization adopt motions that require someone to do something. For example, they may refer a motion to a committee to investigate and report back at the next meeting. Or they may vote to buy a computer and indicate that the finance committee should buy it. The secretary is responsible for taking this information from the minutes and giving it to the proper people. A motion to *refer to a committee* should be typed out and given to the committee chairman with the proper instructions. If the finance committee is to buy a computer, the secretary gives the exact motion that was adopted to that committee. The secretary must be diligent in seeing that the assembly's wishes are carried out.

THE TREASURER

The treasurer is responsible for receiving and disbursing the money of the organization. The bylaws should state the treasurer's general duties and responsibilities; the standing rules should state the treasurer's administrative duties. Depending on the complexity of the organization, the treasurer's duties vary.

The Treasurer's Duty in Small Clubs

In small clubs where dues are the primary source of income and where there are not many expenditures, the treasurer's job is relatively simple. The duties may include:

- Receiving and depositing dues in the club's bank account. (A treasurer should *never* keep club monies in his or her personal account.)

- Giving members receipts for their dues.

- Paying the bills that the club has voted to pay (by writing checks or following whatever other process the organization has set up to pay bills).

- Giving a report at the meetings.

- Keeping records that will allow a committee to audit the books at the end of the fiscal year. For example, the treasurer should record which members have paid their dues and when bills are paid (and the check number of the payment).

- Balancing and reconciling the checking account.

The Treasurer's Report in Small Clubs

In a small club, the treasurer usually gives his or her report orally, and it can be very simple. Here are examples of two ways the treasurer's report can be written (the second itemizes all expenditures):

TREASURER'S REPORT

Balance on hand April 1, 1998	$350.00
Total receipts (income)	$15.00
Total disbursements	$5.00
Balance on hand April 31, 1998	$360.00

TREASURER'S REPORT

Balance on hand April 1, 1998	$450.00
Income/Receipts	$165.00
Dues	$15.00
Fundraising	$150.00
Disbursements/Expenditures	$30.00
Postage	$15.00
Printing	$12.00
Telephone	$3.00
Balance on hand April 30, 1998	$585.00

In either case, the treasurer signs the bottom of the written report.

The treasurer's report is not approved by the assembly but is filed for audit. The auditor's report is then approved. (See Chapter 2, "Calling the Meeting to Order" and "Reports of Officers.")

The Treasurer's Duty in Larger Organizations

In larger organizations with employees, the treasurer is responsible for payroll, including deducting social security and income taxes. If the organization is incorporated and owns property, the treasurer is required to file applicable local, state, and federal taxes.

When working for a larger organization, the treasurer should be versed in bookkeeping and/or accounting practices. The treasurer's reports are probably more detailed than those in a small organization.

Duties may also include preparing and submitting a budget for approval. If the treasurer is to handle large sums of money, he or she should be bonded (insured) to protect the organization from loss.

The budget

Many organizations work from a yearly budget. Usually the treasurer prepares the budget with the help of the financial committee, the committee chairmen, and perhaps the executive board. The budget is then submitted to the members for approval. A budget is a guide for spending; it is not set in stone. It can be amended by the members when it is presented for adoption, and even after it is adopted.

Usually, when a bill is received that is within the budget, the person responsible for that budget item, such as a committee chairman, signs the bill as approved and gives it to the treasurer for payment. For example: The Buildings and Grounds Committee has a budget of $2,000 for painting. When bids were taken for painting, the lowest bid was $1,950. A contract was signed and when the job was completed, a bill was received for $1,950. The chairman of the Building and Grounds Committee approves the bill by signing his name and writing the words "approved for payment," and sends it to the treasurer who then pays the bill. However, some organizations may still require membership approval for the expenditure to be paid even though it is within a budgeted amount.

If the budget has not allotted enough for painting, and the lowest bid is for $2,050, the chairman of the Building and Grounds Committee must get membership approval for the additional expense before contracting for the painting.

If an organization does not work from a budget, each expenditure must have prior approval by the membership unless an organization has a rule stating differently. In this situation, the Building and Grounds Committee would get estimates for painting and submit them to the membership for a vote. After the membership decides on which bid to accept, the Building and Grounds Committee chairman can then enter into a contract with the company, and the work can be done. When the bill is received and the committee is satisfied with the work done, the treasurer pays the bill.

The audit

An audit of the treasurer's books is important to ensure the accuracy of the treasurer's reports. An audit protects both the treasurer and the organization. The auditor may uncover sloppy bookkeeping practices or even recommend a better way of doing things.

The auditor's report is an endorsement of the financial report, and it relieves the treasurer of any responsibility for the period covered by the report, except for fraud. Treasurers should insist that books are audited once a year, and anyone newly elected to the office should not accept unaudited books. Small organizations should appoint an audit committee. In larger organizations, independent accountants should do the audit.

BOARDS

Boards are considered deliberative assemblies. This means that they have the authority to meet to determine courses of action taken in the name of the organization.

Robert's Rules of Order, Newly Revised (Perseus Books) defines a board this way:

> An administrative, managerial, or quasi-judicial body of elected or appointed persons which has the character of a deliberative assembly with the following variations:
>
> (a) boards have no minimum size and are frequently smaller than most other assemblies;
>
> (b) while a board may or may not function autonomously, its operation is determined by responsibilities and powers delegated to it or conferred on it by authority outside itself.

A board may come in any size. It may be a governmental body that makes laws for a village, or it may be the governing body of a corporation. Within a club, it may be a body that has been given administrative powers for the organization.

All boards are set up by some enactment. In public bodies, they are brought into existence by state legislatures or by county and local governments. In incorporated organizations, they are usually brought into existence by the corporation charter. In small unincorporated organizations, they are established in the bylaws.

A board may have various names, such as *board of directors, board of trustees, board of managers,* or *executive board.* For an organization to have a board, there must be a provision in the bylaws. If provisions aren't in the bylaws, no small group of members can act like a board.

Bylaws and Boards

Boards get their powers and duties from bylaws and can only do what the bylaws allow. A board is primarily the administrative arm of an organization, and it transacts the business of the organization between regular meetings.

Board membership is defined in the bylaws. Bylaws should set the quorum of the board, specify how vacancies are filled, define how vacancies are created, set the number of board members, explain their duties, and determine how often the board meets.

The bylaws should also state who comprises the board. Usually, the board consists of the officers and committee chairmen and a few elected directors. Or the board may be composed of members elected by the membership, who in turn elect their own officers from the members of the board. Usually the president and the secretary of an organization serve on the board in the same capacity as they do in the regular membership meetings.

Boards cannot disobey the orders of the assembly or act outside of their prescribed duties. Unless the bylaws specifically give a particular authority to the board, the assembly can counteract any action of the board.

Board meetings

Board meetings are usually held in *executive session* (closed to the membership) unless the bylaws state that the meetings are open to members. The minutes of the board meetings are not made public to the membership unless the board members vote to let the membership read the minutes or unless the membership indicates by a two-thirds vote (or with previous notice a majority vote) to have the board minutes read.

These guidelines, however, do not mean that the board keeps its activities secret. The board should give a periodic report of its activities to the members. When drafting bylaws, an organization should carefully consider how much power it assigns to the board.

For example, in homeowners' associations, the board members usually make all the decisions for the association. Often, the only power the members of the association have is the ability to elect members to the board. This can lead to tyranny. Therefore, members should select board members for their understanding of democratic principles, especially the concept of *consent of the governed. Consent of the governed* means that power rests with the people. The reason those elected can govern is because the members say they can. The members have consented to the way they are governed by the rules they have established. And they can change the way they are governed by amending the bylaws, removing those elected from office, and reversing actions adopted by the board. This concept is the basis for representative democracy.

Everything said at board meetings is confidential, and board members should respect this and not tell other members what has transpired until the entire membership hears the report. Individual board members cannot speak for the entire board.

All board members are equal, but the chairman presides at the meetings. The chair does not have more power than any other board member unless the bylaws give it to him or her. (See Chapter 16 for specific procedures.)

When a board is established so that a portion of its membership is elected each year, in effect it becomes a new board each year. Any business that was pending, or left unfinished, at the meeting prior to new members' assuming their positions does not carry over to the next meeting. It must be presented as new business. If the board chooses its own officers or is responsible for appointing committees, the new board immediately selects its officers and its committees. Neither the previous officers nor committee chairman and committee members carry over.

Those elected to the board, especially in governmental bodies such as school boards or village boards, should remember that compromise is a key element in serving on the board. Board members should work for the good of the entire organization, not for the agenda of one group or special interest. Too often people run on a platform, and when they accomplish their agenda, they lose interest in the rest of the board's proceedings.

Serving on a board is a privilege. Each board member should be thoroughly familiar with the governing documents of the organization, as well as parliamentary law and procedures.

Open meeting laws

Some organizations — for example, homeowner and condo associations and public bodies such as school boards, city councils, and county boards — are subject to open meeting laws in state statutes. When a board is subject to these laws, it means that non-board members can attend the meetings. They do not have the right to participate in the meetings unless the board allows time for them to do so. However, they do have a right to attend the meetings, listen to the discussion, and hear how the board members vote. They also have a right to read the minutes of these meetings. When such boards allow discussion or comments from the audience, it is done under the direction of the presiding officer and the rules that the board has adopted. Debate is often limited and discussion must be kept relevant to the topic under discussion. The board has the right to cut off the public discussion when it sees fit. Those who speak in such discussions must remember to direct their remarks to the presiding officer and not to the audience. Both sides should conduct this part of the meeting with civility.

However, there are times when bodies subject to open meeting laws need to meet in *executive session*. This means that the meeting is closed to the public; only board members can attend. Board members should be familiar with the state statutes that grant this power so they understand under what circumstance they are allowed to go into executive session. These boards can go into executive session only under the conditions stated in the law. If they use executive session as a way to keep the public out of a meeting, they may be sued.

To go into executive session, a member of the board needs to make a motion and state the reason for going into executive session. (The secretary should record this motion in the minutes.) The board members then discuss the motion and take a vote. A majority vote is required to adopt this motion. If the board goes into executive session, it should be for discussion only. Any action a board wants to take should be done when the board members return to the open portion of the meeting. This way the action is recorded in the minutes for all to read. Anything said in executive session is confidential. Members can punish any member who discloses what was said in executive session. See Chapter 16, "Executive Sessions."

Ex Officio Board Members

Many organizations have *ex officio* board members. *Ex officio* means "by virtue of office"; in other words, the member serves on the board because he or she holds a certain office either within the organization or in the community. For example, if the bylaws state that the president of the state organization shall be an ex officio board member of the local branch of that organization, that person becomes a member of the board because he or she is the state president. When the member's term as state president ends, his or her term as ex officio board member also ends, and the new state president becomes the ex officio member. Another way members become ex officio members is by virtue of some office that they hold in the community. Sometimes a mayor is asked to serve as an ex officio member of a board even though he or she is not a member of the organization.

The most frequently asked question about ex officio members is, "Can ex officio members vote?" If an ex officio board member is a regular member of the organization, there is no distinction between the ex officio member and the other board members. The ex officio board member is counted in the quorum and has the right to make motions, debate motions, and vote on all questions. If an ex officio member is not a member of the society, he or she is not counted in the quorum. However, the ex officio member still has the right to make motions, debate motions, and vote on all questions.

When the bylaws state that "the president is an ex officio member of all committees," the president is not counted in the quorum of any committees because it would be too difficult to attend all the committee meetings. But if the president attends the meeting, he or she has the right to make motions, discuss motions, and vote on all questions.

When a person is appointed an ex officio member by virtue of holding a public office (such as mayor), his or her membership on the board or committee ceases when the term in office expires.

Handling Resignations

In the course of an organization's work, boards and officers may be confronted with the resignation of a fellow officer, board member, or committee chairman. There are two reasons people resign from office. The first reason is that something arises in the personal life of the officer that demands his or her time and attention. The officer feels at this time that he or she can't fulfill the duties of the office and do justice to the organization, so the officer submits a resignation. The second reason is that there is a rift or severe disagreement within the organization. An officer may become angry, disheartened, or vengeful, so he or she submits a resignation.

The first thing that the organization should do after it receives a resignation is to figure out why the person is resigning. If the organization really needs this person's active input, it should find a way to keep him or her. If the person is resigning because of lack of time, then perhaps the organization can appoint an assistant to help with the work. If the person is resigning because he or she can't attend the meetings, the organization should consider changing the meeting date and time.

If the person submits his or her resignation because of organizational problems, the organization needs to look at how its members communicate with each other. Perhaps the members need to be more willing to allow disagreements and hear what others are saying. If an organization strictly obeys the principle of majority rule while protecting the rights of the minority, it can resolve problems in an intelligent, kind, and civil way.

A resignation should be a formal letter that includes the date, a name to whom it is addressed, the reason for the resignation, and the person's signature. The person resigning can mail his or her letter to the secretary or hand it to the secretary in person.

Under no circumstance should the secretary or president accept a verbal resignation. If a resignation is given to the officer this way, he or she should talk with the person and find out the reasons for the resignation. Perhaps just talking to the person can solve the problem. However, if the person insists on resigning, the person should put it in writing and submit it to the secretary. This gives the accepting body something to read and consider. Every resignation should be put to a vote. When it is accepted, the office is vacant and should be immediately filled according to the rules for filling vacancies stated in the bylaws.

If an officer submits a resignation and then decides to withdraw it, he or she can do this until a vote is taken. It is unjust for a secretary or governing body not to allow a withdrawal of the resignation before a vote is taken. The only way a resignation can't be withdrawn is if some rule of the organization or a state statute prohibits it.

When submitting the resignation, the member resigning should give it to the secretary only and not mail it to everyone in the organization. (An e-mail resignation is not acceptable because it is not signed.) Sending the resignation to every member only confuses matters and promotes gossip and conjecture in the organization. If the member later decides to withdraw his or her resignation, there is much more explaining to do. The other members may see this person as unstable and not worthy of the position.

PASSING THE TORCH

In each Olympic ceremony, before the games begin, we see the dramatic lighting of the Olympic flame by a torch that was lit in Greece and carried by plane, by boat, and on foot to the location of the present games.

Members of an organization may be fired up with this Olympic flame of enthusiasm when they first start meeting and working, but as the torch passes from one administration to another this enthusiasm often wanes.

How can organizations keep their members and officers alight with enthusiasm? Here are some suggestions:

- Have officer training sessions for new officers.
- Listen to the members and meet their needs.
- Recognize and use the talents of all the members.

Perhaps you are in an organization that elects officers and then says, "Here's last year's file, a list of your duties, and a copy of *Robert's Rules*. Good luck!" The newly elected officer or committee chairman scratches his or her head and says, "Now what do I do?"

How often have you met long-term members who expect everyone to know as much as they know, and who criticize the efforts of those who don't intuitively know what to do? These same long-term members often don't offer any guidance or training to new officers or new members.

Successful organizations know that a productive, happy membership requires investment in the members. These organizations have training sessions for new officers, they appoint mentors to explain the ropes to new members, and they listen to the reasons why people have joined the organization and then try to meet those needs.

An officer training session may include the following:

- A meeting between the outgoing officer and the new officer, so the outgoing officer can go over files, explain duties, and share the things that worked or didn't work.

(It is important for the outgoing officers and committee chairmen to give their files to incoming officers and committee chairmen.)

- A group training session in which the outgoing officers explain to all the new officers how the organization works. It may also include individual officer training.

- On-the-job training in conducting meetings, taking minutes, and writing and giving officer reports.

Each organization should come up with a plan for training new officers. Members are more likely to serve if they feel competent in performing the tasks at hand. By investing time and effort in training officers, the transition from one administration to the next will be less painful.

12

Nominations and Elections

In every organization, the process of nominating and electing officers and board members is very important, and the bylaws should clearly state the procedure. If the procedure is not stated in the bylaws, a member of the assembly can make a motion explaining the procedure to follow. The assembly then decides by a majority vote whether to follow the proposed procedure.

This chapter explains the nominating and election process from start to finish. It discusses the various ways organizations nominate a candidate and take votes. The chapter also describes the duties of the *tellers' committee* — those members appointed to count the vote. Likewise, the chapter takes you step by step through the teller's sheet and report.

NOMINATIONS

An organization can nominate candidates in several ways:

- By a nominating committee
- From the floor
- By ballot
- By mail
- By petition

Most often, a nominating committee presents nominations, and the assembly has the opportunity to present additional nominations from the floor. The nominating process should not be confused with the election to office. *Robert's Rules of Order* states that a person does not have to be nominated to be elected to office. If the vote is taken by ballot, there is always the opportunity to write in a name. In this case, a person can win as a write-in candidate without ever being nominated.

Nominations by Committee

Many organizations have a nominating committee. The bylaws should specify the composition of this committee and how it is selected. The nominating committee is the one committee a president should not be a member of or help to select. If at all possible, the board or the membership should elect the nominating committee.

Duties of a nominating committee

The duty of a nominating committee is to find the best candidate for each office. The bylaws should not tie the hands of the committee to find more than one person to fill each slot; the committee should find the best candidate for each office. Persons serving on the committee can be nominated for office.

The secretary should give the committee a copy of the membership list, the bylaws, a description of the duties of each office, and the eligibility requirements. The committee must carefully review the eligibility requirements for each office and see that the nominees meet these requirements. If anyone is elected, and it is discovered after the election that the person is not eligible, the election of that officer is null and void. The committee then has to find a new nominee, and the members have to vote again.

The committee should meet, carefully review the membership list, and select the people who they think will do the best job in each office. A member of the committee should then be designated to call each nominee to see if he or she is willing to serve if elected. If someone is not willing to serve, the committee needs to meet again and find another candidate.

If no candidate is found, the committee can leave that slot open for nominations from the floor. Or, they can tell members publicly that they do not have a nominee for a certain office; this allows members to volunteer. No one should be nominated without his or her consent because, if elected, the person may decline to serve and members will have to hold another election.

Report of the nominating committee
The report of the nominating committee is usually given under "special orders." When called on to give the report, the chairman of the nominating committee states the nominations for each office.

> ***Chairman of Nominating Committee:*** Madam President, the nominating committee submits the following nominations: for president, Judy Smith; for vice president, Dave Jones; for secretary, Ricky Shores; and for treasurer, Sarah Thomas. *[hands the nominations written on a sheet of paper to the president and sits down]*

Sometimes there is a split in the nominating committee over who to nominate. If a minority of the committee wishes to nominate someone else, the members in the minority can make the nomination when nominations are taken from the floor.

As soon as the committee reports, it is discharged from its duties. Sometimes the committee is revived to make nominations to fill vacancies. After the committee reports, the chair states:

> ***President:*** The nominating committee nominates Judy Smith for president, Dave Jones for vice president, Ricky Shores for secretary, and Sarah Thomas for treasurer. Nominations are now open from the floor. Are there any further nominations for president?

Nominations from the Floor
As soon as the president opens nominations from the floor, any member can bring forth a nomination. However, the rules for a member nominating a candidate are the same as for the nominating committee. A member should know beforehand if the person he or she wishes to nominate is both eligible and willing to serve.

When the nomination is from the floor:

- A member does not have to get recognition, and often in small assemblies, a member can call out a name while still seated.

- A person can nominate himself or herself.

- A nomination does not need a second.

- A member can be nominated for more than one office.

- A member can't nominate more than one person for an office until everyone has had the opportunity to make nominations.

- Nominees do not have to leave the room during the nominations, when the vote is taken, or when the vote is counted.

- The presiding officer can continue presiding, even if he or she is one of the nominees for the office.

- A member can rise and decline the nomination during the nominating process.

- After each nomination, the president repeats the name to the assembly. For example, the president says:

  President: Denise Harmon, for president. Are there further nominations for president?

- A motion to close nominations is usually not necessary unless it is apparent that members are nominating people just to honor them, and that the nominees have no intention of serving.

- Usually the president closes nominations when no further nominations come forward from the assembly.

If at any time during the nominating process a member realizes that he or she will be unable to serve if elected, the member should stand and request that his or her name be removed from nomination. Removing your name during the nomination process is better than waiting until after you are elected.

Nominations by Ballot

Instead of taking nominations from the floor, an organization may take nominations by ballot. In this process, each member is given a nominating ballot and writes the name(s) of one or more candidates on it. The tellers' committee counts the ballots and writes a list of the nominees to give to the president to announce. A vote is then taken for election. The nominating ballot should never become the electing ballot.

Nominations by Mail

When members are widely scattered, taking nominations by mail may be helpful. The secretary is responsible for mailing a nominating ballot to each member, with instructions on how to fill it out. After the members mail back the nominations, the secretary composes the ballot from which the members vote.

Nominations by Petition

Sometimes an organization's bylaws provide for nominations by petition. In this case, a nominee must be nominated by a signed petition of members before the nomination is put on the ballot. The nominating petition may be enclosed with a newsletter or mailed to the members.

Other Nominating Procedures

If the bylaws do not state how to conduct nominations, any member can make a motion proposing a nominating process. This motion is an incidental main motion. It needs a second and is not debatable but is amendable. It requires a majority vote to adopt. The best practice, however, is for the bylaws to state the procedure.

Nominations and the Minutes

The secretary places all nominations in the minutes. If the organization uses a nominating committee and then takes nominations from the floor, the secretary records the nominating committee's report first and then lists nominations for each office in the order they are presented as given by the members from the floor.

MOTIONS RELATING TO NOMINATIONS

When nominations are taken from the floor, usually the president closes the nominations by unanimous consent. However, there may be times when members nominate people just to honor them or to delay the election. In this case, it is appropriate for a member to make a motion to close the nominations. After the nominations are closed, a member can make a motion to reopen them. The following sections discuss these two motions.

Close the Nominations

+ **Purpose:** To close the nominations and take the vote immediately.

+ Is not in order when another member has the floor.

+ Needs a second.

+ Amendable.

+ Not debatable.

+ Requires a two-thirds vote.

+ Can't be reconsidered.

+ **Result:** Nominations are closed and voting begins.

This motion requires a two-thirds vote because it takes away the members' right to nominate. A two-thirds vote also protects the assembly from an abuse of power from a temporary majority who would like to stop the nominating process. A member must make the motion to close the nominations when no one has the floor. A rising vote is always taken on this motion.

Member: Madam President, I move to close the nominations.

Member 2: Second.

President: It is moved and seconded to close the nominations. All those in favor, please rise. Be seated. Those opposed please rise. Be seated.

If the affirmative has the vote, the president states:

> *President:* There is a two-thirds vote in the affirmative. The motion is carried and nominations are now closed. We will now take the vote for . . . *[state the office].*

If the negative has it, the president states:

> *President:* There is less than a two-thirds vote in the affirmative. The motion is lost and nominations are still open. Are there further nominations?

The president continues with the nominations until members are ready to vote. After progress in the meeting, members can make the motion to close nominations again.

Reopen the Nominations

+ **Purpose:** Reopen the nominations so others can be considered for office.

+ Needs a second.

+ Amendable.

+ Not debatable.

+ Requires a majority vote.

+ A negative vote can be reconsidered.

+ **Result:** Members can propose more nominees.

The time at which nominations are to be closed or reopened can be stated in the motion or added by amendment.

Because members' rights are not infringed upon by reopening the nominations, this motion requires only a majority vote, and a voice vote is taken. To reopen the nominations, a member can make the motion when no one has the floor. The member states:

Member: Madam President, I move to reopen the nominations.

Member 2: I second it.

President: It is moved and seconded to reopen the nominations. All those in favor say "Aye." Those opposed say "No."

The president then announces the vote. If the ayes have it, the president says:

President: The ayes have it and the motion is carried. We will reopen the floor for nominations. Are there further nominations?

If the noes have it, the president says:

President: The noes have it and the motion is lost. Nominations are closed and we will take the vote.

UNDEMOCRATIC PRACTICES IN THE NOMINATION AND ELECTION PROCESS

Members should be alert to some undemocratic political practices in organizations. One example occurs if a person is elected and then resigns, the office is considered vacant, and the president or board fills it by appointment instead of having another election. Doing this may allow an unpopular or hand-picked candidate to get the office even though he or she was not elected.

In writing the nomination, election, and vacancy conditions in the bylaws, the organization should make sure that if a vacancy is created early in the term of office, the vacancy is filled by election instead of by appointment, whenever possible. However, in some national organizations that meet yearly or biennially (every two years), this is difficult.

Another problematic practice to watch out for is nominating someone for office who is not eligible. When nominations are taken from the floor or when a nominating ballot is used, a good practice is to provide the members with an eligibility list so that they are not nominating people who will not be able to serve. When the secretary mails the members a notice about the nomination and election meeting, the letter can include a request that members who do not wish to be considered for office notify the secretary in writing. When the secretary prepares the eligibility list for the meeting, only those members who are willing to serve are on the list.

ELECTIONS

After the nominating process is finished, the members must vote on the proposed candidates. If the bylaws do not state how the vote is to be taken, a member can make an incidental motion regarding how to take the vote.

If the bylaws state that the vote must be taken by ballot, even if there is only one candidate for each office, members must nevertheless vote by ballot. A ballot vote allows members to write in a candidate's name. Asking one person (for example, the secretary) to cast the electing ballot for the entire assembly is out of order. Such a motion takes away members' rights to write in a candidate.

Members can take the vote for election by

- Voice
- Ballot
- Roll call
- Cumulative voting

Election by Voice Vote

When there is only one candidate for office, election by voice vote is a good method to use if the bylaws do not stipulate how the election should take place. However, any time an election occurs by voice vote, members forfeit their right to write in a candidate.

When more than one person has been nominated and the election is by voice vote, the chair takes the vote on the candidates in the order in which they were nominated. Members must remember to vote *yes* for the candidate that they want and vote *no* for the other candidates. The first candidate to receive a majority vote wins.

The presiding officer takes the vote this way:

> **President:** All those in favor of Member G for president, say "Aye." Those opposed say "No."

The president then announces the vote:

> **President:** The ayes have it, and Member G is elected president.

If Member G loses, the chair announces the result this way:

> **President:** The noes have it, and Member G is not elected. All those in favor of Member X for president say "Aye." Those opposed say "No."

The president then announces the results of this vote. The procedure continues until someone receives a majority vote. When electing officers, if there is a tie vote or no one receives a majority vote, members keep voting until someone is elected.

When more than one candidate is nominated, the problem with a voice vote is that those nominated first are more likely to get elected. If there is a motion to make an election by voice vote unanimous, that vote must be by ballot. If there is one "no" vote, the election is not unanimous.

Election by Ballot Vote

Organizations can take a ballot vote two ways:

- A slate of all the officers can appear on one ballot.
- Individual ballots can be provided for each office after nominations for that office are closed.

Slated ballots

Large organizations, such as conventions, usually prepare a printed ballot listing the names of all the candidates, with room for further nominations or write-ins from the membership.

Members go to the polls once. When no candidate receives a majority vote for a particular office or for several offices, members must continue to vote on those offices until someone is elected. With this kind of ballot, having the election early in the meeting is best. In the event that another vote is needed, members can vote again before the convention or meeting adjourns.

Individual ballots

In the second way of taking a ballot vote, the tellers' committee gives members a blank piece of paper after nominations have been closed for an office. The members write the name of the person they wish to see elected for that office on the blank piece of paper. The tellers then collect the ballots and count them, and the chair of the tellers' committee reads the report. The president declares who is elected and proceeds to take nominations for the next office. After nominations are closed, the tellers again give members blank ballots to write the candidate of their choice. They collect the ballots and count them, and the chairman reads the report. This goes on until the members elect someone to each office.

Individual balloting works well in small organizations where members can pause briefly to count the ballots without taking a recess or proceeding with other business.

Members do not proceed to the next office until they elect someone for the unelected office. For example, if no one receives a majority vote for the office of president, the members keep voting until they elect someone. They proceed to vote on the office of vice president only after they have elected a president.

In cases where members are voting on several directors at one time, those receiving a majority are elected to office. If any positions are not elected on the first ballot, the members keep voting on the rest of the candidates until the positions are filled. If more candidates receive a majority vote than there are positions available, those candidates receiving the highest votes are considered elected. For example, the Soccer Club has an executive board of five people. Seven people are nominated, and the members are instructed to vote for five candidates on the same ballot. There are 20 people present and voting. It takes 11 votes to elect. The following candidates received this number of votes:

> Candidate Smith, 14 votes
>
> Candidate Jones, 15 votes
>
> Candidate Baker, 19 votes
>
> Candidate Torry, 16 votes
>
> Candidate Green, 13 votes
>
> Candidate Frank, 12 votes
>
> Candidate Bates, 11 votes

Although all candidates received a majority, only five can be elected to the board. In this case, the five candidates who received the most votes are the winners:

> 1. Baker with 19 votes ⎫
> 2. Torry with 16 votes ⎪
> 3. Jones with 15 votes ⎬ top 5 candidates
> 4. Smith with 14 votes ⎪
> 5. Green with 13 votes ⎭
> 6. Frank with 12 votes
> 7. Bates with 11 votes

If three candidates had received the same vote — for example, if Smith, Green, and Frank had each received 13 votes — the membership would have to hold another election. Even though Candidate Bates received the lowest vote, his name would remain on the ballot. No one is removed from the ballot unless the bylaws state that the member with the fewest votes should be removed, because that person may end up being the compromise candidate.

The tellers' committee (members who are appointed to count the vote during a meeting) counts and records the ballots. For information on this aspect of the voting process, see "Counting and Recording the Ballots by Tellers' Committee," later in this chapter.

Election by Roll Call Vote

If members take the vote by roll call, the organization can follow the same methods used for a ballot vote — either voting for all candidates at once or voting for one at a time. The presiding officer should explain the procedure. Each member states who he or she is voting for as the secretary calls the roll. The secretary records the vote and repeats it to make sure that it is accurate.

Election by Cumulative Voting

When an organization has elections for positions in which more than one candidate is elected (for example, the Soccer Club), the bylaws may provide for cumulative voting. (Note that cumulative voting cannot take place unless it is stated in the bylaws.) *Cumulative voting* is the ability to cast all your votes for one candidate or to weight your vote in some way. In the earlier example of electing the five board members, the membership voted for five different candidates. In cumulative voting, a member can give two votes to Mr. Smith and three votes to Mrs. Baker. This allows a minority group to get together and elect one of their candidates. However, this practice is not in accord with the parliamentary principle of one person, one vote.

Election by Other Types of Voting

If an organization's membership is spread over a large distance, the bylaws can provide for a vote by mail ballot. In this case, it is wise for the bylaws to allow candidates to be elected by a *plurality vote* because, if no one receives a majority vote, the vote is difficult to retake.

In a plurality vote, the winning candidate must receive the most votes but not necessarily a majority of those cast. For example, let's say an organization has 500 members, and three candidates run for president. Of the 500 ballots sent to the members, 375 ballots are returned in the mail. Electing by majority vote takes 188.

Candidate A receives 180.

Candidate B receives 125.

Candidate C receives 70.

No one receives a majority vote, but Candidate A received a plurality (the most votes) and is therefore elected president.

MOTIONS CONCERNING ELECTIONS

When taking the vote by ballot, the president usually declares that the polls are closed after asking the members if everyone who wants to vote has voted. This means that no one else can vote and the tellers can count the votes. A member can also make a motion to close the polls, which requires a second and a two-thirds vote to adopt, or the motion can be adopted by unanimous consent. The president should not admit a member's motion to close the polls if people are still voting.

If members come into the assembly and want to vote after the polls are closed, a member must make the motion to open the polls. This motion takes a majority vote to adopt. Members can reopen the polls until the tellers give their report and the presiding officer announces the results. Keep the ballots that come in during the reopening of the polls in a separate pile until the other ballots are counted. After the separate ballots are counted, add them to the tellers' report.

COUNTING AND RECORDING THE BALLOTS BY TELLERS' COMMITTEE

A tellers' committee is a small group of members appointed to count the vote during a meeting involving a ballot vote or a rising counted vote. Depending on the size of the group, the committee is usually comprised of two to three people.

In many small organizations, the presiding officer appoints several members to count ballots or to count a rising vote when the time comes. In a case such as this, where an organization does not have a tellers' committee, a secretary who is well versed in counting the ballots can be very helpful. The secretary can assist those appointed to act as tellers during the counting of the ballots.

Tellers who are appointed at a meeting to count a ballot vote should be appointed because of their accuracy and dependability, not because they have something to gain from the outcome of a vote. They should have the confidence of the assembly. If the issue is a controversial one, the tellers should include members on each side of the issue and a neutral person to count the ballots. If a tellers' committee is needed to count ballots for an election of officers, the committee should be appointed before the meeting and trained in the correct procedure for counting the ballots.

In larger organizations or at national conventions, a tellers' committee, which is usually large and headed by a chairman, is appointed for the entire convention or the entire year. The chairman is in charge of the ballots and ballot boxes and is responsible for training the tellers on the proper way to count the ballots and on the various methods of counting a rising vote. The tellers' committee is present during the entire session to count any doubted voice vote, when requested to do so by the presiding officer or the membership.

Teller's Sheet and Report

For each ballot vote taken, the tellers should have a sheet of paper that helps them tally the ballots. A teller's sheet may look like this:

TELLER'S SHEET AND REPORT

Office_____

Number of votes cast_____

Number of votes to elect_____

Number of illegal votes_____

Candidates:

1._____

2._____

3._____

4._____

5._____

Signed Tellers' Committee:

1._____

2._____

3._____

4._____

Counting the Ballots

Following are the procedures that the tellers' committee should follow to count ballots:

1. When three tellers are appointed to count the ballots, Teller One should open each ballot and determine whether it is a legitimate ballot. All blank ballots are put aside because they are not counted in the total number of votes cast. *Illegal ballots,* those that have writing on them but are not readable or that contain the name of a person who is not eligible for election, or two ballots with names on them folded together, are put in another pile.

2. Teller One counts the legal ballots and writes the total on the teller's sheet on the line "Number of votes cast." If there are illegal ballots, these are counted and the number put on the line "Number of illegal votes." The number of illegal and legal ballots is then totaled. This number is used to establish the number for the majority vote. The majority vote number is written on the line "Number of votes to elect."

3. Teller One reads aloud the names on each ballot. The other two tellers each keep a separate teller's sheet, recording each candidate's name on the teller's sheet the first time it is read, and placing a tally mark next to a candidate's name each time Teller One reads that name aloud. So that there is no doubt who should receive the vote, Teller Two repeats each name as it is read by Teller One. When a candidate receives five votes, Teller Two calls out "tally." If Teller Three's report doesn't agree with Teller Two's, then the count stops at this point to see where the mistake was made in recording the vote.

4. When all the ballots have been read aloud, the tellers' committee totals the votes for each candidate and writes the number of votes received by each name. The tellers' committee then writes the word "elected" by those receiving a majority vote. If no one receives a majority vote, the phrase "no election" is written on the teller's report or is written near any office for which no candidate has received a majority vote.

5. Each member of the tellers' committee signs the teller's report, and the chairman of the committee (Teller One) reads the report to the assembly and gives it to the presiding officer.

   In the election of candidates for the Soccer Club board, there were no blank ballots, so the tellers write on their sheets "20" for the number of ballots cast. There were no illegal ballots, so they write "0" on that line. On the line that gives the number to elect, they write "11."

Filling Out the Teller's Report

TELLER'S SHEET AND REPORT

Office: Executive Board_____
Number of votes cast__20__
Number of votes to elect__11__
Number of illegal votes__0__

The tellers' committee then fills in each name as the member opening the ballots called it.

For example, Teller One reads off the names on the first ballot:

Teller One: Smith, Jones, Baker, Torry, Green.

Teller Two repeats the names. Then Tellers Two and Three write those names in the blanks under "Candidates" and make a tally mark after each name.

Candidates:

1. Smith_____I_____
2. Jones_____I_____
3. Baker_____I_____
4. Torry_____I_____
5. Green_____I_____

The next ballot is opened. This ballot has two names that were not on the first ballot. On this ballot, Teller One reads the following names:

Teller One: Frank, Bates, Smith, Baker, Torry.

Teller Two repeats the names. Then Tellers Two and Three add the two new names, Frank and Bates, to the bottom of the list, and make a tally mark by each candidate. The teller's sheet now looks like this:

Candidates:

1. Smith_____II_____
2. Jones_____I_____
3. Baker_____II_____
4. Torry_____II_____
5. Green_____I_____
6. Frank_____I_____
7. Bates_____I_____

This process goes on until all the ballots are cast and recorded by the two other tellers. As soon as one candidate receives five votes, Teller Two calls out "tally." Teller Three then checks to see if his or her sheet matches Teller Two's. If it doesn't, the committee should immediately stop and recount the ballots to see where they made the mistake.

When the count is finished, the report should look like this, with the word "elected" written by those who received a majority vote.

TELLER'S SHEET AND REPORT

Office: Executive Board_____
Number of votes cast __20__
Number of votes to elect __11__
Number of illegal votes__0__

Candidates:

1. Smith THL THL IIII 14 elected
2. Jones THL THL THL 15 elected
3. Baker THL THL THL IIII 19 elected
4. Torry THL THL THL I 16 elected
5. Green THL THL III 13 elected
6. Frank THL THL II 12
7. Bates THL THL I 11

Signed:

1. Joyce Bell, Chairman

2. Robert McGregor

3. Bill Walsh

Giving the Tellers' Committee Report

The chairman of the tellers' committee rises, addresses the chair, is recognized, and reads the teller's report. The chairman reads the entire report including the number of votes cast, number to elect, any illegal votes, and all names and the vote totals for each candidate who received votes (even those who are not elected). The members have the right to know who received what number of votes. The report does not include the number of eligible voters (only the officer responsible for the membership roll is able to give this number if needed).

The teller reading the report does not indicate who has been elected. Instead, after the tellers' committee report, the presiding officer announces those people elected.

> ***Tellers' Committee Chairman:*** The Tellers' Committee Report for Election of Board Members:
>
> Number of votes cast were 20.
>
> Number to elect is 11.
>
> Mr. Smith received 14 votes. (elected)
>
> Mrs. Jones received 15 votes. (elected)
>
> Mrs. Baker received 19 votes. (elected)
>
> Mr. Torry received 16 votes. (elected)
>
> Mr. Green received 13 votes. (elected)
>
> Mrs. Frank received 12 votes.
>
> Mr. Bates received 11 votes.

Joyce Bell

Chairman

Note: The words in parentheses are written on the report but not read aloud. The committee chairman then gives the report to the presiding officer and sits down.

The presiding officer repeats the report and announces the election of each candidate:

President: The Tellers' Committee Report reads:

Number of votes cast were 20.

Number to elect is 11.

Mr. Smith received 14 votes. (elected)

Mrs. Jones received 15 votes. (elected)

Mrs. Baker received 19 votes. (elected)

Mr. Torry received 16 votes. (elected)

Mr. Green received 13 votes. (elected)

Mrs. Frank received 12 votes.

Mr. Bates received 11 votes.

Note: The words in parentheses are written on the report but not read aloud.

President: The members have elected Mr. Smith, Mrs. Jones, Mrs. Baker, Mr. Torry, and Mr. Green to the executive board. Do these members accept the position? *[All members nod yes; no one rises to reject election.]*

The presiding officer states when the election is effective, according to the bylaws:

President: Thank you. You will take office at the close of our annual meeting. *[as stated in the Soccer Club's bylaws]*

Those elected take office immediately unless the bylaws state differently. In this organization, the newly elected board members take their places at the close of the annual meeting.

If an organization usually has an installation of officers but fails to hold it, those elected still take office unless the bylaws provide that those elected take office when installed. An *installation* is only a ceremony and is not the activity that enables those elected to take office. Also, because an installation is considered a ceremony, a quorum is not needed to conduct the installation.

The complete teller's report is then entered into the minutes. If a recount isn't necessary or requested, the ballots can be destroyed or filed with the secretary for a certain number of days and then destroyed.

OTHER POINTS ABOUT ELECTIONS

Here are some other things to consider during the election process:

- A quorum needs to be present throughout the election meeting. If members leave during the meeting so that a quorum is not present, those offices not yet elected must be put off until an adjourned meeting or until the next meeting.

- Tellers should cast their ballots at the same time that the assembly votes.

- If a member is elected and not present and has not previously said that if elected he or she will serve, someone should call the member to see if he or she will accept the office. If not, the members can vote again during that meeting for another candidate.

- If an elected candidate declines the office after he or she is elected and after the meeting has adjourned, another election needs to take place, if at all possible. If the bylaws specifically address this situation, members should follow the bylaws.

- If it is discovered after an election that the person elected does not meet the eligibility requirements, and even if the person has begun to serve, the election is void. The organization must have another election.

- A member can't make the motion to adjourn while the assembly is occupied with taking a vote, verifying a vote, or announcing a vote, except when the vote is by ballot. In a ballot vote, after the tellers have collected all the ballots, a member can make the motion to adjourn. If the motion is adopted, the assembly can adjourn before the vote is announced if it has another meeting scheduled. The tellers' committee can still count the ballots. When the next meeting begins, the first order of business is to hear the report of the tellers' committee and for the presiding officer to announce the vote that was taken at the previous meeting.

- If counting ballots takes some time, it is best for the assembly to take a recess instead of adjourn.

- In counting the votes, the tellers' committee must not confuse a majority vote with the highest number of votes. The person who gets the most votes may not have a majority of the votes. In this case, the members must vote again until one candidate receives a majority vote.

- If there is a question about the way a ballot is marked, the tellers should take it to the presiding officer. He or she should present it to the assembly to decide what to do with the vote — whether to count it and toward what name to credit the vote.

- When presenting the nominations or taking the vote for a list of offices, the president should follow the order of offices that appears in the bylaws.

- If a person has been nominated to more than one office and is elected to two offices, he or she can choose which office he or she wants. The assembly then votes again on the other office.

  If a member is not present to choose which office he or she wants to serve, the members vote on which office they want him or her to serve. Members then vote on a candidate to fill the remaining office.

- If members adjourn before an election is complete, they should set the time for an adjourned meeting to finish the election. If they don't set a for an adjourned meeting, they can call a special meeting (if the bylaws allow this). Or, members can also finish the election at the next regular meeting if the meeting falls within a quarterly time period.

- If members are voting for offices that have staggered terms or that last more than a year, the secretary should include in the minutes when the term expires. The minutes may say, for example, "Kenneth Baker was elected to the board for three years. His term expires April, 2004."

- If electronic machines are used for voting, they should be programmed so that each segment of the ballot is treated as if it were a separate ballot. Tellers present during the voting should be carefully instructed in their duties and should be able to explain to other members how to use the machine. If members haven't used the machine before, it may be wise to show them how to use it the day before the election.

ELECTION IRREGULARITIES

During an election, especially when tellers are not trained or when candidates are running in opposition, members may become aware of mistakes or illegal procedures in collecting or counting the ballots. If a member notices a mistake in procedure, he or she should immediately make the chair and assembly aware of his concerns.

The best thing an organization can do is adopt rules that tell how to proceed if a member challenges an election or if a person is illegally elected to office and has begun to serve. Rules may include how long the organization saves ballots and how long members can wait to challenge an election. These rules supersede the adopted parliamentary authority. It is important to remember that once someone is elected, the election can't be rescinded unless there is some provision for it in the bylaws. It is possible that because of a mistake in counting the ballots, or another procedural mistake, someone can be declared elected to office when he or she did not receive the majority votes. Organizations can create and write election rules to correct this mistake.

A common mistake in elections is having too many ballots cast for the number of members present. If this occurs and it does not affect the outcome of the vote, the election is still valid. Often the extra ballot comes from someone who has entered the assembly but has not signed in to the meeting.

Because fraud does happen in the election process, members need to be alert and watchful of the election process. Some practices to watch out for include:

- Ballot boxes being stuffed or written ballots being changed.
- Mail or absentee ballots not arriving on time or mysteriously disappearing when the time comes to count them.
- Voting machines having wedges inserted to prevent the lever from going down all the way.
- Polls closing or opening at times different than the times posted.

The most important thing associations or governments can do is appoint conscientious and honest people to serve on the tellers' committee and to watch the polls.

TAKING A RECOUNT

If members question the validity of an election or the procedure in taking the vote, a member should make a motion to recount the votes within a reasonably brief time after the president announces the election outcome. The motion to have a vote for a particular office recounted needs a second, is not debatable, and takes a majority vote to adopt.

After the person elected to office assumes the position, it is too late to nullify an illegal election. For this reason, members should listen carefully to the report of the tellers' committee. If something doesn't quite add up, a member should question it during the meeting. If officers assume their duties immediately after the meeting is adjourned, it is then too late to question the election.

13

Committees

Committees are considered the workhorses of any organization. Much business is discussed, investigated, and carried out in committees. This chapter concentrates on the two types of committees found in organizations: standing committees and special committees. It explains the purpose of each and the important role of committee chairmen.

THE ROLE OF A COMMITTEE

A committee can do only what the organization asks it to do; it cannot act independently of the organization. However, if a committee originates an idea that it feels will benefit the group, it can bring the idea to the assembly in the form of a motion.

The bylaws should state who has the power to appoint the members of committees. Whoever has the power to appoint members of a committee also has the power to appoint the chairman and to fill vacancies.

The secretary lets members know of their appointment to a committee and gives the committee chairman the proper documents so that the committee can accomplish its assigned work. If a motion is referred to a committee, the secretary needs to give the chairman a copy of the motion and the instructions that go with it.

The committee chairman should preserve all documents given to him or her and return them to the secretary in the same condition in which they were received. In standing committees, the committee should keep a record of its activities and place them in a file. This file becomes a continuous record of the activities of the committee and is given to the new committee chairman each year.

STANDING COMMITTEES

Standing committees are listed in the bylaws and are considered a permanent part of the organization. Members of a standing committee usually change when new officers are elected, but the purpose of the committee and its functions and duties do not change.

The standing committee has certain functions to perform that are essential to the harmonious operation of the organization. When the board or the membership receives business that is connected with the work of a standing committee, it usually refers that business to the committee. The committee investigates and then reports back to the board or membership. Examples of standing committees may include finance, program, or membership committees.

SPECIAL COMMITTEES

The other type of committee is a *special committee,* also called a *select* or *ad hoc* committee. This committee is created to perform a specific task and is dissolved when the task is completed and the final report is given. The membership should not create a special committee to do something that is within the designated function of a standing committee.

Special committees have two functions. One function is to *investigate*. For example, if an organization wants to buy a piece of property to build a permanent clubhouse, a member could make a motion to create a committee to research this possibility. The other function of special committees is to *carry out* what the assembly has adopted. For example, if the motion to buy a piece of property is adopted, then a member could make a motion to create a committee to carry out the purchasing of the property.

The purpose of a committee determines its size as well as who is appointed to serve on it. If a special committee is created to investigate a question, it is important that all the different views of the membership be reflected in the committee members. This practice allows many differences to be resolved in the committee instead of at the assembly meeting, where they take up a lot of time. Such a committee is thus usually a large one in order to represent all viewpoints.

If a special committee has been created to carry out something the membership has adopted, only those in favor of the membership's wishes should be on the committee. If members who are opposed to the action are on the committee, the action may not be carried out or could be delayed. This type of committee is usually a small one so that the members can easily meet and get the work done.

APPOINTMENT OF THE COMMITTEE CHAIRMAN

The committee chairman is the most important member of a committee. He or she is responsible for calling the committee meetings, overseeing all the work, and completing the work. Most committee chairmen are appointed by either the president or an executive board. Sometimes the assembly elects a chairman and committee members after it has voted to establish a special committee.

When selecting a committee chairman, those who do the appointing should select someone who is enthusiastic about the committee work, has the time to devote to the committee, and knows how to do the work. This person should also be able to work with others and inspire them to do the work. The other committee members should be appointed for what each can contribute to the work of the committee and for their ability to work with others on the committee. Committee work is teamwork, not a one-man band.

14

The Role of the Member

So far this book has discussed the roles of officers, boards, and committees, but what roles do the members play? After all, the members are the ones who run for office, serve on boards and committees, and come to meetings to present ideas. Unless members take an active role in the organization, it can't function or even exist.

In organizations there are members who seek active roles and those who sit on the sidelines and "let the next person do it." It is important for the betterment and advancement of the organization to engage all the members in active participation in all the functions of the club. Unfortunately, in many organizations only a few people are allowed to rise to the top. This causes cliques to develop, creating division among the membership. When only a few members are considered leaders or are asked to serve on committees, resentment and ill will are created, and, worst of all, other members' talents are left untapped.

For an organization to grow, to be successful, and to be truly democratic, all the talents of the members need to be recognized, cultivated, and used. An organization should allow the cream to rise to the top, but it should also recognize that everyone can be trained and cultivated for leadership roles in organizations.

This chapter looks at ways to involve new members, the duties of a member, and situations requiring a member to assume special responsibility.

MEMBERSHIP INVOLVEMENT

Here are proven techniques for incorporating new members immediately into the organization and making them feel welcome and useful:

- Make sure that each new member receives a copy of the bylaws and other documents that govern the club.

- Listen to the member. Why did he or she join the organization? If the member's needs are not being met, he or she will probably not renew the membership.

- Assign the new member a mentor, someone to explain how the organization operates and to advise where the member can best use his or her talents.

- Give a training session on parliamentary procedure and explain that at meetings all members are encouraged to present ideas to the club in the form of motions.

- Immediately appoint the new member to a committee where his or her talents are useful and where the member is interested in the work.

Toastmaster's International is an example of an organization that immediately includes all new members. At every meeting, each member is assigned a task or is able to participate in some way. This practice trains all members for leadership roles. If the same people always do the work, always are elected to office, or always get the limelight, the result is a schism in the organization, which may ultimately destroy the organization.

The biggest mistake an organization can make is to have a probationary period for new members or to set up barriers to service. If you wait too long to include the new member, eventually you may not have new members.

DUTIES OF THE MEMBERS

Members have many duties and responsibilities. Here are a few:

- Members should attend meetings, be on time, and know the rules of parliamentary procedure. It takes two to tango, and to make a meeting go smoothly, both the presiding officer and the members need to know the parliamentary rules.

- Members need to prepare themselves for leadership roles.

- Members should accept committee assignments and perform the tasks given to them in a timely manner.

- Members need to work harmoniously with other members even though they don't always agree with them.

- In debate, each member has the right to sway the membership to his or her point of view. If a member votes with the losing side, the member must respect the fact that the majority rules and cheerfully carry out the membership's wishes.

- Members must be impartial, fair, and courteous in meetings. This means respecting the rights of others, especially in debate. Members should call out a *point of order* only when a serious breach of the rules has taken place. Members should listen attentively and courteously to the other members and wait in turn to speak. All members must ensure that majority rule does not become mob rule by protecting the rights of the minority and by not gaveling through or railroading through any business. It is important that each member diligently follow this principle, because today one member might side with the majority, and tomorrow side with the minority.

- When the bylaws or other rules of the organization are not being followed or when members' rights are being taken away in a meeting, members have a responsibility to courteously call the violation to the attention of the membership.

A SPECIAL RESPONSIBILITY FOR MEMBERS

Every now and then a presiding officer does not respect the rights of the members and will not entertain a legitimate, seconded motion because he or she does not agree with it. In such situations, a member can pursue the following actions:

1. Raise a point of order.
2. If the chair rules the main motion out of order, appeal the decision. (See Chapter 9, "Appeal from the Decision of the Chair (Appeal).")

    If the chair ignores the point of order, the member can make the motion again. If it is seconded and the chair still ignores it, the member can place the motion before the assembly, ask for debate, and take the vote. This means that the member stands in his or her place and takes over during this part of the meeting until the main motion is disposed of — either permanently or temporarily. The member has a right to do this under *Robert's Rules of Order.* This is a good example of the principle that power is vested in the membership, not in the leadership.

15

Discipline

Every organization has the right to enforce its rules and expect ethical and honorable conduct from its members. Most organizations have discipline problems from time to time. A discipline problem may be something as simple as a member misbehaving at a meeting or an officer overstepping the boundaries of his or her office. If the problem is not corrected when it arises, it can escalate into something more serious, requiring that someone be removed from office or membership. However, the organization can often solve discipline problems by taking the member or officer aside and talking with him or her about it, which saves both the member and the organization embarrassment.

This chapter explains common discipline problems that organizations encounter and how to handle them. Many problems that cause difficulties in organizations are the result of inflated egos, personality conflicts, or ignorance of proper procedures. If egos or personalities are the root cause, it takes diplomacy, patience, and skill to solve these problems.

THE UNRULY MEMBER AT MEETINGS

In meetings where controversial issues are debated, some members may get so excited that they talk out of turn and continually seek the floor to rebut those who don't agree with them. In a case like this, the chair should remain calm and firmly remind the member of the proper rules of debate. If the member is reasonable, nothing more may need to be said.

If the member doesn't heed the remarks of the chair and continues his or her behavior, the chair's next step is to *call the member to order*. The chair states, "The member is out of order and will be seated." If the member refuses to be seated and continues with his or her obnoxious behavior, the next step the chair can take is to *name the offender.* This action, in essence, prefers charges against the member and should be used as a last resort. Before this action is taken, the chair instructs the secretary to record the obnoxious behavior or words. In naming the offender, the chairman uses the member's name and states what he or she has done wrong.

> ***President:*** Mr. Smith! The chair has asked you repeatedly not to speak after each speaker. The chair has ordered you to sit down four times and you have continued to speak.

If the member sits down at that point, the assembly can choose whether to drop the matter or ask for a penalty.

PENALTIES

The chair cannot impose a penalty for misbehavior; only the assembly can do so. A member can rise and make a motion proposing a penalty, or the chair can ask, "What penalty should be imposed on the member?" Possible motions that assemblies can make include:

- A motion that the member must apologize
- A motion that the member must leave the hall during the remainder of the meeting
- A motion to censure the member
- A motion to suspend the member's rights for a designated period of time
- A motion to expel the member from the organization

If the assembly wants the member to leave the hall while they discuss the penalty, someone must present this option in the form of a motion, which takes a majority to adopt. If the assembly does not ask the member to leave during the discussion, it should allow that person to speak briefly in his or her defense. If the member denies the charges, the secretary can read back what he or she has said or done.

Any penalty other than expulsion requires a majority vote to adopt; expulsion takes a two-thirds vote. At the request of a single member, the vote on a penalty motion must be taken by ballot.

Removing an Offender from the Assembly Hall

Anyone attending a meeting can be removed from the assembly hall. The chair has the power to remove a nonmember at any time during a meeting, and this person has no right to appeal the chair's decision. (However, a member can make an appeal on behalf of the nonmember.) An assembly vote is required to remove a member from the hall.

If a person is asked to leave the assembly and refuses, the chair should take the steps necessary to see that order is enforced. The chair must carefully appraise the situation and act wisely. The chair can either appoint a committee to escort the person to the door or ask the sergeant-at-arms to remove the person. (The sergeant-at-arms is the person who acts as a doorkeeper, maintains order at the direction of the presiding officer, and is responsible for the comfort of the assembly.) Those escorting someone to the door must be careful how much force they use, because they can be liable for damages or be sued. If those appointed to escort the person to the door can't persuade the person to leave, they should call the police. However, the police may not want to get involved unless the organization is willing to press charges.

Making a Motion to Censure

To *censure* a member or an officer is to warn him or her that if a certain behavior continues, the next step is suspension or expulsion.

Censure

✦ **Purpose:** To reprimand the member with the hopes of reforming him or her so that he or she won't behave in the same way again.

✦ Needs a second.

✦ Amendable.

✦ Debatable.

✦ Requires a majority vote.

✦ Can't be reconsidered.

✦ **Result:** The member is put on notice that if he or she repeats the offense, he or she can be suspended or removed from membership or office.

This is an incidental main motion and can be made only when no business is pending. All subsidiary and incidental motions can be applied to this motion. The member or officer being censured may come to his own defense during the debate but can't vote. Taking the vote by ballot is wise. A member can not be censured twice for the same offense.

Censuring a member

Members can be censured for misconduct at meetings, violating confidentiality, moral misconduct outside the meeting, absenteeism, bribery, fraud, lying, disloyalty, working against the organization, conspiracy, and violating other values that an organization holds dear.

A motion to censure a member can occur in two circumstances. First, if the chair has named the person (as a result of that person's poor behavior), a member can make the motion to censure when the chair asks for a penalty. Second, if members know of another member's bad behavior and want to bring it to the attention of the assembly in the form of a motion to censure, that can be done under new business or under the part of the agenda called *for the good of the order.*

In the first situation, when the chairman asks for a penalty, a member rises and states:

> ***Member:*** I move to censure Member Gates.
>
> ***Member 2:*** I second the motion.
>
> ***President:*** It is moved and seconded to censure Member Gates. Is there any discussion?

After discussion, the chair takes a vote. If the members want to take the vote by ballot, a member makes a motion to do so, or the chair can ask, "Is there any objection to taking the vote by ballot?"

If the assembly votes to censure the member, the chair states:

> **President:** The affirmative has it. The motion is carried. Member Gates, you have been censured by the assembly. A censure indicates the assembly's displeasure of your conduct at meetings. A censure is a warning. If you don't act according to the rules, you can be suspended or expelled from membership.

In the second situation, if a member knows of another member's serious misconduct, he or she can make the motion to censure during new business or under the good of the order. Here is an example:

> **Member:** Mr. President, before I make the motion to censure, may I call to the attention of the assembly that Member Johnson has been telling members what has gone on in executive session of the board meetings, thereby breaking the rule that everything said in executive session is confidential. This is causing great harm in the organization and we must show our disapproval of this behavior. I therefore move that we censure Member Johnson.

Censuring officers
Officers can be censured as well for behavior such as not performing duties, doing things beyond what the bylaws or organization has assigned the officer to do, and fraud.

A presiding officer can also be censured for not following parliamentary rules in meetings, and for denying members their basic rights to make motions, participate in debate, and vote.

In censuring a presiding officer, a member informs the chair that he or she is going to do so, and then turns to the vice president to make the motion. If the vice president refuses to entertain it or is not present, the member then presents the motion to the secretary. If the secretary declines or is absent, the member can present the motion to the assembly from where he or she stands on the floor. If the vice president or secretary conducts the censure, they do so from where they are in the assembly and not from the president's position. The president can speak in his or her defense but cannot vote on the censure.

To censure the chair, a member presents the motion in the following fashion:

> **Member:** Madam President, I am going to propose a motion to censure you, which I have a right to do. When a motion to censure the president is made, it is addressed to and entertained by the vice president. *[The member turns to the vice president and presents it as a resolution.]*
>
> Mr. Vice President, I move the following resolution to censure:
>
> "*Whereas,* The president has repeatedly denied members their right to make motions and debate; refused to entertain points of order and proper appeals; recognized only those who have upheld her views and denied the opposition the right to speak; and
>
> *Whereas,* she has been obnoxious, rude, and arrogant; and
>
> *Whereas,* such conduct is detrimental to the organization; now, therefore, be it
>
> *Resolved,* that the president be censured.

This motion needs a second. The vice president places it before the assembly:

> **Vice President:** It is moved and seconded to censure the president. Is there any discussion?

After discussion, the vice president takes a vote by ballot. If the affirmative has it, he or she states:

> **Vice President:** There are 35 votes in the affirmative and 5 in the negative. The affirmative has it and the motion is carried.

The vice president then turns to the president and states:

> **Vice President:** Madam Jones, you have been censured by the assembly for the reasons contained in the resolution. I now return control of the meeting to you.

If the president persists in the behavior, the next step is to remove him or her from office. Members must follow the bylaws for this procedure. If the bylaws contain a provision on how to remove someone from office, follow that proce- dure. If the bylaws state that someone is elected to office for _____ years *or* until their successor is elected, the members can then rescind the election. If the bylaws state "elected to office for _____ years or "elected to office for _____ years *and* until the successor is elected," the members must have a trial. The difference between "or" and "and" in this part of the bylaws is substantial.

Holding a Trial

Because a trial is a serious event for any organization and should rarely be used, there are specific procedures to follow to protect the rights of the accused:

- A trial is held in executive session.

- The accused has a right to *due process* — to be notified of the charges, given time to prepare a defense, and allowed the right to appear and defend himself or herself.

Several steps must happen before a trial can take place. The first step when members hear of misconduct by another member is to choose a committee to investigate the validity of the reports and to see if charges should be made. The members of this committee should be chosen for their integrity and good judgment. To establish such a committee requires that a resolution be made, seconded, discussed, and voted on. This resolution should avoid as much detail as pos- sible to protect the parties, who may be innocent.

In the second step, the committee should quietly conduct its investigation and make a sincere effort to get the facts.

Any information collected is confidential. The committee should also talk with the accused to hear his or her side of the story. If the committee members find that the reports of misconduct are untrue, they should prepare a report and resolution for clearing the accused. If they find substantial evidence that the report of misconduct is true, the next step is to report the findings and prefer charges.

Next, the investigating committee prepares several resolutions. The first resolution includes setting a date and time for the trial meeting. It states that member X is to appear to show why he or she should not be expelled from the organization; it also states the specific charges. A second resolution establishes the trial committee and its members. The trial committee should have different members than the investigating committee.

If the members adopt the resolutions to have a trial, the secretary immediately sends by registered mail a letter notifying the accused of the time, date, and place of the trial, as well as the charges against him or her. (The letter should include a copy of the exact charges.) At the trial, the secretary should have on-hand a copy of the letter that was sent to the accused and a signed return receipt to prove that he or she received the letter.

The trial is a hearing. Members of the organization appointed to present the evidence against the accused are called *managers*. They should not be thought of as prosecuting attorneys; their intent should be to get at the truth and see that the outcome is just. The accused has a right to be represented by counsel and to speak and present witnesses in his or her own defense. The defense counsel may be an attorney but must be a member of the organization, unless the organization agrees by a vote to allow a nonmember to represent the accused.

At the beginning of the trial, the charges are read and the accused is asked how he or she pleads. If the accused answers "guilty," there is no reason to proceed with the trial. If he or she pleads not guilty, the members proceed with opening statements by the managers and then by the accused. Next, witnesses are presented by the managers and then by the accused. Rebuttal of witnesses by the managers and then by the accused is followed by closing arguments on both sides.

After closing arguments, the accused leaves the room and the assembly discusses and takes a vote. Each charge is read, debated, and voted on. If the accused is found guilty, the next business in order is determining the penalty. Usually the managers propose the penalty, and the members can debate and amend that motion. One member can demand that the vote be taken by ballot. Removing the person on trial from membership requires a two-thirds vote. After the penalty is decided, the accused is brought back into the assembly and told the results.

A trial is an extreme measure. The best policy is to talk to the member and see what can be resolved before the situation ever reaches this proceeding.

SOME FINAL THOUGHTS

President Lyndon B. Johnson's favorite expression when trying to get opposing groups together was "Come let us reason together." Consider this expression when confronted with disruptive members and overbearing officers. Often the best solutions come when members try to resolve problems first by talking with the member or officer in question. One wise parliamentarian said, "If you're having a problem with someone, take him out to lunch." This man believed that gently talking with someone in a friendly atmosphere could resolve the difficulty without embarrassment to the person or the organization.

This method certainly isn't new. Jesus told his followers that when they had problems with their fellow church members, one member should go and talk to the troublemaker. If the troublemaker didn't change his ways, then two members should go and talk to that person. If there still wasn't a change, the matter should go before the entire church body to solve.

Keep in mind that members and officers make mistakes because of ignorance, lack of training, or miscommunications.

Censuring a person or using other disciplinary procedures may not solve the problem or may even make matters worse. By talking with the member or officer first, you may gain a friend and a good member.

"Come let us reason together" should be a motto for solving all organizational problems. This idea even works well in the middle of a meeting when tempers are running high. In this case, the chair can recess a meeting to let members cool down and to take the opportunity to speak with the disruptive members.

Part IV

MEETINGS AND STRATEGIES

16

Meetings

A *meeting,* as defined by *Robert's Rules of Order,* is a single
official gathering of the members of an organization in one
room, with a quorum present to transact business. The members do not leave the meeting, except for a short recess, until
the business has been completed or the chair declares the
meeting adjourned. This chapter covers the many types of
formal meetings (including conventions and mass meetings)
and informal meetings (small board and committee meetings), and it discusses the pros and cons of electronic meetings. It also explains how to manage and evaluate meetings
and how to form strategies — and counterstrategies — for
meetings.

THE BASICS

All meetings, regardless of size or purpose, have some things
in common:

- A quorum must be present.
- Someone is in charge of conducting the meeting.
- Someone is responsible for taking the minutes.
- Business is conducted according to specific rules that
  state who can attend, who can participate in the discussion of business, and who can vote.
- All members are notified of the meeting's date and time
  and the purpose for which the meeting is called. The
  parliamentary term for this procedure is the *call to the
  meeting.*

Most organizations have both formal and informal meetings. A *formal meeting* is one in which the entire membership meets to hear reports of officers, boards, and committees, and to propose business, discuss it, and vote on it. An *informal meeting* is one in which a small group of the organization meets, in either committee meetings or small boards, to help the organization carry out its goals.

Meeting procedures vary according to the meeting type. The primary difference between formal and informal meetings is the chair's role in the meeting. In formal meetings, the members usually follow strict parliamentary procedures, which means that the chair stands while presiding and while stating a motion and taking the vote. He or she does not participate in the debate unless he or she leaves the chair. Members must rise and be recognized in order to obtain the floor, make motions, and debate. Debate is restricted to ten minutes each time a member speaks unless there is a rule to the contrary, and each member may speak twice to a motion.

In informal meetings, the person presiding is usually seated and takes an active role in making motions, discussing them, and voting on all issues. There are usually no limits on debate, and members can discuss an issue without a formal motion.

FORMAL MEETINGS

Formal meetings range from annual meetings and regular periodic meetings to conventions and mass meetings, plus less-common types such as adjourned (continued), executive, and special meetings and sessions. This section defines each type and explains its particular requirements.

Annual Meetings

The term *annual meeting* can refer to two things:

- The meeting of a society that has only one meeting a year.

- A regular, periodic meeting of a society, designated by the bylaws as the annual meeting. The bylaws may prescribe this meeting as the one in which members hear the annual reports of officers, boards, and committees; elect officers; and perform other such once-a-year business.

In organizations with regular meetings, business not completed at the annual meeting can carry over to the next regularly scheduled meeting, if the time interval between meetings is quarterly or more often. When organizations meet only once a year, business can carry over to the next annual meeting only if the assembly refers the business to a committee.

Regular Meetings

A *regular meeting* is the periodic meeting of an assembly, which is held weekly, monthly, quarterly, or at similar intervals. The bylaws should state the day of the meeting (for example, "the first Monday of each month"), and the standing rules should state the hour of the meeting (for example, "8:00 p.m."). If an organization meets quarterly or more frequently, main motions can carry over to the next meeting through each of the following procedures:

- Postponing a main motion to the next meeting
- Referring the motion to a committee
- Laying the motion on the table
- Reconsidering the motion

If meetings are held semiannually or less often, the organization can carry over a main motion to the next meeting only by referring it to a committee, with instructions to report at the next meeting.

Adjourned Meetings

An *adjourned meeting* is a continuation of a meeting. When an assembly can't finish the business of a regular or special meeting during the designated time of the meeting, it can provide for an adjourned meeting at a time before the next regularly scheduled meeting. The adjourned meeting is established by a motion to *fix the time to which to adjourn* or by a main motion to *adjourn until a specified time*. This sets the time (and place if it is not already established) to continue the meeting. In an adjourned meeting, the minutes of the meeting being continued are read first, and then business is taken up where the previous meeting left off.

Executive Sessions

An *executive session* is a meeting of an assembly that is closed to all but the members. In some organizations, all meetings are closed. (An example is the *lodge system*.) In an ordinary assembly, board and committee meetings are usually held in executive session. Other members may be invited to attend when they have important information to share, but they do not have the right to attend unless the bylaws provide for it.

In many organizations, guests can attend meetings in order to observe the business proceedings of the organization. However, members may not want the guests present to hear the discussion at times. In these situations, a member can make a motion to go into executive session. This motion is a privileged motion and is adopted by a majority vote. If the motion is adopted, all nonmembers are requested to leave the meeting, until the members vote to end the executive session.

Business conducted in an executive session is confidential and known only to its members. Members are not supposed to divulge the proceedings of an executive session and can be punished under a disciplinary provision if they violate the secrecy. Anyone who is not a member but is allowed to stay during the executive session (for example an executive director or employee of the organization) is honor-bound not to tell what happened in the executive session. Minutes of an executive session are read and approved only in an executive session.

Most disciplinary action against a member must be held in executive session.

Special Meetings

A *special meeting* (or a *called meeting*) is a separate meeting of a society held at a time different from the regular meeting. The bylaws must provide guidelines for special meetings. If the organization is incorporated, or if state laws have authority over it, a special meeting provision may be in the corporate charter or the state laws. If an organization's governing documents do not provide for the calling of special meetings, the organization can't hold them.

The bylaws or other governing documents should specify the proper procedures for calling a special meeting, including who can call it, the conditions under which it can be called, and the number of days notice that members must be given. Notice of the time, place, and purpose of the meeting must be sent to all members in advance of the meeting. At a special meeting, members can discuss only the business that was stated in the notification (which is referred to as the *call to the meeting*). If some emergency business is transacted for which no notice was given, the organization must ratify that business at a regular meeting or at another special meeting.

Sessions

A *session* is a series of connected meetings held by a group and devoted to a single order of business or program. Each meeting in a session is scheduled to continue business from the point where it left off in the preceding meeting. Sessions are very common in conventions.

Conventions

Conventions differ from regular meetings in that they are assemblies of delegates chosen from the units of an organization, which may be scattered over a large geographical area. The delegates are sent as representatives of these units. Usually a convention is held once every year or two and lasts about a week, although it could last longer if necessary, as in a constitutional convention, where the constitution of the organization is being revised or brought into existence.

The voting members at a convention are those who hold proper credentials as delegates or those who in some other way hold membership and voting rights. Before delegates can participate, they must report to the credentials committee.

This committee gives them the necessary documents to enter the convention floor and to participate in the convention business.

Other names sometimes used for conventions are *congress, conference, convocation, general assembly, house of delegates,* and *house of representatives.*

Of the various types of conventions, the most common is the convention of an established state or national society. The delegates are chosen by and from the local chapters of the society. Sometimes a convention is called for the purpose of forming a new association of persons to address a common problem or concern. This type of convention is handled like a mass meeting (discussed later in this chapter).

Conventions vary in terms of how often they are held and how long the sessions last. A convention can last anywhere from a day to a week or more. Many conventions are held annually, but some are held less frequently. The variation depends on the size of the organization and the amount of business that needs to be done. The rules relating to a society's convention are stated in the bylaws.

In its bylaws regarding conventions, a state, regional, or national society should have provisions that do the following:

- Authorize a periodic convention.
- Define its powers and duties.
- Fix the quorum.
- Specify the voting members (who can vote and who can't).
- Define the qualifications of delegates and alternates, how they are elected, and how many there are.
- Explain how the convention should be organized and operated.

The procedures of a convention differ from those of a regular meeting. After opening ceremonies and any presentations, such as inspirational speakers, the first business in order is the report of the credentials committee.

The credentials committee

The *credentials committee* is one of the most important committees in the convention. This committee is responsible for registering the delegates, giving each delegate the proper identification to enter the assembly, and providing the delegates with copies of the program (the order of business) and other information such as times and places of workshops or other meetings.

The credentials committee is the first to report at the convention, and business can't begin without the credentials committee report. This report states the number of delegates in attendance and establishes the membership of the meeting and quorum. At a convention, the quorum is the number of members present. Members present at the beginning of the meeting adopt the credentials committee report, which must be revised and adopted again when new delegates arrive and register. Because delegates continually arrive or leave the convention, the credentials committee report changes and must be voted on as it changes. It takes a majority vote to adopt the credentials committee report. The committee usually reports at the beginning of each meeting within the session and before an important vote if new delegates have registered or delegates have left.

The credentials committee mans the registration table, and its members are present at stated times during the entire convention to register delegates as they arrive or arrange for alternates to replace those delegates who must leave the convention.

Standing rules for the convention

The convention adopts standing rules, which a committee on standing rules prepares. These rules contain both parliamentary rules and standing rules for this particular convention. Parliamentary rules may include those that set a time limit on debate (for example, each speaker can speak for three minutes) and establish the voting process (such as members shall use voting cards instead of voice votes or rising votes). There may be standing rules particular to the convention, such as all speakers shall come to the microphones and must wear badges to come into the assembly. The committee drafts these rules, which are presented immediately after the credentials report. The rules may be amended by the assembly and are adopted by a two-thirds vote.

Program

A convention usually adopts its own order of business. This order of business is called the *program* and specifies when certain issues are to be taken up and when certain events are to occur. The program, or *agenda,* is developed by the program committee and adopted after the standing rules of the convention. The program chairman presents it as a main motion. It is debatable and amendable and is adopted by a majority vote. After the program is adopted, it takes a two-thirds vote to change it.

Resolutions or reference committee

Some organizations have a resolutions committee or a reference committee whose basic purpose is to screen all main motions before they are presented to the assembly. The reference committee invites members to an open meeting for the sole purpose of getting the members' input before resolutions or proposed bylaw amendments go to the entire assembly.

In some organizations, a standing committee, such as the bylaws committee, functions as a reference committee. The bylaws committee usually acts as a reference committee to help expedite the amending of bylaws. The bylaws committee can provide an informal setting where members can raise questions, state their objections, or give suggestions for improvement of proposed bylaw changes. The committee can then reevaluate the proposed amendments and make changes that are more acceptable to the membership. Because members have already raised questions and given suggestions to the committee, much time is saved during the regular session when the bylaw amendments are presented. In most cases, the controversial issues can be resolved because the bylaws committee can then propose a compromise amendment during the business meeting.

Adjournment sine die

After the convention finishes its business and program, it adjourns *sine die,* which means adjournment "without a day." In other words, this particular group of delegates will not meet again. The next convention is a "new" convention where delegates start all over by adopting standing rules and a program. A convention is a complete unit in and of itself, which is why it always adjourns *sine die.*

Mass Meetings

A *mass meeting* is a meeting of an unorganized group. It provides a meeting place and an orderly way to bring people of the same interests and concerns together for the purpose of forming an organization or solving a community problem.

Because a mass meeting has no written rules regarding meeting conduct, some basic parliamentary principles govern it:

- The individuals sponsoring the meeting have the right to restrict the discussion and any proposals to the purpose that they have announced.

- Those attending have the right to determine the action taken by making motions, debating, and voting on proposals.

- The sponsors have the right to keep out of the meeting anyone who is opposed to the purpose or would try to subvert the purpose. (After all, the organizers have invested both time and expense in calling the meeting.)

Calling a mass meeting

Those who want to have a mass meeting have a variety of ways that they can notify those interested, such as via telephone or mass mailer, or through media announcements and posters. The call to the meeting should state the purpose of the meeting; the date, time, and place; and who is invited to attend. For example, the meeting may be for residents of a certain neighborhood, registered voters, or those interested in a certain issue.

Preparing for a mass meeting

Like other meetings, a mass meeting must have structure. The people calling the meeting need to prepare an agenda and decide who is going to call the meeting to order; who they want to nominate as a temporary chairman and secretary; who will explain the purpose of the meeting and what the sponsors want to accomplish; and, finally, by which rules they will abide.

Conducting a mass meeting

Although a mass meeting has no governing documents to provide structure, the basic parliamentary rules of conducting a meeting apply. In *Robert's Rules of Order, Newly Revised* (Perseus Books), specific rules are given for conducting a mass meeting. The following rules are for the first mass meeting that a group calls. If a series of mass meetings is held, those meetings should follow the order of business as outlined in Chapter 2.

The first item of business in a mass meeting is electing a chairman and secretary. When the time arrives for the meeting to begin, the person selected by the meeting organizers to preside calls the meeting to order and requests nominations for a chairman. Those sponsoring the meeting should be ready to nominate a candidate for the office. The nominee can be the person who called the meeting to order. Another way to accomplish this is for the person presiding to immediately nominate the candidate that the sponsors want to be chairman. After the sponsors nominate their candidate, the person presiding asks for nominations from the floor. He or she then takes a voice vote.

After someone (ideally the sponsors' candidate) is elected chairman, the next business in order is to elect a secretary. The sponsors again nominate a candidate for this office and follow the same procedure as electing a chairman. After the election of the secretary, the chairman asks the secretary to read the call to the meeting. The chairman then recognizes the person who is designated to explain the purpose of the meeting.

After the purpose of the meeting is explained, one of the meeting sponsors can propose a resolution or a series of resolutions to accomplish the purpose. Those present are considered members of the assembly and have the right to propose amendments to the resolution or present any other motions that would help expedite the purpose of the meeting. The only motions not allowed are those contrary to the purpose of the meeting, and the chairman has the responsibility to rule those motions out of order. For example, if the meeting is called to oppose the construction of a shopping mall in the neighborhood, it is out of order to propose a motion in favor of the shopping mall.

Adjourning a mass meeting

Here is a word of caution about adjournment: If the assembly needs to have another meeting, the assembly needs to establish the date, time, and place of the meeting prior to adjournment. If members adjourn without adopting a motion to set the time for another meeting, the assembly dissolves and has to start again from the very beginning if another meeting is called.

Using a mass meeting to establish an organization

A mass meeting can be used to bring an organization into being. The procedures are the same as those explained in the "Conducting a mass meeting" section, except for the following:

- The chairman and secretary elected are considered chairman *pro tem* and secretary *pro tem,* and they serve until permanent officers are elected. *Pro tem* means "for the time being."

- A motion must be presented to establish the organization.

- A bylaws committee is appointed to draft bylaws for the new organization.

- A time and a place are set for the next meeting, the purpose of which is to consider the proposed bylaws.

- After the bylaws are adopted at the next meeting, the members recess in order to enroll the members.
- After the membership is established, permanent officers are elected.

INFORMAL MEETINGS

Informal meetings are specifically designed for boards and committees whose membership is under 12. They are called "informal" because the rules are less formal than rules for larger bodies. The person presiding is usually seated and can make motions, discuss motions, and vote on motions. The members do not have to rise to address the chair, and members can often discuss ideas before they make a motion. However, even though an informal meeting has a more relaxed approach, members should still follow an agenda and limit discussion to the subject of the meeting. If these techniques are not practiced, time is wasted and things do not get accomplished. The two most common types of informal meetings are *board* and *committee meetings*.

Board Meetings (Under 12 Members)

In board meetings, business is conducted largely the same way as in other deliberative assembly meetings. All boards must transact business in a properly called meeting. For example, members must be notified of the meeting in advance, and a quorum must be present. The secretary keeps the minutes of the board meeting. The minutes are accessible only to members of the board, unless the board votes to release them to the general membership or two-thirds of the general membership votes to have them released and read to all members. At board meetings, the executive committee (if one exists) should report to the board what it has been doing since the last board meeting.

The formality of the rules in board meetings is determined by the size of the board. *Robert's Rules of Order* sets the dividing line between large and small boards as 12 members. Large boards operate under the same rules as other deliberative assemblies. Small boards can use more relaxed procedures, which differ from the procedures of large boards in several respects. In meetings of small boards:

- Members do not have to stand up and obtain the floor before speaking. They can speak while seated.

- Motions do not need to be seconded.

- Members can speak any number of times, and there is usually no motion to close debate.

- Members can discuss a subject while no motion is pending.

- When all the members know what they are voting on, having a formal motion before voting is not necessary. (However, for the sake of having a clear record in the minutes of the issue being voted on, putting the discussion in the form of a formal motion before taking a vote is always best. By doing so, there is no question about what everyone is voting on.)

- Unless they agree by unanimous consent, members must vote on proposed board actions just like other assemblies. However, a vote can be taken by a show of hands, which is often more convenient than other ways of voting.

- The chairman doesn't have to stand up to put a question to a vote.

- The chairman can enter into the discussion and usually remains seated while conducting the meeting. He or she usually makes motions and votes (unless board custom dictates otherwise).

If a board meeting ever disintegrates into chaos, or a lack of order prevents business from being accomplished, a wise presiding officer returns to the formal rules of conducting a meeting and advises the members that parliamentary rules are in place. (Examples of parliamentary rules are getting recognition from the chair before speaking, making a main motion before beginning to speak, observing the formal rules of debate, and stating the question before taking the vote.)

Committee Meetings (Under 12 Members)

The chairman (or the first member named to a new committee, who usually acts as the chairman) is responsible for calling together the committee. This means that he or she sets the time, date, and place of the meeting and notifies all the committee members. The chairman can be appointed by the presiding officer of the assembly or can be elected by the committee.

If for any reason the chairman won't call a committee meeting, two members can call the committee meeting. A quorum is a majority of the committee's total membership.

The rules in a committee meeting are the same as those specified for small boards. The chairman usually acts as the secretary of a small committee. In a large committee, someone else is usually chosen to act as the secretary.

Committees operate under the same bylaws, parliamentary authority, standing rules, and special rules that govern the organization creating the committee. Committees do not make their own rules (except when authorized by a higher authority — the bylaws or the assembly — to do so).

The chairman of a committee plays a very active role in the committee. He or she can make motions, debate, and vote in the committee. Because debate is not limited in a committee, it can continue as long as necessary to reach an acceptable conclusion.

A committee doesn't really decide anything (unless it has been given power by the assembly to make certain specific decisions). Usually a committee just makes recommendations, which are then discussed and voted on by the parent assembly. (The committee is basically a "child" of the organization that created it.)

Should the committee wish to take action beyond the scope of its powers, it can report to the assembly that it seeks empowerment to do so. If the assembly assents, it can empower the committee to take the action requested.

When committees are about to decide on an important issue, they should invite members of the organization to appear and offer their views on the subject being discussed. They can also invite nonmembers who have expertise in the subject. This is called a *hearing*. After everyone who has an interest in the proceedings has been heard, the committee deliberates privately. During committee deliberations, only committee members have the right to be present. Any vote taken to decide the will of the committee, including information to include in committee reports, requires a majority vote.

In a committee, the motion to *reconsider the vote in committee* allows members to revisit an issue that has been voted on. This procedure is handled differently than in regular meetings of assemblies. In a committee:

- Members can make and take up the motion to reconsider any number of times. Also, there is no limit on the amount of time that has elapsed since the original motion was considered and voted on.

- Any member who did not vote on the losing side can make the motion to reconsider in committee. This means that the person could have been absent or abstained when the committee originally took the vote.

- A two-thirds vote is required to adopt the motion to reconsider in committee, unless all the members who voted on the prevailing side are present or have been notified, in which case a majority suffices.

ELECTRONIC MEETINGS

Many organizations today have officers and members scattered across the globe and choose to conduct meetings via the telephone, e-mail, or videoconferencing. Remember that the reason organizations have meetings is so members can hear about issues, respond to what others are saying, and give suggestions to evaluate them all at the same time. Telephone and video conferencing meetings allow members the means to accomplish these goals. If members want to hold telephone or video conferencing meetings, the bylaws must include a special provision. Members should adopt rules of order concerning basic parliamentary procedure about how to obtain the floor, make motions, and handle the debate in telephone and video conferencing meetings.

However, meeting via e-mail or electronic chat room does not allow members to fully participate in the democratic process. Many organizations today try this approach to meetings and find that it creates confusion rather than order. They have difficulty keeping order, having members understand where they are in the process, and getting business done.

E-mail is quickly replacing many other forms of communication. Many people find it a fast, inexpensive way to inform and communicate with others. However, because of its convenience, a temptation of e-mail is for some disgruntled officer or member to e-mail everyone with their concerns, or even a resignation, and then later have to withdraw the resignation or apologize for off-the-cuff remarks. Another problem is that members send e-mail messages intended only for boards and committee members to those who are not members of the boards or committees. Because the information is shared with the members in general before any decision is made, this can cause dissension in the organization.

E-mail is a quick way to get announcements, agendas, committee reports, and minutes to members. However, e-mail is not always effective when used during a decision-making process. Some e-mails get read immediately, and some don't. Occasionally, e-mail is not delivered to the proper recipient, or it is not delivered at all.

One problem with deciding an issue by e-mail is that members often respond to the remarks of one member at a time, instead of responding to all of them at once. Plus, two or more members may be typing a response at the same time, and if conflicting responses to an issue are sent simultaneously, it can be difficult to determine the response from which to work.

Often the entire group becomes confused with who said what, who responded to what, and what was finally decided. As a result, organizations must still have a standard meeting to get everything sorted out. What begins as a potential timesaver can result in wasting a lot of time. If the members were in a room together, they would all hear the discussion at the same time, know who is speaking and what side they are on, and know the outcome of a vote. Because there is not much order in electronic meetings, essential elements of democracy are sidestepped (see Chapter 1).

E-mail meetings may be helpful for organizations whose members are scattered, but it should not be used as a medium for decision-making in organizations whose members can easily meet in person. For this reason, the organization's rules should clearly define any use of e-mail.

Until someone designs a good computer program for having online meetings, using e-mail for sharing newsletters or factual information or for correcting the minutes is best. If members want to use e-mail for official notification of meetings, the bylaws should contain this information, but keep in mind that not everyone has a computer or Internet access.

MEETING MANAGEMENT

Every organization has goals that it wants to accomplish, which require that its members work together. But anyone who works with a group knows that one of two things generally happens: either one person in the group is willing to do all the work, so it gets done; or a meeting is called about the work to be done, which leads only to more meetings. Many people are being "meeting-ed" to death these days, and the meetings don't accomplish all that they should.

Is there a way to solve the meeting dilemma but still preserve democracy and not waste everyone's time? Yes, through *meeting management.* Many of the techniques previously explained in this book, such as preparing and following an agenda, rotating debate and keeping debate within its limits, and insisting that members keep to the topic at hand are elements of meeting management.

The following suggestions apply mainly to informal meeting settings, such as board and committee meetings, where organizations waste the most time because people don't stay on the subject. Often a committee meeting turns into a social event, or the members get sidetracked by discussing or deciding something that is not within the scope of the meeting or the duties of the committee or board.

Here are some helpful techniques for managing a meeting so that you can accomplish what you set out to do in an efficient, timely manner:

- Don't have a meeting if you can accomplish the objective some other way. Perhaps phone calls, e-mails, faxes, or letters will suffice.

- If you need to meet, minimize attendees and time spent. Only call those people who really need to be there. Give attendees as much notice as possible. Include time, place, start and end times, subject, and agenda in the call of the meeting. If visual aids are needed (charts, videos, overheads, and so on), set them up well in advance and test to ensure that they function properly.

- Start the meeting on time. Don't allow latecomers to waste the time of those who arrive promptly.

- Allot a reasonable amount of time to accomplish the meeting's objectives and stick to the schedule. Follow the agenda to cover each item as quickly as possible. Don't allow discussion to get off the subject of the agenda.

- Have someone take minutes or notes on what the committee or group decides to do. The chairman should keep a list of assignments and target dates for action. In recurring meetings, discuss issues from previous meetings and give progress reports.

- Before ending the meeting, have the recorder summarize plans that were agreed upon as well as target dates. End the meeting on time.

- Know what your responsibility and authority is in the meeting. This should be stated in the bylaws. Be sure that you have the authority to make decisions about the issues being discussed at the meeting. Foresee what is likely to happen in the meeting and prepare for it.

- Use committees. Delegate responsibility and work to smaller groups. If you are the chair of a committee, break up the work among the members. A wise meeting manager uses committees to get a lot of work accomplished for the organization.

- When giving directions or assigning tasks to others, make sure that they understand what they are expected to do and when it is to be done.

- Make sure that the leader of the meeting does what a leader is supposed to do: He or she should know the agenda items as well as what decisions and action plans are going to be proposed. The leader should be impartial but have the facts surrounding any proposed action plans. The leader should allow debate on the agenda items but make sure that discussion sticks to the agenda and doesn't wander and waste time on irrelevant issues. The leader should follow the agenda and keep the meeting moving.

- Use general consent instead of a vote on noncontroversial issues, such as:

  - Paying bills

  - Approving the minutes of the previous meeting

  - Answering correspondence

  - Closing nominations

  - Considering reports and recommendations

  - Adjourning

  To determine if general consent is possible, the chairman says, "If there is no objection, we will do . . . ." If no one objects, the action can be done in the name of the organization. The chairman says, "Hearing no objection, we will do . . . ."

Managing Meetings at the Office

Can a business use these same techniques at the office? Can a knowledge of democratic principles and formal rules and procedures help in conducting meetings in the business world? Most definitely yes! Incorporating meeting management techniques and the basic principles of parliamentary procedure in business meetings saves time, encourages input from all the participants, and gives structure to the meeting.

The basic principle of taking up one item of business at a time is applicable in any meeting. The person planning or facilitating the meeting should have an agenda or a list (arranged in the order of priority) of things to accomplish at the meeting. Everyone attending the meeting should receive a copy of the agenda.

The principle of impartiality is also applicable. The key question the meeting planner should ask is, "Do I really want the ideas of others, or do I just want to tell them what to do?" How the meeting planner answers this question determines how the meeting proceeds.

If the person conducting the meeting really wants the input of employees or colleagues, he or she will be impartial — refraining from passing judgment on what is said and allowing all to speak. In this kind of meeting, it is important to alternate the discussion in order to bring out the best ideas. The meeting leader will not allow one person or a small group of people to dominate the discussion; he or she also solicits opinions from those who are not participating in the discussion.

Here are some other important points to remember when conducting a meeting:

- When calling the meeting, explain its purpose and what you hope to accomplish. An example may be "how to cut down the time between when an order is received and when it is shipped."

- Include in the meeting all the people involved in solving the problem.

- Set a meeting time and place that is convenient for all attendees.

- If several departments in a large organization are involved, have the meeting in a neutral place and choose a facilitator who is impartial.

- Prepare for the meeting. Gather information in advance and send it to those who will attend. Ask them to consider the information and to come with solutions.

- Start and end the meeting on time. If more work needs to be done, set another meeting and encourage the members to continue thinking about solutions.

The most effective meetings in the business world are those in which employees know that their ideas are taken seriously and implemented. When employers call meetings just to talk *at* their employees, no one takes these meetings seriously, and everyone will make excuses not to attend.

The Meeting Environment

Another factor of meeting management is the meeting room itself. Check the obvious factors in advance. For example, is the room large enough to seat the group comfortably? It should not be too large or too small. Is it temperature-controlled so that the members won't get too hot or too cold? Is it quiet enough for the audience to hear the speakers and the leaders? Does it have audio and video equipment, overhead projectors, computers, or whatever else speakers may need to present their information?

Does the room have a properly functioning public address system (if needed)? Are there enough exits into and out of the room for safety, but not so many that the organization can't control admission? Are there enough tables and chairs? Check all these matters in advance to ensure that the room is properly prepared.

The seating arrangement can facilitate the meeting. For smaller meetings (fewer than 30 people), some experts suggest that circular or semicircular seating helps focus the members' attention on the leader and on each other. This arrangement is good for promoting interaction. The circular seating pattern fosters a sense of equality (like the Knights of the Round Table). Although it is good for intense face-to-face interaction, it may not be good for problem solving. When using the semi-circle, make sure that the door to the room is at the bottom of the U so that meeting participants are not distracted by persons coming and going. The diameter of the semicircle should be about 15 feet for a 15-person meeting. If there are more than 15 people, set up a second row of chairs. This way everyone can easily see each other, the leader, and any visual aids at the front of the room.

No matter what seating arrangement you choose, encourage people to sit close together. Sitting close together promotes a feeling of group cohesiveness. If you know that someone has left the meeting and will not return, take away the empty chair and move the group together to fill the empty space. Avoid empty spaces because they suggest something missing or a vacuum — psychologically negative suggestions for a group that is trying to accomplish something together.

Evaluating Your Meetings

After a meeting, evaluate what happened so that you can plan better meetings in the future. The following checklist helps you identify mistakes and avoid future ones:

- Was a detailed meeting agenda provided so that everyone knew what was supposed to happen?

- Did everyone receive sufficient notice of the meeting so they could plan to attend?

- Did the presiding officer follow the agenda?

- Did the chairman announce the results of the votes and the effect that the votes would have?

- Did the chairman keep the discussion on track? Or, did members raise and discuss unrelated issues?

- Was there adequate time to conduct the business on the agenda?

- Did members listen to the discussion and wait their turn to speak? Or, was cross-talk allowed to disrupt and distract the business at hand?

- Did the members and the chairman follow the rules of parliamentary procedure? Or did they make up the rules as they went along?

- Did the chair allow the speakers to make their statements? (The chair should interrupt only to call the meeting to order, to call time, or to redirect the discussion to the business at hand.)

- Did everyone speak and participate? Or was discussion dominated by one, two, or a few members?

- Did the chairman enter the discussion without stepping down from the chair? Did the chairman try to *railroad* an issue or stifle discussion on an issue?

- Were any decisions made in haste and without sufficient consideration?

- When a decision was made, were there clear instructions regarding what was to be done, who was to do it, when they were to complete it, and when they were to report back to the organization?

- Were any hidden agendas at work in the discussion?

- Was there discord in the meeting? Was it resolved? If so, how was it resolved?

- Did the members see alternative courses of action? Were any presented?

- Did all members participate in the discussion? If some didn't, did the chairman try to bring them into the discussion? If they still didn't participate, did anyone try to find out why?

- Regarding committee reports, did committees report on what they had done rather than what they were going to do?

- Was the room comfortable for the meeting? Or was it too hot, too cold, too large, too small, too noisy, too bereft of chairs or tables, or deficient in any other way?

- Was the seating arrangement appropriate for the meeting?

- Did the audio and video equipment (if any) operate properly?
- Were there any other problems that could be identified and corrected in future meetings?

MEETING STRATEGIES

This section offers plans of action for either adopting a motion or defeating a motion while preserving the highest ideal of democratic proceedings in meetings. Although the word *strategy* has a favorable definition — a careful plan or method to achieve a goal — it can also connote a plan of action to defeat an enemy by trickery.

The intent of this discussion is not subterfuge but information. This section describes the procedure or procedures that counteract any motion presented in a meeting. There are always two sides (sometimes many sides) to each issue, and if one group prevails by subverting the democratic process and preventing the other side(s) from being heard, the action is doomed to fail. Often such action leads to the breaking up of the organization. However, each side of an issue has the right to use parliamentary procedures in a fair, just, and honest way to obtain its goal.

Here is a word of advice from Henry Robert:

> Where there is radical difference of opinion in an organization, one side must yield. The great lesson for democracies to learn is for the majority to give to the minority a full, free opportunity to present their side of the case, and then for the minority, having failed to win a majority to their views, gracefully to submit and to recognize the action as that of the entire organization, and cheerfully to assist in carrying it out, until they can secure its repeal.

All members should know fully the rules of procedure, their rights as members, and how to protect those rights. Remember that if an opposition sleeps on its rights, it may be too late to correct the action. Therefore, members must pay attention to what is happening in the meeting and point out to the chair and the assembly any mistakes when they happen — not after the meeting has adjourned and everyone has gone home.

Strategies for Members

When organizations have to consider a controversial issue, both sides commonly come to the meeting with a plan to achieve their goals. If the organization is divided on the issue and the presentation of the debate was equal, usually the side having the best understanding of parliamentary procedure wins. Therefore, all members should understand the types of strategies and how to counter each one.

There are several types of meeting strategies: those necessary to adopt, delay, or defeat an action; to bring a compromise; and to change an action.

One of the most important strategies is to come prepared for the meeting. The person who will make the motion should already be assigned and rehearsed, have the motion carefully worded, and be prepared for the debate. During rehearsal for debate, ask someone to play devil's advocate so that members can counter the opposition's objections. Plan what you will do when motions are made to defeat the proposed action; if possible, work with a parliamentarian. The same advice goes for those opposing the action.

If you are the person who has to preside during a controversy, think about all the situations and motions that can arise, and prepare for them. Be ready to keep order and handle points of order and appeals from the decision of the chair. Seek advice from a parliamentarian before the meeting and, if possible, hire a parliamentarian to help you during the meeting.

Strategy to adopt an action

Often a proposed action comes from a committee or the board of an organization. If this is the case, the great advantage is that the proposal comes from an official organ of the organization. In the eyes of the membership, such a proposal usually carries more authority than if an individual member makes the motion. There is also more than one person supporting the idea. The other advantage is that in presenting the idea to the members, the committee or board gives a report explaining the whys and wherefores of the motion. The committee can meet many objections in the report by providing enough information. The other advantage that a board or committee has is the ability to give to the assembly written information attached to the agenda or sent out with the call to the meeting.

An individual presenting a motion isn't able to give a report or attach printed materials to the agenda without the permission of the assembly. Nor is an individual likely to have a small group of supporters already in favor of the action. However, one way to get more information to the group about the motion is to present it in the form of a resolution. In this form, the preamble can state the reason for the proposed action.

A defensive strategy in adopting a motion is to watch for those who may try to shut off debate prematurely, or those who try to kill a motion by laying it on the table instead of making the motion to postpone indefinitely. During the meeting, if you feel that you are losing ground or you need to consult with others, make a motion to recess. If the members seem to need more time to think about the motion, or the committee needs to gather more facts, use a delaying strategy.

Strategy to delay an action

Delaying an action is sometimes the wisest move to make. There are two ways to delay an action: first by referring the motion to a committee and second by postponing it to a later time. (Sometimes the motion to reconsider the vote delays the action if this motion is not taken up at the meeting but is called up at the next meeting.)

A delaying strategy is helpful if a member makes a motion that no one is prepared to discuss or has even thought about. In this instance, the motion to postpone to the next meeting enables the members to gather information, formulate their reasons pro or con, and get the absent members to attend the next meeting. In cases where the members are uncertain because they don't have enough information, or when they want to know how the details are going to be worked out, it is best not to push for a decision at that meeting but to make a motion to refer to a committee.

Strategy to defeat a motion

Members don't always agree, and those who oppose an action have the right to try to defeat it. The most obvious ways to defeat an action are to:

- Debate against it.

- Postpone it indefinitely.

- Postpone it to another meeting, hoping that members can gather more support to vote against it.

However, if something detrimental to the organization or a member is proposed, the wisest action is to object to consideration of the question immediately after the chairman states it. This motion should seldom be used, and only when something would truly harm the organization even to discuss it. (For information on making this motion, see Chapter 9.)

Compromise as a strategy

An alternative to defeating a motion is to compromise. Very rarely is an issue a *yes* or *no* question. Most issues are negotiable and can be resolved through discussing, carefully listening to others, and then using the amending process. For example, say that the membership is divided about the time of the meetings. Group A wants the meetings changed to an earlier time, but Group B wants to keep the current time. After much discussion and proposing of amendments, the members vote on a time that neither one really wants but that is between the current meeting time and Group A's suggestion. It is a compromise that everyone can accept.

Other strategies

Besides the strategies already discussed, there are others that an organization can use to effectively change an action, correct a mistake, cool down tempers, keep a motion alive, or deal with various situations arising in a meeting:

- **A point of order:** A point of order can correct a multitude of errors. If the chair does not correct a serious mistake in a meeting, a member can raise a point of order. Members should use this motion only when a serious mistake has been made in the meeting; for example, when members' rights are being taken away. The chair always rules on the point of order before proceeding with any further discussion or motions. If a member does not agree with the chair's ruling, he or she should appeal the decision of the chair.

- **Parliamentary inquiry:** If a member realizes that the assembly doesn't understand what is going on, he or she can rise to parliamentary inquiry, which he or she can do at any time. This is not considered debate, so the member can make it while a nondebatable question is pending. This action may help, for example, when someone has moved the previous question to try to cut off a member's right to debate. A member can rise and ask the chair what will happen if the members vote for the previous question.

- **Point of information:** A member can raise a point of information anytime during debate to ask for factual information. It is not considered debate, so a member can lead the discussion without debating by asking all the right questions.

- **Motion to recess:** A motion to recess can help cool things off in debate or can provide time to plan strategies with those who are of like mind. Or, it can buy time to call in additional support from members not present. If someone moves the previous question early in debate, a motion to recess can rally votes to stop this motion. If things aren't going your way, move to take a recess.

- **Move the previous question:** When nothing new is being said but debate is lingering, make the motion to stop debate by saying "I move the previous question." If adopted, this closes debate and brings the motion to a vote.

- **Lay the pending motion on the table:** If there is a motion being debated on the floor and a member needs to leave the meeting early but wants to make a motion before leaving, he or she can move to lay the pending motion on the table. If adopted, the pending motion will be temporarily laid aside and the member can now make the new motion. Once this issue is decided, someone can move to take the original motion from the table. If the motion is adopted, the assembly proceeds with the meeting where it left off.

- **Postpone to later in the meeting:** If a motion is being discussed and a member who has important information about the subject has not arrived, a member can move to postpone the motion to later in the meeting.

   Or, if a member is not at the meeting but another member knows that the member would come to the meeting with a simple telephone call, he or she can make a motion to recess. During the recess, this person can call the member and find out when the member will arrive at the meeting. He or she can then make the motion to postpone until later in the meeting to give the member time to arrive. If the member can't make the meeting, another member can make a motion to postpone the vote to the next meeting.

- **Reconsider and enter on the minutes:** When a temporary majority resulting from an unrepresented attendance at the meeting pushes through a motion that many absent members would have opposed, the best strategy is to vote on the prevailing side and then move to reconsider and enter on the minutes (see Chapter 17.) This motion needs a second. It stops all action on the motion, which members can bring up only at the next meeting. The call letter for the next meeting must include a notice about this motion.

- **Fix the time to which to adjourn:** If members want to go home but important business still needs to be discussed which may die if the meeting adjourned because of a time element, set the time for an adjourned meeting.

To do this, make the motion to fix the time to which to adjourn. Set the hour, date, and place for the meeting. You can then make the motion to adjourn. At an adjourned meeting, business is taken up where the members stopped at adjournment.

- **Consider the intent of a motion:** When a motion is not worded in proper parliamentary terms, consider the intent of the motion. For example, a member may move to table something to the next meeting. This is really the motion to postpone to the next meeting. If the chair places it before the assembly as the motion to lay on the table, a member should raise a point of order because it is taking away the members' right to debate, and it only requires a majority vote. Another example is if a member makes a motion that would, in effect, rescind something previously adopted where no previous notice was given. Alert members will point out that the vote needed to adopt this motion is a two-thirds vote or a majority of the entire membership. By understanding intent, the membership knows the proper rules governing any situation.

Voting strategies

If a voice vote is taken and a member feels that the vote is not decisive, he or she should call for a division. The chair must retake the vote by asking the members to rise. If a question is controversial and a member thinks having a secret vote would deliver the most honest and representative vote, he or she should move to take the vote by ballot. This motion needs a second, is not debatable, and requires a majority vote.

Requests for clarification

When you don't understand what is going on in a meeting or you've gotten lost in the procedures, the best strategy is to ask the chair by rising to a parliamentary inquiry. If more members use this tool, organizations can prevent much misunderstanding in meetings.

Another way to use a parliamentary inquiry is to ask the chair if it is in order to do something. The chair's duty is to assist the members in presenting business.

Still another way of asking for help in a meeting is by requesting a point of information. If you want more facts about the subject being discussed or don't understand what someone has just said, ask. For example, a member may say,

> **Member:** Mr. Chairman, I rise to a point of information. Did I understand the previous speaker to say . . . ?

Be assured that if you didn't understand something or are lost in the procedures of a meeting, others are probably having the same problem.

Paying attention pays off

Members can often stop illegal actions before they occur in a main motion by remembering these points:

■ A main motion can't conflict with national, state, or local laws. It can't conflict with the bylaws (constitution) or rules of the assembly. If such a motion is adopted, even by a unanimous vote, it is null and void.

If such a motion is made, the presiding officer should rule it out of order. If the presiding officer does not rule it out of order, a member should call a point of order, stating that it conflicts with the existing laws, bylaws, or rules.

■ Members can't make a motion that presents substantially the same question as a motion that was previously rejected during the same meeting. Members can renew a motion if there is a change in wording or a difference in time or conditions.

However, if a member votes on the prevailing side, he or she can move to reconsider the vote on the motion that was defeated. If the motion to reconsider is adopted, the motion is again before the assembly as if it were never voted on, and the members can amend it or substitute something more to the liking of the membership.

Here's an example: The assembly voted against having a booth at the county fair because no one had the time to man the booth. After some progress in the meeting, a member who voted against the motion comes up with a creative solution, so the member moves to reconsider the vote. The vote is reconsidered, and the motion is now before the assembly again. It is then amended to everyone's satisfaction and adopted.

- A motion can't conflict with a motion previously adopted and still in force. However, a member can move to rescind the action or to amend the action (which is called *amend something previously adopted*). If an action is rescinded, it is no longer in force.

- A main motion can't conflict with, or present substantially the same question as, a motion that is temporarily set aside. For example, if a motion is postponed, laid on the table, or referred to a committee (or if a reconsideration is moved and not taken up), someone can't make a motion that conflicts with the motion that has been temporarily put aside. If such a motion is made, the chair should rule it out of order and state the proper procedure. If the chair does not rule the motion out of order, a member can raise a point of order.

The correct procedures for handling motions that conflict with or present substantially the same question as a motion that has been temporarily set aside are:

- If a motion is laid on the table, make the motion to take it from the table.

- If a motion has been postponed, move to suspend the rules and take up the motion.

- If a motion has been made to reconsider the vote and has not yet been called up, call up the motion to reconsider.

- If a motion has been referred to a committee and the committee has not yet reported, move to discharge the committee.

- A main motion that proposes action outside the organization's purpose (as defined in the object of the bylaws or corporate charter) can be considered only by a two-thirds vote.

Strategies for Presiding Officers

The presiding officer's duty is to ensure that all meetings proceed in a democratic fashion and that all procedures and proposed actions are in accord with the governing documents of the organization and parliamentary rules. Therefore, a presiding officer should be thoroughly familiar with the following:

- The bylaws and other governing documents of the organization

- The organization's adopted parliamentary authority

- The agenda and any controversial issues that may be coming before the assembly

- Procedures for presiding, the ranking of motions, and the rules of debate

Should a presiding officer have a meeting strategy? Yes, in the sense that he or she is well prepared to conduct the meeting. An effective presiding officer is thoroughly familiar with the agenda and presides from a meeting script. (See Appendix B for a sample meeting script.) The officer has reviewed different procedures from the organization's parliamentary authority and has consulted beforehand with the parliamentarian about any tricky items that may come up.

The presiding officer's goal should be to expedite business in a timely fashion while still allowing members to present it in a fair manner. He or she should not try to push things through solely to get things done in record time.

Most presiding officers are familiar with the members and know which issues are hot-button issues. When a presiding officer knows that an agenda item is one of those issues, the officer should thoroughly prepare to keep control of the meeting so that it doesn't get out of hand.

Techniques for keeping order in a meeting are:

- Read up on how to handle debate and any motions that members may use to block the democratic process, such as *previous question, lay on the table, points of order,* and *appeals from the decision of the chair.*

- Before debate begins, remind the members of the rules of debate:

  - The member making the motion has the first right to speak to the motion.

  - Everyone gets a turn to speak, and debate is alternated between the pros and cons.

  - Members must rise, address the chair, and be recognized before speaking.

  When members know that the chair is impartial and in control of the situation, they are more likely to behave.

- If things start to get out of control, declare a recess. If a brawl begins, adjourn the meeting to protect the membership. (You can't adjourn the meeting because you think it is going on too long or because you don't like the members questioning your decisions.)

- Know when and how to use general consent in taking a vote, as well as when to assume a motion and take the vote. Instead of waiting for someone to move to pay the bills, say:

  President: All those in favor of paying the bills say "Aye." Those opposed say "No." *[Announce the vote.]*

  To vote by general consent, say:

  President: Is there any objection to paying the bills? Hearing none, the treasurer will pay the bills.

- Keep the meeting going forward! If members don't rise to debate an issue, take a vote. Don't wait for someone to move the previous question. When debate is going on, alternate between those who are in favor and those opposed. Ask:

President: Does anyone want to speak for the motion?

Then,

President: Does anyone want to speak against the motion?

If members make substantially the same points, ask:

President: Is there anything new to add to the discussion?

If no one rises to speak, take the vote. Or ask if there is any objection to closing debate and taking a vote. If one person objects to closing debate, you must take a rising vote. If two-thirds of the assembly votes to close debate, you can take a vote on the motion.

The chair should be good at reading the assembly and knowing when they are ready to vote. The chair can use this procedure of closing debate when the members aren't readily rising to debate. By asking "are you ready for the question?" or "is there any objection to closing debate and taking a vote?" the chair tells the members that if they don't rise to discuss the issue further, the chair is taking the vote now.

- When handling debate, remember that the member who made the motion has the first right to speak to the motion. *Robert's Rules of Order, Newly Revised,* says, "The chair should turn toward the maker of the motion to see if he wishes to be assigned the floor first in debate . . . ." Be watchful in this situation. Many times members who are opposed to a motion will move the previous question as soon as the motion is made in an attempt to force an immediate vote. If this happens, you do not have to entertain the motion *previous question* because there has been no debate. If the motion at hand is a controversial question, you have an obligation to see that debate is not stopped before the minority has been able to present its side.

- Remember to remain impartial and courteous at all times and conduct the meeting in a democratic way. If you feel strongly about an issue, step down and let another officer preside until the vote is taken. (However, this officer must not yet have debated the issue.)

  One way to handle this situation is to find someone in the membership who feels the same as you do and have that member speak to the motion. If you know that something is coming up at the meeting, you can give facts and information to that member to present to the membership. By remaining impartial and unbiased, you retain the respect of the members.

- If in doubt about why a member has risen and addressed the chair, especially when a nondebatable question is pending, say:

  President: For what purpose does the member rise?

- You don't have to wait for someone to make the motion to adjourn. If no further business is coming forward, take a vote on adjourning the meeting by saying:

  President: Is there further business? *[pause]* All those in favor of adjourning the meeting, say "Aye." Those opposed say "No." The ayes have it, and the meeting is adjourned.

  Or you can say:

  President: Is there any objection to adjourning the meeting? *[pause]* Hearing no objection, the meeting will adjourn. *[pause]* The meeting is adjourned.

- When you anticipate a complicated procedure (such as adopting bylaws) or a series of motions, the most efficient way to conduct the meeting is to instruct the members in the correct procedures for that part of the meeting.

17

Strategies for Individual Motions Illustrated

This chapter provides strategies that you can use with various classes of motions. It explains in brief the purpose of each strategic motion and how members can use that motion in a meeting to help adopt — or defeat — another motion. This chapter also explains the countermotions for each strategic motion.

As you read about the various classes of motions and their countermotions, keep in mind the fundamentals about main motions. Recall that before a member can discuss a topic at a meeting, he or she must state it as a main motion and second it. If the motion does not get a second, it is not placed before the assembly. However, if members begin debating a motion that does not have a second, the fact that it was never seconded is a moot point. After discussion begins, no one can stop the discussion on the motion nor prevent a vote on it because it was not seconded. A second does not mean that someone is in favor of the motion, only that another member wants to hear it discussed. The maker of the motion has the first right to discuss the motion. After the chair states the motion, it belongs to the assembly, not to the maker of the motion, and members can alter the motion as they see fit.

Members can take an immediate counteraction when a motion is proposed by objecting to its consideration. Or, they can apply subsidiary motions to the main motion to change or defeat it. The following sections explain these strategies. The motions are given in the same order as in *Robert's Rules of Order, Newly Revised* (Perseus Books) according to each motion's rank. (For additional information on any of these motions, see Part II.)

OBJECT TO A MOTION'S CONSIDERATION

If a member believes that a main motion would be detrimental to the organization or a member to discuss (for example, if a very controversial issue has the potential to split the membership in half), he or she can immediately object to its consideration. A two-thirds vote in the negative (that is, against consideration) is required to sustain the objection and not consider the main motion. In taking the vote the president asks,

> **President:** Shall the motion be considered?

SUBSIDIARY MOTIONS

The following subsidiary and privileged motions can help either adopt or defeat the main motion. Countermotions are given for each motion.

Postpone Indefinitely

The *motion to postpone indefinitely* has three purposes: to kill the main motion, to test the strength of opposition on the motion, and to enable a member to speak two more times to the main motion. It requires a second and is debatable. During debate of this subsidiary motion, members can discuss the main motion. If the motion to postpone indefinitely is adopted, it kills the main motion for the duration of the meeting. However, members can bring up the main motion again at the same meeting by a motion to reconsider the vote. (An affirmative vote to postpone indefinitely can be reconsidered.) Or, members can bring up the motion again according to the rules of renewal of a motion. Members can also bring up the main motion before the assembly at another meeting.

Strategies for countering a motion to postpone indefinitely are:

- **Amend:** If members are against killing the main motion, they can move to amend it to make it more agreeable to the opposition. If the motion to amend is made, it takes precedence over postpone indefinitely.

- **Refer to a committee:** If the main motion is referred to a committee to investigate, postpone indefinitely does not go to the committee. However, the committee can recommend that it be killed.

- **Postpone to a certain time:** If members want to gather support for or against the motion, they can postpone it until the next meeting. Or, members can fix the time to which to adjourn (set a time for an adjourned meeting) and then postpone the motion to the adjourned meeting.

Amend

The purpose of the motion to amend is to change the main motion either to make it more agreeable or to defeat it. In the latter case, the motion may be a hostile amendment. For example, if someone moved to give the secretary a raise, someone else can propose an amendment to give the secretary a decrease in salary.

Another way members can use an amendment to defeat a motion is to substitute another motion for the main motion, which the following section discusses.

Strategies for countering a motion to amend are:

- If a motion is poorly worded and fixing it with amendments would take too long, someone should suggest that the motion be withdrawn. If the assembly agrees, start again with a new motion.

- If you are unhappy about how your main motion is being amended, move to refer it to a committee to investigate and come up with a solution.

Each member can always speak and vote against any proposed amendment with one exception: If the main motion is amended, the maker of the main motion can vote against it but cannot speak against the motion.

Substitute

If a member does not like a motion, he or she can make a motion to strike out all or part of the motion and replace it. This is the motion to substitute. Members can use this method to strike out a paragraph, a section, an article, or even the entire motion or resolution. In the case of a main motion, *substitute* replaces one main motion with another main motion. Members can also use this motion to make more than one change at a time.

There are specific procedures for using the motion to substitute. For example, say a member makes the following main motion:

> **Member 1:** I move to buy a new word processing typewriter.

Another member can amend the motion by substitution:

> **Member 2:** I move to amend the motion by striking out the entire motion and substituting "to buy a computer and a laser printer."

The motion to substitute needs a second and is debatable. It is considered a primary amendment (see Chapter 6), and members cannot make it when another primary amendment is pending. Debate can focus on the merits of both the original main motion and the substitute. Through debating, the membership decides which motion is the main motion.

The chair states the motion to substitute this way:

> **President:** It is moved and seconded to amend the motion by striking out the main motion and substituting "to buy a computer and a laser printer." Is there any discussion?

> **Member 2:** I believe that buying a computer and a laser printer would be a better investment for us than a word processing typewriter because it does more than word processing. The treasurer could keep all the financial records on the computer. Others could use it too and have their own files. A word processing typewriter will soon be obsolete.

Member 1: I speak against the substitute motion and for the typewriter. Right now this is all the organization needs, and we need to think of our budget.

Debate goes on until the members are ready to vote. The chair takes the vote this way:

President: The question is on the motion to substitute. Shall the motion to buy a computer replace the motion to buy a typewriter as the main motion of the assembly? As many as are in favor say "Aye." Those opposed say "No." The ayes have it, and motion to substitute is adopted. The pending question (to be considered now) is to buy a computer and a laser printer. Is there any discussion?

If the noes have it, the chair would say:

President: The noes have it, and the motion to substitute is lost. The question is on buying a word processing typewriter. Is there any discussion?

Remember that during this process, members vote to determine which motion is the main motion. The vote taken does not adopt either the main motion or the substitute motion. After the motion to substitute is decided by a vote, the main motion is considered by the membership just like any other main motion.

The perfecting process

During the substitution process, members can amend both the main motion and the substitute motion. This is the *perfecting process*. It allows members, if they wish, to make the pending main motion more attractive to the group. Those in favor of the substitution may want to amend to compromise, so that the motion to substitute will be adopted.

If members want to amend either the pending main motion or the substitute motion, the chair must first take amendments on the pending main motion — the motion that was made first. After the members finish amending the pending main motion, the chair takes amendments on the substitute motion. When this is finished, the chair takes a vote to determine which of these motions is the main motion.

In the perfecting process, members must remember this rule: If the substitute motion is adopted as the main motion, members can't amend it further except for adding non-modifying matter. For example, if the substitute motion has been amended to "buy a computer and a laser printer not to exceed $2,000," no one may strike out and insert anything further in the motion — to strike out "laser" and insert "ink jet" is out of order. But a member can add at the end "by July 1." It is important that members make all changes to the substitute motion in the perfecting process. If the motion to buy a typewriter is voted the main motion, members can further amend it because it was the original main motion.

Fill in the blank

Another helpful form of amending that members can use as a strategy to get more input from other members is the incidental motion *fill in the blank*. This motion is a way to consider more than a primary and a secondary amendment at the same time. When members have many different ideas about specifics in a motion, such as dollar amounts, dates, times, places, names of nominees, and so on, this is a helpful procedure.

Fill in the blank allows members to strike out the specific piece of information in question, such as a date, place, time, or number, and to create a blank in the motion. The blank lets members consider many alternatives without having to go through a long amending process. This motion must be seconded, is not debatable, and must be voted on immediately.

For example, a member makes a motion to "buy a computer and a laser printer not to exceed the cost of $2,000." A second member moves to strike out "$2,000" and insert "$3,000."

What if several members had other ideas about the cost? Someone can move to create a blank.

> ***Member:*** Madam President.
>
> ***President:*** *[assigns the member the floor]*
>
> ***Member:*** I move to strike out "$3,000" and create a blank.
>
> ***Member 2:*** Second.
>
> ***President:*** It is moved and seconded to strike out "$3,000" and create a blank. As many as are in favor say "Aye." Those opposed say "No." *[None are opposed.]* The ayes have it, and a blank is created. The chair will now take suggestions on filling the blank.

Any member can rise and, without recognition, insert an amount to fill the blank. These proposals do not need a second. Each member can give only one suggestion to fill the blank and cannot give a second suggestion unless he or she has unanimous consent to do so. The suggestion that was struck out to create the blank also becomes one of the suggestions to fill the blank.

When members have finished giving their suggestions, debate is open on all pending suggestions. After debate ceases, the chair takes a voice vote or, in small assemblies, takes a vote by a show of hands on all the suggestions until one suggestion receives a majority vote. It is important for members to vote for or against all suggestions because the first suggestion to get a majority vote is adopted and fills the blank. The chair should begin the voting with the least likely suggestion to be adopted. Here is an example of filling the blank:

> ***President:*** The motion to fill the blank has been created. Are there any suggestions?
>
> ***Member 2:*** One thousand five hundred dollars.
>
> ***President:*** One thousand five hundred dollars. *[writes it down]*
>
> ***Member 3:*** Two thousand five hundred dollars.
>
> ***President:*** Two thousand five hundred dollars. *[writes it down]*
>
> ***Member 4:*** Four thousand dollars.

President: Four thousand dollars. *[writes it down]* Are there any more suggestions? *[looks around and sees no one rising]* Is there any discussion on the proposed suggestions?

Member 2: Madam President.

President: *[assigns the floor]*

Member 2: I believe we can get the computer and printer that we need for $1,500, and anything over that would be unnecessary for our needs.

Member 3: Madam President.

President: *[assigns the floor]*

Member 3: I am for the amount of $2,500. Most laser printers cost between $500 and $600, and to get a computer that has all the programming we need will cost more than $1,500.

Member 1: Madam President.

President: *[assigns the floor]*

Member 1: I am for $3,000. If we buy one that costs less, we will have to install it ourselves. I know of a good computer system that we can buy from a company who will install it and teach us how to use it.

President: Is there any further discussion? *[pause]* If not, the question is on filling the blank.

Before members vote, the president should explain the voting procedure and then repeat all the suggestions for filling the blank.

President: The suggestions proposed, beginning with the largest amount, are $4,000, $3,000, $2,500, $2,000, and $1,500. The chair will take the vote beginning with $4,000 and work to the smallest sum until an amount receives a majority vote. Each member needs to vote yes or no when each amount is presented. Voting will continue until one of these amounts receives a majority vote. As many as are in favor of $4,000 say "Aye." *[One person says "Aye."]* Those opposed say "No." *[The rest say "No."]* The noes have it,

> $4,000 is defeated, and the question is on $3,000. As many as are in favor say "Aye." *[A majority says "Aye."]* Those opposed say "No." *[Two say "No."]* The ayes have it, and the blank is filled with $3,000.

When the blank is filled, voting on the proposals to fill the blank stops. The president then takes a vote on the amendment.

> **President:** The question is on the amendment "not to exceed $3,000." As many as are in favor say "Aye." Those opposed say "No." The ayes have it, and the amendment is adopted. The question is on the motion as amended, "to buy a computer and a laser printer not to exceed $3,000."

The president continues the discussion of the motion as amended or takes a vote.

Presiding officer's prerogative to propose creating a blank

If a member does not call for creating a blank and the presiding officer thinks that one is needed, the president can say:

> **President:** The chair suggests creating a blank by striking out "$2,000." If there is no objection to creating a blank *[pause and look to see if there is an objection]*, the blank is created. *[pause]*

The presiding officer should pause and wait to see if there is an objection. If there is an objection, he or she can take a vote on creating a blank. Members can make the incidental motion to create a blank when either a primary or a secondary amendment is pending.

Special note about filling the blank

The presiding officer should keep the following rules in mind when calling for a vote to fill in a blank:

- When buying something or spending money, arrange the proposed amounts from the highest to the lowest.

- When selling — or accepting a sum of money in settlement — start with the lowest amount and proceed to the highest.

- In filling the blanks with names or colors, arrange the suggestions in the order in which they were given.

- When there is no apparent reason for an increase or decrease, begin with the largest number, the longest time, or most distant date.

Refer to a Committee

One of the purposes of the motion to refer to a committee is to appoint a small group to investigate the motion and bring back their findings. In meetings where people are undecided about a motion or where a lot of amending goes on, the motion to refer to a committee is helpful. It lets a small group work out the details and then present those details to the assembly, which can ultimately save time.

In organizations that have semiannual or annual meetings, to refer a motion to a committee keeps the motion within the control of the assembly and ensures that it will be put on the agenda of the next semiannual or annual meeting.

However, if a member does not want the motion referred to a committee because he or she wants the organization to decide it now, the member can move that the assembly act as the committee. Doing so takes away the limits on debate and allows for flexibility in the discussion.

If one member moves to refer a motion to a committee but another member wants to consider it now, the second member can either debate against referral or amend it by striking out "the committee" and inserting that "the assembly act as the committee." If this amendment is adopted and the motion that the assembly act as the committee is adopted, then a solution may be reached at the meeting.

When members have many conflicting viewpoints about a matter, another helpful use of the motion *refer to a committee* is to establish breakout groups of 10 to 12 people who meet during a recess. Each group has an appointed moderator, and the groups meet in informal discussion to come up with solutions. After the meeting reconvenes, the moderators of each group give their reports. The reporting is a form of debate.

The breakout group must then return the motion to the assembly for a final decision.

Strategies for countering the motion to refer to committee are:

- Strike out the name of the committee and insert that "the assembly go into a committee of the whole (or quasi-committee of the whole for informal consideration)."

- Stipulate the date when the committee is to report back.

- Stipulate the committee's duty.

If the organization meets quarterly or less frequently and a member wants a motion decided before the next meeting, he or she can make the motion to fix the time to which to adjourn. (In other words, set the time for an adjourned meeting and then have the committee report back at that meeting.) Alternatively, a member can make the motion to recess and then have breakout groups meet to see if it can resolve issues without having to refer the motion to a committee.

The assembly needs to be alert to the possibility that some members will refer a motion to a committee with the intention of letting the issue *die in committee.* Members should pay attention to when the committee is to report back to the assembly, as well as to who is appointed to serve on the committee. For instance, say that a member moves that a committee be appointed to do a feasibility study of selling the organization's building and building a new facility. If many of the members appointed to the committee do not want to sell the building, the committee may not do what it was instructed to do. As a result of inattentive selection of committee members for this committee, the whole issue may die in committee. The proper procedure for correcting such a problem is to discharge the committee and appoint a new one.

Postpone to a Certain Time

The motion to postpone to a certain time is very useful when a member believes that too few members are present to make a representative decision. For example, say that there are just enough members present to conduct the meeting, and a controversial motion is made. A member can move to postpone it to the next meeting, arguing in debate that this motion is best discussed when more members are present.

Members can also use *postpone to a certain time* to delay a motion until later in the meeting, especially when it's known that members who may be informed about the subject are arriving late.

Likewise, members can use this motion to postpone a pending motion until later in the meeting so that the members can take up other business first. Another use is to postpone to the next meeting so that members have more time to think about an issue.

If a motion is controversial and members are getting angry in the debate, a member can make this motion. If adopted, it gives the members time to think about the issue and to cool off.

If a member is concerned about a motion being postponed until either later in the meeting or the next meeting and then not being taken up, he or she can amend the motion to make it a special order for a definite time. The special order ensures that the assembly takes up the motion at that specifically designated time.

Strategies for countering motions to postpone to a certain time include the following:

- If someone moves to postpone a motion to the next meeting but the motion includes a time that occurs before the next meeting, postponing to a certain time is out of order. For example, if a motion is to sign a lease by August 16 and the next meeting is September 1, the motion to postpone to the next meeting is out of order. If the chair does not rule it out of order, a member can raise a point of order.

- To prevent someone from trying to delay the decision, members can amend the time element of the motion. If a member moves to postpone the motion to the next meeting, another member can amend it by striking out "the next meeting" and inserting "later in this meeting." Or, members can amend it by making the motion a special order and adding the phrase "at 8 p.m. and make it a special order." This amendment ensures that the motion will come up again at that exact time. (See "Postpone to a Certain Time" in Chapter 7 for more details.)

- If members want more discussion time for the motion than the current meeting allows, someone can move to fix the time to which to adjourn. If the motion is adopted, someone can move to postpone the motion until the adjourned meeting.

- If a member does not want the motion postponed, he or she can debate against it, amend it to an earlier time than the time proposed in the motion and make it a special order, or vote against it. For example, if a member moves to postpone the motion to the next meeting, another member can amend the motion by adding at the end, "and make it a special order for 7 p.m." Doing so ensures that the motion is taken up promptly at 7 p.m. and interrupts pending business at that hour.

Limit or Extend the Limits of Debate

The motion to limit debate is useful when a lot has to be accomplished at a meeting and members are long-winded. Before any business is proposed, a member can make an incidental main motion that limits debate to, say, 5 minutes per person, or that limits the debate for each subject discussed to 15 minutes. During debate, members can make a motion "limit debate to 10 more minutes and take a vote."

After members adopt a motion to limit debate, they may change their minds later in the meeting and want to extend the debate. They can either reconsider the vote on the motion to limit debate or suspend the rules and extend the debate.

When you need to keep a debate brief, the most useful form of this motion is to limit the amount of time each member can speak. Most people can get their points across in 5 minutes.

Strategies for countering the motion to limit debate are:

- After a member makes the motion to limit debate, another member can propose an amendment to the amount of time.

- If a member wants to stop debate now, he or she can move the previous question.

- If a member does not want debate limited, he or she can move to recess and talk to other members to vote this motion down.

- Because this motion is not debatable, a member can raise a parliamentary inquiry, asking the chair what the implications of this motion are and what effect it will have on the discussion. This action allows members to think about how they will vote.

Previous Question

The purpose of the motion *previous question* is to stop debate immediately and take the vote. It is one of the most misunderstood and misused motions in a meeting, and members need to know how to defend themselves from its abuses.

The first abuse occurs when members call out "question" and the chair immediately stops debate and takes a vote on the motion. If this happens, a member can call out "point of order" and remind the chair that someone needs to make a formal motion to close debate, the motion needs a second, and the vote must be two-thirds in the affirmative to close the debate.

Another abuse in meetings occurs when a member makes a main motion and then someone immediately moves the previous question to try to force an immediate vote. If the chair allows this tactic, a member should raise a point of order, stating that members have the right to debate. Because no debate has been allowed, this motion is out of order.

Another often-used tactic occurs when the maker of the motion speaks for the motion and then another member immediately moves to close debate. Again, the chair should rule this motion out of order. If the chair does not, a member should raise a point of order. Debate means just that: All sides must be heard. If someone is allowed to debate for the motion, the opposition should have the right to debate against it.

One motion that is most helpful in counteracting *previous question* is *recess*. *Recess* is a higher-ranking motion and takes precedence over *previous question*. If *recess* is adopted, members have the opportunity to persuade the other members to vote against closing the debate.

Strategies for countering *previous question* are:

- Make the motion to recess.

- Raise a parliamentary inquiry to let members know the implications of closing debate.

- Make sure that members follow the correct procedures with this motion and that the vote is taken as a rising vote (where everyone stands up to be counted).

- Vote in the negative.

Lay on the Table

Lay on the table is another frequently misused motion in meetings. Because people have seen it misused so often, its misuse becomes acceptable.

Members often say, "Let's table this motion to the next meeting." Technically, there is no such motion in *Robert's Rules of Order*. To "table to the next meeting" is the motion to postpone to the next meeting. If the chair does not restate this as the motion to postpone to the next meeting and call for debate, a member should raise a point of order.

Lay on the table is correctly used to set aside an order of business in order to take up a more urgent item of business or to hear a speaker who can't stay for the completion of the pending business. However, the motion *suspend the rules* is the preferable motion to use. If members can't get a two-thirds vote to suspend the rules, they can move to lay each order of business on the table until they get to the order of business that they want to take up. After that business is completed, they then have to go back and take each order of business off the table. Using *lay on the table* to kill a motion or delay it to a later time is incorrect. Its only purpose is to temporarily put business aside so that the members can take up a more urgent matter.

Strategies for countering the motion to lay on the table are:

- Raise a point of order when *lay on the table* is misused.

- Make a motion to recess when members want to get support to defeat it.

- Raise a parliamentary inquiry when a member wants the other members to understand the implications of adopting this motion.

- If the motion to lay on the table is adopted, remember to make the motion to take from the table after the more important business has been decided. That way the members can again discuss and vote on the motion that was laid on the table.

PRIVILEGED MOTIONS

Privileged motions do not relate to the main motion or to subsidiary motions but to special matters of immediate importance that come up in a meeting.

Raise a Question of Privilege

The motion to raise a question of privilege is most useful when a member can't hear what is being said or when the room is too hot or too cold and you need to take care of these environmental problems immediately. This is a good motion for members to have in their parliamentary vocabulary.

> **Member:** Mr. President (or Madam President), I rise to a question of privilege of the assembly.

This is one of the higher-ranking motions, which members can make at any time during a meeting, even when another member is assigned the floor. However, this motion can't interrupt voting or the verification of a vote.

Another form of raising a question of privilege is to go into executive session when the members need to have a confidential discussion or when members have sensitive information to give to the assembly concerning the subject under discussion. This motion is especially helpful in city government meetings, such as school board meetings, when members must discuss sensitive issues like hiring and firing. (Government meetings operating under *open meeting laws,* however, need to abide by the state laws for going into executive session.) If members want nonmembers to leave the room, a member can move to *go into executive session.*

Strategies for countering the two forms of this motion are:

- Use the higher-ranking motions such as *recess, adjourn,* and *fix the time to which to adjourn.*

- To counter *go into executive session,* debate against it and vote against it.

Recess

Members can use *recess* in a multitude of ways. It can be used to cool off a heated argument in debate, to caucus with other members before a vote is taken, to give time to count ballots, or to let members get up and stretch. Likewise, members can use this motion to counteract the motions *limit debate, close debate,* and *lay on the table.*

Strategies for countering motions to recess are:

- Amend the amount of time for the recess.

- Adjourn the meeting instead of taking a recess.

- If someone proposes to take a recess of a day or several days, a member should raise a point of order indicating that a recess means a short duration of time, not a day or several days. The correct motion in this case is fix the time to which to adjourn.

- Raise a parliamentary inquiry and ask the chair to explain the implications of a recess. Because a parliamentary inquiry is not a debatable motion, it allows the members to decide whether they want to take a recess.

- To prevent an amendment to recess, someone can move the previous question. (There are two times when members can apply *previous question* to a higher-ranking motion than itself: *recess* and *fix the time to which to adjourn*.)

Adjourn

When the assembly has no set time to adjourn, members have the right to make the motion to adjourn. If this motion is made and defeated, members can make it again after there has been progress in the debate or business.

If a business meeting is getting out of hand, *adjourn* is a good way to put an end to it.

This motion is out of order when the assembly is engaged in voting or in verifying a vote, or if it is made before the result of the vote is announced by the chair. However, there is one exception to the rule that you can't adjourn while the assembly is engaged in voting. That exception occurs when a ballot vote has been taken and all the ballots have been collected but the result has not yet been announced.

Strategies for countering the motion to adjourn are:

- *Fix the time to which to adjourn.* If a member thinks the members are going to vote to adjourn the meeting and important business has not yet been taken care of, the member can move to set the time for an adjourned meeting. He or she can make this motion after the chair announces that the motion to adjourn has passed and before the chair declares that the meeting is adjourned. (See Chapter 8, "Adjourn.")

- Raise a parliamentary inquiry. Ask what will happen to the important business if the meeting adjourns.

- Raise a point of order. Anytime a member believes that this motion is out of order or would dissolve the assembly, he or she can raise a point of order.

- Vote against adjourning.

Fix the Time to Which to Adjourn

Members use the motion *fix the time to which to adjourn* to set the time and place for the continuation of this meeting (an adjourned meeting). This motion is helpful if the bylaws do not allow for the calling of special meetings. For example, say an organization is revising or amending bylaws and needs a series of meetings to do so. The organization's bylaws either do not allow for special meetings or state that members can amend bylaws only at the annual meeting. At their meeting, the members can move to fix the time to which to adjourn in order to set another meeting for continuing their work with the bylaws. This process can go on at each meeting until all the bylaws are proposed and voted on.

Strategies for countering motions to fix the time to which to adjourn are:

- Amend the time, date, place, or any other variable.

- Move the previous question. If *previous question* is adopted, members cannot make amendments. However, this strategy may not serve any good purpose.

- Raise a parliamentary inquiry and ask the chair what effect this motion will have if adopted. This is a way to get the information to the assembly. By having the chair explain the purpose of the motion, members can decide whether they want to have an adjourned meeting.

INCIDENTAL MOTIONS

The preceding discussions of counteractions have mentioned several incidental motions: point of order, parliamentary inquiry, and point of information. One motion not mentioned as a strategy is *appeal from the decision of the chair.*

Members need to realize that anytime the chair makes a ruling, a member can appeal the ruling. The purpose of an appeal is to let the assembly decide. Presiding officers do make mistakes, and the assembly has the right and obligation to correct them. Correcting a mistake in the meeting procedures may even determine how the assembly decides an issue.

Another helpful incidental motion is the motion to withdraw. Members should use this action only when it is apparent that the motion being discussed is poorly worded or that something has changed so that the motion is not relevant anymore.

A situation that assemblies need to be aware of, however, is one occurring when a member gets mad because "his" or "her" motion is being amended, and the member is unhappy and wants to withdraw it. If members are not informed, they may allow the motion to be withdrawn. If you want the motion to continue to be discussed and voted on, you can object to its withdrawal. This way the presiding officer has to take the vote on the motion to withdraw.

MOTIONS THAT BRING A QUESTION AGAIN BEFORE THE ASSEMBLY

Rarely is it ever too late to revisit an issue or for the assembly to change its mind after it takes a vote. This section discusses the motions that enable the assembly to do so.

Reconsider the Vote

Reconsider the vote is an important motion to use when the assembly has already adopted a motion but new information comes to light during the meeting. By reconsidering the vote on a motion, members can change their minds about what they have adopted, or at least consider it again by taking into account the new information. To prevent a misuse of this motion, only a member who voted on the prevailing side can move to reconsider.

If a member did not vote on the prevailing side but wants the motion to be reconsidered, he or she can rise when no business is pending and briefly state reasons for reconsidering the motion. If a member who voted on the prevailing side agrees with the reasons, perhaps he or she will then make the motion. While business is pending, a member can request permission to state his or her reasons for reconsideration. Another tactic a member can use is to make the motion to recess. During the recess the member can approach members who voted on the prevailing side and try to convince one of them to make the motion to reconsider.

For example, in one organization, a bylaw amendment was defeated. A member who did not vote on the prevailing side wanted it reconsidered. A recess was taken, and the member was able to convince another member who had voted no (the prevailing side) to make the motion to reconsider. The members voted to reconsider the vote. The member gave persuasive reasons why the amendment should be adopted, and it was.

An important point to remember is that members must make the motion to reconsider on the same day that the motion it is reconsidering was adopted, unless the organization has adopted rules to the contrary. City and county government officials frequently misuse this motion, believing that they can reconsider a vote on a motion a month later. In such cases, if the action is adopted, it must be rescinded. If the motion was defeated, the motion can be renewed; that is, presented again. However, city and county governments may have statutes or laws concerning the presentation of business — the approval of building permits, zoning, and other public issues, for example. Government bodies need to check with their attorneys about such laws and proceed carefully concerning these parliamentary rules. Some government organizations have adopted rules of order that allow members to reconsider the vote on a motion at the next meeting.

Rescind

Should a member want to rescind an action, the key strategy is to give previous notice. By giving previous notice, either in the call to the meeting or at the previous meeting, only a majority vote is needed to rescind an action. If a member does not give previous notice, rescinding requires either a two-thirds vote or a majority of the entire membership. Members need to be alert to situations where members move to rescind an action without giving previous notice and the vote is then approved only by a majority. This action violates the principle of protecting the rights of the absent members. Members must also be aware of the rules regarding rescinding the motion. (See "Rescind and Amend Something Previously Adopted" in Chapter 10.)

OTHER HELPFUL MOTIONS

Many members believe that after they adopt a motion or after a motion is defeated, no one can do anything about it.

A common misconception is that once a motion is defeated at a meeting, members can't bring it up again. People leave the meeting upset because they think they are helpless. The rule is that members can't bring up a motion again at the same meeting unless the vote on the motion is reconsidered. However, a motion that is defeated can be brought up again later in the meeting if changed by time or circumstances, at the next meeting, or at later meetings. It is known to happen that if a persistent person keeps bringing up a motion at every meeting, it ultimately gets adopted.

If a motion is adopted and the members change their minds afterward, they can rescind or amend the action; or, during the same meeting, they can reconsider the vote.

If an unrepresentative temporary majority at a meeting ramrods something through, two members can stop the action by moving to reconsider and enter on the minutes.

Reconsider and Enter on the Minutes

Reconsider and enter on the minutes is an unusual form of the motion to reconsider. By making this motion and seconding it, two members can stop action on an adopted motion.

The same rules apply to this motion that apply to the motion to reconsider. The maker of the motion must have voted on the prevailing side. The only purpose of this motion is to prevent an unrepresentative temporary majority in attendance at a meeting from taking advantage of its position and adopting a motion that a majority of the membership would normally oppose.

For example, say that a small group has been trying at each meeting to get the organization to buy a new stove for the clubhouse. The motion has been defeated at every meeting at which it has been presented. However, at this particular monthly meeting, many of the members can't attend, but a quorum is present. The majority of those present are those who want to buy a new stove. They see this as the only opportunity to adopt this motion, and they succeed.

To stop the action, a member who is opposed to buying the stove needs to vote on the prevailing side — with those who voted yes. (This may seem like an unusual thing to do, but only a member who has voted on the prevailing side may make the motion to reconsider.) Immediately after the vote is announced, this member should make the motion to reconsider and enter on the minutes. It needs a second. This act suspends all action on the motion until the next meeting. The absent members must be notified of the proposed action. To reconsider and enter on the minutes can't be called up on the same day, but members can bring it up on the next day or another day as long as the time between meetings is within a quarterly time interval.

This motion is sometimes subject to abuse. It is possible for two members to hold up a legitimate action. The strategy for countering this motion is:

- *Fix the time to which to adjourn.* Set the time for an adjourned meeting so members can take up the motion before the next regular meeting.

There are two conditions under which *reconsider and enter on the minutes* is not in order:

- If delaying it would defeat the object of the motion.
- If there is more than a quarterly time interval between meetings.

In such cases, a member should raise a point of order if the chair does not rule the motion out of order.

18

Most Frequently Asked Questions

Members of organizations generally ask the same questions about parliamentary procedure and meetings. Most questions concern voting, a quorum, the motion *lay on the table*, the agenda, minutes, bylaws, and what to do about a tyrannical presiding officer. If you have a question or a problem, the best advice is to look in your organization's bylaws and governing documents and then consult your parliamentary authority. The bylaws and other governing documents always take precedence over the parliamentary authority.

This chapter provides answers for commonly asked questions about parliamentary procedure and issues in meetings. The questions are grouped by topic: voting, the secretary and minutes, the president, nominations and elections, other officers, ex officio officers and members, quorums, meetings, and motions.

VOTING

Q: I am trying to find some sound guidelines to establish our method of proxy voting. Are there minimum requirements in order for proxy voting to be valid?

A: *The first thing you should do is consult the statutes regarding proxy voting in the state in which your organization is incorporated. If the state statutes allow proxy voting for your kind of organization, they may require certain procedures for conducting and counting the proxies.*

If you are not incorporated, check the statutes for the state in which you reside to see what they say about proxy voting.

Second, check to make sure that your bylaws provide for proxy voting. Proxy voting is not permitted unless the bylaws state that it is, except in states whose statutes say that proxy voting must be allowed.

Note that Robert's Rules of Order indicates that most organizations should not use proxy voting. However, proxy voting is an advisable method to use in organizations in which members have a financial interest, such as business corporations, homeowner's associations, and neighborhood associations.

Here are questions to consider as you write your bylaws concerning proxy voting:

- Are proxies counted in the quorum and how?

- Will the proxy be a general proxy or a limited proxy? A *general proxy* gives the person holding the proxy the right to vote as the holder sees fit on all issues and motions. A *limited proxy* is a signed proxy in which the signer stipulates the way that the holder is to vote on specific issues; the proxy holder must cast the member's vote the way the signer designated on the proxy. The difference between a general proxy and a limited proxy is that a general proxy gives the proxy holder the discretion to cast a vote based on information discussed in the meeting.

- Who is in charge of validating the proxy?

- What is the procedure for counting the proxies with voting members present?

- What is the form of the proxy?

- Does your organization really need proxy voting? Will it complicate your meetings, or allow members to stay away so that they don't participate in the discussion? Can this method of voting ultimately put control of the organization into the hands of a few people?

- Is the proxy valid for one meeting, or does it expire after a short period of time?

- Is the proxy revocable?

As you consider the preceding questions, remember why organizations have meetings — so members can meet face to face, discuss and debate the issues, and arrive at a reasonable agreement through a vote. Members often come to meetings thinking that their minds are already made up about certain issues, but after hearing the discussion, they change their minds and vote differently. Proxies cut out that process.

Q: **If a quorum is not present at a meeting, can the organization use proxies to make up the quorum in order to take a vote?**

A: *If an association's bylaws authorize voting by proxy, the quorum should be based on attendance at meetings in person or by proxy.*

Q: **Yesterday at our church, these questions arose. Can the chair of a committee vote? Can ex officio members of a committee vote?**

A: *The answer to your first question is yes. The chairman of a committee is a member of the committee and has all the rights of other members. Usually, the chairman is the most active participant in the committee and is selected because of his or her knowledge or interest in the committee work.*

The answer to the second question is also yes. Ex officio members of a committee can vote. According to Robert's Rules of Order, Newly Revised, "If the ex officio member of the board is under the authority of the society (that is, if he is a member, officer, or employee of the society), there is no distinction between him and the other board (or committee) members." If the ex officio person is not a member, he or she has all the rights and privileges and none of the obligations, and the ex officio person should not be counted in the quorum of the committee or board.

Conferring ex officio status on members is a way to have people serve on committees or boards without having to appoint or elect them. The bylaws of an organization may state that the president (or other leader of an organization, such as a pastor) is an ex officio member of a committee. Instead of someone being appointed to a committee by a board or elected to the committee by the membership, the person is appointed by virtue of his or her position or office in the organization or the community. Therefore, the ex officio person is a member of that committee with all the rights of membership unless your bylaws state differently.

Q: At a zoning board meeting, five votes were necessary to obtain a variance. By what authority was it specified that five votes were necessary to obtain a variance? I assumed that if an organization has no bylaws, any abstaining votes go to the majority vote, which means the majority opinion wins.

A: *If there is a state, city, or municipal law that says five votes are necessary for a variance, you follow that law. If not, a simple majority should be enough to adopt the variance.*

If an organization has no bylaws and its parliamentary authority is Robert's Rules of Order, any abstentions count as zero. If your state, city, or municipal laws indicate that it takes five votes to obtain any variance, it takes five votes in the affirmative. If only six members attend a meeting and the vote is four in favor and one opposed, the variance does not pass because an abstention is not a vote and is not counted either way. In this case, the person abstaining impacts the vote, in essence casting a no vote.

Q: What is the proper way to break a tie during an election of officers? Should the president cast the tie-breaking vote? We recently had our yearly election, and there was a tie for one office. The president cast the tie-breaking vote after the ballots were counted. Should he have waited until the meeting came back to order, or was he right in casting the tie-breaking vote before the meeting resumed?

A: *According to Robert's Rules of Order, the president always votes in a ballot vote. Therefore, he cannot break a tie vote because he cannot vote twice. Your president should have announced that the vote was a tie vote and that the members would keep voting until someone received a majority vote. If an organization wants their president to be able to cast the* tie-breaking ballot, if such a situation occurs, he or she must hold his or her ballot until the result of the vote is announced. The president then announces the result of the vote with his ballot.

Q: When a roll call vote is taken on a motion, what is the order of the roll call vote? In other words, who votes first, second, and so on? Does this order change from motion to motion?

A: *The secretary takes the roll call in alphabetical order, but the president's name is read last, and only when it will affect the vote. When a member's name is called, he or she can vote yes, no, abstain, or present (which also means to abstain). If a member is not ready to vote, he or she answers "pass." Once the secretary reads the roll, the secretary calls again the names of those members who answered "pass," giving them one more opportunity to vote.*

As the secretary calls each member's name, the secretary repeats how each member votes and marks it by the member's name. At the conclusion of the roll call, the president can ask if everyone who wants to vote has voted. At this time, members can also change their votes before the secretary tallies the votes and the president announces the result.

The secretary gives the final number of those voting on each side and the number of those abstaining to the president. The president announces the result and declares the motion adopted or defeated.

Q: I am the president of a volunteer fire company. We have recently had many discussions about the value of abstaining during the vote. We feel that an abstaining vote is actually a vote against the motion. Can you please provide the rules for how to handle this and tell us what alternatives we have?

A: *You need to find out the rules of your fire department regarding what constitutes a majority vote. If the rules state that all motions are adopted by a majority vote, that means a majority of those voting. An abstention means, "I am not voting." In this situation, an abstention does not affect the vote at all.*

If your rules say a "majority vote of those present," or a "majority vote of the entire membership," then an abstention can affect the vote.

For example, say that you have ten members at your meeting. Your rules state that a vote can pass only by a "majority vote of those present." In this case, it takes six votes in the affirmative to adopt. So if five members voted for a motion, two voted against, and three abstained, the motion is lost.

However, if the rules state "a majority vote," then, using the results of the previous vote, the motion carries because the majority is determined by those who voted, not by those present. The majority in that case is four.

In taking the vote, the presiding officer takes only the aye and no votes. He or she does not ask for abstentions. If the meeting is a big one, how can you tell who abstained? The only way is to take a counted vote, roll call, or ballot vote.

It is highly recommended that you have your rules or bylaws state "a majority vote," meaning a majority of those voting. However, if your group is a small board of fewer than ten members, having a rule that requires a majority vote of the entire board membership prevents a small group from getting together and pushing through business. For example, say a board has nine members, which means that five members is the quorum. If your rules require only a majority vote, then at a meeting of five members, it is possible for one or two people to adopt motions if others abstain. Having all action adopted by a majority of the entire membership guarantees that at least five members are always in agreement, and this fact can solve problems that arise during controversial issues.

Q: When a main motion is before the assembly, can an assembly require more than a majority vote in order for the motion to be approved, even if more than a majority vote is not required by either parliamentary law or the rules of order of the assembly?

A: *If an assembly wants to change the vote required for the adoption of a main motion, someone has to make a motion to suspend the rules. This needs a second. It requires a two-thirds vote because it is taking away rights from the members.*

The member making the motion can state:

Member: I move to suspend the rules and have the vote taken on this main motion by a two-thirds vote.

Member 2: Second.

President: It is moved and seconded to suspend the rules and have the vote taken on this main motion by a two-thirds vote. All those in favor please rise. Be seated. Those opposed please rise. Be seated. The affirmative has it and the vote on this main motion will require a two-thirds vote.

If the negative wins, the president says:

President: There are less than two-thirds in the affirmative and the motion is lost. We will not suspend the rules and require a two-thirds vote on this main motion. The motion will be adopted by a majority vote.

Q: Is it correct that abstentions are not counted as votes in determining the winner of an election requiring a majority? Are there any conditions where an absolute majority of eligible voters is necessary to declare a winner? In that case, can abstentions actually prevent a winner from being declared? Is the situation the same with invalid ballots, for example, someone voting for Robin Hood?

A: *You are correct that abstentions are not counted. An absolute majority of eligible voters is required only when your organization has rules to that effect. For example, such a rule may say that a vote requires "a majority of the entire membership." In this case, an abstention may prevent someone from getting elected. Look at this example:*

Your membership is 50.

A majority of the membership is 26.

Member X receives 25 votes.

Member Y receives 23 votes.

Two members abstain.

No one is elected because no one has a majority of the entire membership. It takes 26 votes for election.

Robert's Rules of Order considers invalid ballots illegal votes. A vote is illegal when:

- It has the name of someone who is not eligible to serve in the office. An obvious example is a fictional character such as Robin Hood. A not-so-obvious example is a member who does not meet the requirements for office.

- The tellers can't read the name on the ballot.

- Two ballots are folded together, and each ballot has a name written on it. In this case, both ballots are counted together as one illegal ballot. If two ballots are folded together and one is blank, the blank is ignored.

An illegal ballot can affect the outcome of an election because it is counted in the total number of votes cast. Consider this example:

30 votes are cast.

16 is the majority.

Member A receives 15 votes.

Member B receives 14 votes.

There is 1 illegal ballot.

Members have to vote again because no candidate received a majority vote. In this case, the illegal ballot did make a difference; it may have been cast for member A.

Q: **I am aware that the president may vote to break a tie vote on a motion. Does the president have voting privileges on any other occasion or for any other reason?**

A: *The president can vote to make or break a tie vote, can cast a ballot vote, and can vote in a roll call vote. The president does not vote at other times because his or her vote can influence the other members and how they vote. The president is to remain impartial. Because a ballot vote is secret,* *the president's vote can't influence others, which is why the president can vote at the same time as the members. In a roll call vote, the assembly demands that each member vote and that each state how he or she is voting for the record. When the president's vote will affect the result, the president has no choice but to vote in this vote, and his or her name is called last. However, he or she can choose to abstain.*

Keep in mind that the president can only make or break a tie vote if he or she has not already voted. For example, if the president participates in a ballot vote and the vote results in a tie, he or she cannot break the tie because he or she cannot vote a second time.

Q: What happens when the president's vote will cause a tie to occur on a motion? If the president's vote causes a tie vote to occur, how is the matter resolved at that point?

A: *If the president's vote causes a tie vote, the motion is defeated. Robert's Rules of Order allows a president to vote to make a tie vote or break a tie vote. The president can also vote whenever his or her vote will affect the result. For example, the president can vote to cause a two-thirds vote or to prevent the attainment of a two-thirds vote. However, members can't force the president to vote if he or she wants to remain impartial. If the motion is a tie and the president does not want to vote, the motion is defeated. A tie vote is not a majority.*

A tie vote means that the motion is lost. What can you do in this situation? Another rule in parliamentary procedure is that members can't be asked to decide the same question twice at the same meeting unless they reconsider the vote. To reconsider the vote, a member must have voted on the prevailing side (in this case, the negative vote can move to reconsider). However, anyone can bring the motion before the assembly again at the next meeting; it is handled as if it is a new main motion.

Q: Recently, at our monthly meeting, we had a member come in late in the middle of a vote that we were taking. We had voted the yea's and were about to vote the nay's. Everyone stopped and explained to her all about the motion and our discussion, which took about 15 minutes. The member then added her yea vote to the others. We continued on to the nay's. Her interruption created a bit of confusion for everyone, and later people complained that they lost track of what we were doing. What is the proper procedure when someone comes in during the middle of a vote?

A: *The proper procedure is to continue to take the vote. An interruption of a vote can happen only before any member votes. However, an exception is that members can transact other business during the counting of a ballot vote.*

It is unfair for a member to arrive late and then hold up the other members. This person knew what time the meeting began and chose to arrive late. That member should not expect other members to stop everything and explain what has transacted. A basic principle of democracy is government by the majority, not by one person.

THE SECRETARY AND MINUTES

Q: What is the main job of the secretary? If the secretary isn't cooperating with the board, does the board have any controls over him or her? Can the board dismiss the present officer and elect a new one? If so, how do you carry that out?

A: *The role of a secretary is very important in any organization. Your organization's bylaws should state the duties of the secretary, but Robert's Rules of Order also lists the secretary's duties. In general, the secretary is responsible for:*

- Keeping the list of all the members and all the records of the organization, including committee reports, on file.

- Notifying members of their election to office or appointment to committees and furnishing them with the proper documents.

- Notifying members of election or appointment to be a delegate at a convention and furnishing them with credentials.

- Signing all the minutes and other certified acts of the organization, unless the bylaws specify differently.

- Maintaining the official documents of the organization, including the bylaws, rules of order, standing rules, and minutes. The secretary keeps the bylaws and other governing documents up-to-date with any changes made through the amendment process and brings these documents to the meetings.

- Mailing to each member meeting notices.

- Taking minutes at all business and board meetings, handling the correspondence, and preparing the agenda for the meetings unless the president prefers to do so. The secretary must know how to call a meeting to order if the president and vice president are absent and know how to preside until the assembly elects a temporary chairman.

The secretary should cooperate with all members and be of service to the entire organization. Your bylaws should provide you with the procedure to remove a secretary who is not cooperative (or any officer not performing his or her duties). If there is no provision for removing this officer, and if your bylaws do not state that the officer serves a certain period of time "or until the successor is elected," you must hold a trial for removal.

If the bylaws provide for removal, follow that procedure. If your bylaws state "or until the successor is elected," you can rescind the election. This requires previous notice and a majority vote, or without previous notice, a two-thirds vote or majority of the entire membership. If the officer is removed, the members can fill the vacancy created by holding an election at the same meeting.

Q: **With the advent of new technology, what is the appropriate method to use in binding minutes?**

A: *You can purchase secretary's books of blank pages that secretaries can print on a computer and, when the book is finished, bind at a printer's. One of these books costs approximately $75. It includes the original hardcover book with* *paper, which is why it is expensive. It is refillable, however, so after the initial purchase, you only have to buy paper. After you type the minutes into the computer, remove the necessary number of blank pages in the book and use your printer to print the minutes on them. Replace the printed paper into the book. When you use up the paper, take all 150 pages to the printer's and have the book bound and labeled with a date. You can then order more paper and put it in the book. Any office supply store should be able to show you product options.*

Q: Do you have any information on the proper form of minutes? What should they include? What can the secretary leave out? Is there a difference between a formal meeting and an informal one as far as minutes are concerned? I am the secretary responsible for the minutes of four different types of meetings: a private company's board of directors' meetings, a private company's stockholders' meetings, the Kiwanis club's general meetings, and the Kiwanis club's board meetings. Where can I find out the proper and legal requirements of the minutes for which I am responsible?

A: *For the most part, the form of the minutes is the same. Minutes record what is done at the meeting, not what is said. However, if any of these organizations publish their minutes, you need a tape recorder because everything goes into the minutes word for word. Check with the Secretary of State's office in the state in which your company is incorporated to see if there are any specific guidelines for the legal requirements of minutes. If so, you need to follow them. The important thing to remember about minutes is that they are the legal document of the meeting. Ask yourself, "If we went to court, what would be most helpful to the judge or jury in deciding an issue?" Sometimes putting background information into the minutes is important because doing so helps explain why the assembly took a particular action. Recording a counted, roll call, or ballot vote may provide proof that a quorum was present.*

THE PRESIDENT

Q: Does a president of the board of directors have the authority to refuse to let an issue come before the board?

A: *No, a president does not have this authority unless your organization has a written rule that says otherwise. The president can rule a motion out of order if it conflicts with your bylaws; corporate charter; or national, state, or local laws. He or she can also "object to consideration of the question," but that does not prevent the motion from coming before the board. The rest of the board must vote on this motion.*

Q: Does the president of the board of directors have the right to deny a guest permission to speak at a board meeting? The guest is a club member.

A: *Board meetings are usually conducted in executive session, which means that only members of the board can attend. A guest would not be allowed to come to the meeting unless your board meetings are open meetings, or unless he or she was invited by the board to give input on an issue because the guest had special knowledge about the subject. In that case, after the guest had spoken and answered any questions, he or she would leave and would not be allowed to participate in the debate.*

Q: Our committee has seven members, and an extra person has just shown up. Can I refuse to let that person speak or take part in the discussion?

A: *Committee meetings are conducted in executive session, and only members of the committee can attend. Unless a member is an ex officio member of the committee, he or she has no right to just show up and ask to participate in the committee meeting. Politely escort the member to the door and explain that only committee members are allowed to attend. (This is true unless your organization has rules to the contrary.)*

Q: One of our members constantly causes problems because he and his wife don't like the club president.

What can we do to stop him? This problem wastes our time and energy.

A: *Your president was voted in by a majority of the members and deserves everyone's support. It sounds to me as if you have a democracy problem in your organization — members who don't understand the concepts of democracy, which require all members to abide by the majority rule even if they did not vote with the majority. The most diplomatic tactic is for you to talk with these people and try to persuade them to be cooperative and encourage them to work with the president. These members need to see how detrimental their actions are to the entire organization.*

Q: **How can a member of an organization bring items to the floor if the president refuses to put them on the agenda? The agenda does not include "old or new business" or "unfinished business." It is also not customary for the association to approve the agenda at the beginning of the meeting. Can I ask for the approval of the agenda? Or can I make a motion at any time to include an item or items on the agenda?**

A: *Yes, a member can bring items to the floor if the president does not put them on the agenda. The agenda is designed to serve the entire organization by bringing order to the meeting and helping members keep on track. It is not the president's agenda or his or her idea of what should go on at the meeting. The president has not been elected to enforce his or her will on the assembly. He or she has been elected to lead the organization and to be impartial and fair in conducting the meetings.*

The agenda should follow a standard order of business such as the one found in Robert's Rules of Order. It should include unfinished business if there is any. Unfinished business is business left pending at the last meeting or postponed to the current meeting. You can find any unfinished business in the minutes of the previous meeting. The secretary should read the minutes at the beginning of the meeting so that members know whether there is any unfinished business. If the president does not bring it up (the president and the secretary are responsible for putting it on the agenda), a member can bring up unfinished business by rising to a parliamentary inquiry:

Member: Mr. President (or Madam President), I rise to a parliamentary inquiry.

President: Please state your inquiry.

Member: The minutes state that X motion was postponed to this meeting. I noticed that the agenda doesn't list any unfinished business. Will the president kindly inform this member when it will be presented to the assembly?

The president is now responsible for telling you when motion X will be brought up. By using this technique, you alert the members that something has been left off the agenda, and you do so in a nice way.

Is your president a dictator or just uninformed? If the president is uninformed, perhaps you can privately show him or her the order of the business meeting in your parliamentary authority. If the president is a tyrant who wants to do things his or her way, you have a bigger problem.

After the minutes are read and before members transact any other business, rise to a parliamentary inquiry and ask why no unfinished business or new business is on the agenda. You can then ask that the following items be added to the agenda. If the president does not do this, make a motion to adopt the agenda with unfinished business and new business added to the agenda. This motion needs a second and requires a majority vote to adopt.

If the president continues to ignore you, raise a point of order. If he or she ignores the point of order, make the motion again. If your motion is seconded, and the president still ignores the motion, you have the right to place the motion before the board, ask for discussion, and take the vote.

You can use this technique anytime the president ignores a legitimate motion that has been seconded. However, you must exactly follow all the steps previously given.

Q: What can members do when the president oversteps
his or her role as facilitator, and how do you correct
the mistake? Also, is the president solely responsible
for appointing members of committees from the
board?

A: *To correct the president during a meeting, the procedure is to
stand and say:*

Member: Madam President (or Mr. President), I rise to a
point of order.

Or just stand and say:

Member: Point of order.

The president should respond:

President: Please state your point.

*You now state the correct procedure. The chair then rules on
your point. Either the chair agrees with your point and corrects what he or she is doing wrong, or the chair does not
agree with your point and proceeds with what he or she is
doing.*

President: Your point is well taken.

or

President: Your point is not well taken.

*If you don't agree with the chair's ruling, you can appeal
from the decision of the chair. This needs a second. However,
if the chair doesn't know the proper procedure, you should
speak with him or her outside the meeting and share helpful
information.*

*You can find the answer to your second question in your
organization's bylaws or standing rules. For the president to
have the power to appoint committees, the bylaws must give
him or her that authority. If the bylaws do not say who
appoints committees, the assembly appoints them.*

Q: Can members conduct business after a meeting is officially adjourned? In this case, the meeting was adjourned, the office manager went to the door to ascertain that a certain leader left, and then the manager reconvened the meeting to do business.

A: *What was done was unethical, undemocratic, and unkind. Any business transacted after the meeting adjourned is null and void. When a meeting adjourns, it is over. Robert's Rules of Order states that the chair can call a meeting back to order in only one situation — when a member was trying to obtain the floor, before the chair declared the adjournment, for the purpose of*

- Giving an important announcement.

- Making the motion to reconsider.

- Making the motion to reconsider and enter into the minutes.

- Giving previous notice about a motion to be made at the next meeting.

- Setting the time for an adjourned meeting.

When the manager tried to reconvene the meeting, someone should have stopped him or her immediately. This group can't function harmoniously if members are purposely being left out of business and discussion.

Q: Can a president make a motion or second a motion?

A: *It depends. In a board meeting of fewer than 12 members (unless you have rules to the contrary), a president can make motions, second motions, discuss motions, and vote on motions. In a general membership meeting, the president is to remain impartial; he or she should not make a motion or second it. However, there is an exception. For example, say the treasurer presents a bill to be paid. The president can assume a motion and say:*

President: The treasurer has presented a bill for X dollars. Is there any discussion? All those in favor say "Aye." Those opposed say "No."

The president then announces the vote. This is a great way to expedite business.

The other situation in which a president can make a motion is when he or she steps down from the chair and lets the vice president preside until the motion is dispensed. However, the best practice is for the president to find another member who is willing to present the motion.

When someone is elected to the office of president, that person must remember that he or she serves all the members. The effective president in any organization is one that remains impartial in conducting the meetings.

Q: At a recent city council meeting, the mayor said, "As chairman, I always have the last word in any discussion." He also said that he looked this up in *Robert's Rules of Order*. I have been a member of a board of education for the past 17 years and have used *Robert's Rules* — I do not remember ever seeing that the chair always has the last word. Maybe I don't have a complete copy. Maybe he is not accurate. Is there such a reference?

A: *Oh, if we could all have the last word! There is one time when the chair has the last word, and that is on a debatable appeal to the chair's ruling. According to parliamentary rules, in a debatable appeal, the presiding officer has the first right to speak to the appeal and the last right to speak to the appeal. The other time the presiding officer has the last word is when saying, "The meeting is adjourned" (and then only if the other members agree about adjourning!).*

NOMINATIONS AND ELECTIONS

Q: Do you need a second on a nomination? For example, I nominate John Smith as chairman. Do I need a second before his name can be put on the ballot for this position?

A: *No second is required. On a ballot, you can write the name of any member who is eligible to serve. Also, Robert's Rules of*

Order clearly states that a person does not have to be nominated to be elected. Thus, on a written ballot someone can gain election through a write-in campaign.

Q: Are there any rules, in *Robert's Rules of Order* or elsewhere, that forbid a person from running for two offices at the same time, such as president and vice president, or president and senator? This situation has come up during nominations for officers and directors at our conservation club, and we need clarification.

A: *There is no general parliamentary prohibition against a person being nominated for more than one office unless the bylaws of an organization prohibit it. However, it is usually understood that members hold only one office at a time. If a member is elected to two offices and he or she is present when the election takes place, the member should choose which office he or she wants to serve. If the member is not present, the other members can decide which office they want him or her to serve.*

If you can await the logical sequence of events, the situation may resolve itself. Perhaps the member will be elected to only one office. If not, the preceding information will help you decide what to do next.

Q: After the floor is closed for nominations, can the president reopen the floor for nominations? And if so, in which cases or circumstances?

A: *Robert's Rules of Order says that a majority vote can reopen nominations for any reason. A member needs to make the motion to reopen the nominations, or the chair can assume a motion by stating:*

Chairman: Is there any objection to reopening the nominations? Hearing none, nominations are now reopened.

If there is an objection, the chair takes a vote.

Chairman: All those in favor say "Aye." Those opposed say "No." *[Announce the vote.]*

One case for reopening nominations is when someone is elected to office and then immediately declines the position. Another case is when the assembly voted many times but no one received enough votes to be elected, and the members want to consider adding someone else's name to the list.

Q: **Does the nominating committee have the only right to nominate an officer, or can a member also nominate someone? And if a member can do it, what is the procedure for getting the floor and nominating someone?**

A: *Check your organization's bylaws for specifics on the nominating and electing process. Those are the rules that the members must obey. However, in general parliamentary terms, any member should be able to nominate an officer. For example, if the nominating committee disagrees about a nomination, those on the committee who are in the minority may propose other nominees for some or all of the offices when the presiding officer asks for nominations from the floor (from the members).*

In Robert's Rules of Order, this is the general procedure for nominations:

1. The nominating committee gives its report by stating the nominees for each office.

2. The presiding officer repeats the nominations of the committee for each office and asks,

   President: Are there further nominations?

   At this time, any member can rise and nominate someone (a nomination does not need a second), unless your organization's bylaws state differently.

3. The presiding officer repeats the nomination and asks if there are any further nominations. This continues until no one responds, and the presiding officer closes the nominations for that office and goes on to the next office. *Robert's Rules of Order* says that bylaws or standing rules should clearly state the procedure an organization follows.

If your organization is not following this procedure of taking nominations from the floor, check the bylaws or standing rules to see whether they prohibit it. If there is no prohibition and the presiding officer does not ask for nominations from the floor, you can raise a point of order. However, talking to the presiding officer before the meeting and showing him or her the pages in Robert's Rules of Order that explain the procedure is better.

If your organization takes the vote by ballot, you can also wage a write-in campaign. According to Robert's Rules of Order, a member does not have to be nominated to be elected, but the member does have to be eligible to serve. So, in the case of a ballot vote, writing in the name of someone who has not been nominated is possible.

Q: **Our church bylaws require the nominating committee to present "a slate of candidates" for the board of trustees (among other bodies). In terms of parliamentary procedure, does "a slate" mean *only* the number of candidates equal to the number of vacancies, or may it mean *at least* a number of candidates equal to the number of vacancies? (Webster's defines *slate* as "a list of candidates. . . .")**

A: *A slate means a nominee for each office. If you have three offices to elect — president, secretary, and treasurer — a single slate is one nominee for each office. A multiple slate is more than one nominee for each office. From a parliamentary law point of view, it is best for the nominating committee to choose only one nominee (the best one) for each office. If the committee members are required to come up with more than one candidate, they may have to choose someone who isn't as qualified. If they choose two who are equally qualified, one is sure to lose, and the loser may decline to be nominated again. Electing officers in organizations is different than national elections where citizens always have two candidates from which to choose. In organizations, it is best not to make members compete against each other. Organizations need to promote cooperation. However, if the members feel that the nominating committee is playing politics and is not nominating the best candidate, the members should nominate someone else.*

OTHER OFFICERS

Q: We are a small neighborhood association (20 members) with a president, vice president, recording secretary, corresponding secretary, treasurer, and chairman of the board. The bylaws don't spell out the chairman of the board's duties. Just what does a board chairman do?

A: *If your bylaws don't give the chairman any duties, his or her primary duty is conducting the board meetings; the association president conducts the membership meetings.*

Q: Does the parliamentarian have a vote on motions, and can he or she speak to motions?

A: *If the parliamentarian is not a member of the organization, he or she is not entitled to vote or debate motions. If the parliamentarian is a member and sits in front by the president, he or she is not entitled to make motions, discuss motions, or vote. People look to the parliamentarian as an authority (and therefore impartial), and it is improper for him or her to sway the vote. However, the parliamentarian, if a member, can vote in a ballot vote just as the president can.*

If a member is considered the parliamentarian and sits with the assembly during the meetings (and does not advise the chair during the meetings), that person may have the right to make motions, discuss them, and vote.

Q: Can you please give me some insight as to how the parliamentarian should act during a meeting? I want to know how much input this person is allowed during discussion on a particular matter.

A: *How the parliamentarian should act during a meeting is dependent on several things. If the parliamentarian is a member of the organization, he or she has all the rights of the members — to make motions, debate, and vote — except when he or she is seated in the front next to the president. When the parliamentarian is seated by the president, he or she gives up the right to make motions, debate, and vote (except in a ballot vote). The parliamentarian is there only as* an advisor. Any comments made to the president should be inconspicuous. He or she only gives advice; the president still makes the rulings.

If the parliamentarian is a member of an organization that wants him or her to serve in that role, the member can choose not to sit by the president when serving as the parliamentarian. In this way, he or she doesn't give up the right to speak and vote. Note that this decision does not prevent the parliamentarian from meeting beforehand with the president to go over the agenda. In many cases, the parliamentarian can write a meeting script for the president to follow if the officer is not familiar with conducting meetings. Before the meeting, the parliamentarian can discuss with the president any controversial issues or any procedures with which the officer is unfamiliar. The parliamentarian and the president can then discuss ways to handle any problems that may arise during the meeting. If the members get lost in the meeting, the president can ask the parliamentarian to clarify the correct procedure. The parliamentarian can speak from where he or she is seated and tell the assembly the correct procedure. It is then the president's duty to decide what to do. (The president always makes the rulings.)

A parliamentarian is an advisor; the position is not one of power. Unfortunately, this office is misused in many organizations.

EX OFFICIO OFFICERS AND MEMBERS

Q: I am the recording secretary for the Parking Advisory Board. We are trying to set up some bylaws. We are looking for a definition of *ex officio member* and need to know whether such a member has voting rights.

A: You need to first adopt a parliamentary authority. Robert's Rules of Order is an example of a parliamentary authority. When you adopt an authority, it will help you define *ex officio member*. A person usually becomes an *ex officio* member of an organization by virtue of his or her office. Many times *the president of an organization is an ex officio member of a board or committee. Perhaps you want someone in the community who works in a related field to be an ex officio member of your board. If that person leaves his or her position, he or she is no longer a member of your board, but whoever follows that person then becomes a member ex officio.*

An ex officio member has all the rights of membership: the right to make motions, debate, and vote. Members who are ex officio and who are also regular members of the organization are counted in the quorum. Those who are not members of the organization are not counted in the quorum, but they still have the rights of membership.

Q: My church's bylaws provide for ex officio members on the various governing boards and committees. The bylaws are silent, however, regarding the voting rights of these ex officio members. Do ex officio members count toward a quorum?

A: *If the ex officio members are church members, they count in the quorum and have the right to make motions, debate, and vote. If the ex officio members are not members of the church, they have the right to make motions, debate, and vote, but they are not counted in the quorum.*

QUORUM

Q: I am interested in the rules about quorums as set forth in *Robert's Rules of Order*. What is the least number needed to open the board of directors' meeting? Is it just one more than 50 percent?

A: *Your bylaws should specify the quorum. If they don't, Robert's Rules of Order states that a quorum is a majority (more than half) of all the members.*

In boards or committees, if the quorum is not established in the bylaws, by rule of a parent organization, or by state statutes, the quorum is a majority of the members of the board or committee. A board or a committee does not have the power to establish its own quorum unless the bylaws give that power. So, look at your bylaws carefully to make this determination.

Q: I am looking for information on how many members must vote to form a quorum with committee sizes of five, seven, and nine.

A: *The members do not vote to form a quorum. Your governing documents, preferably your bylaws, should state the quorum of your committees. However, if no quorum is stated, Robert's Rules of Order says that the quorum is a majority of the members of the committee:*

The quorum of a five-member committee is three.

The quorum of a seven-member committee is four.

The quorum of a nine-member committee is five.

MEETINGS

Q: What is the procedure for ensuring that items are not added to the agenda during the actual board meeting? Or, how do you prevent this from occurring?

A: *If the agenda is not adopted at the beginning of the meeting, any member can add items by making a motion to add an agenda item at the time when the chair calls for new business. If a majority vote adopts the agenda at the beginning, amending the agenda by adding something to it requires a two-thirds vote.*

The purpose of an agenda is to keep order, keep the meeting on track, and expedite business. The agenda should be flexible, enabling members to bring business before the assembly, not preventing them from bringing business. Only items requiring notice cannot be added.

One reason for adopting an agenda may be that the meeting time is short; adopting the agenda thus expedites the business so that the organization can complete it all. An agenda should not be adopted for the purpose of excluding ideas.

Likewise, the president should not impose his or her own agenda on the members. The president is to preside and see that the members' wishes are carried out and that all members have the right to bring business before the board. The chairman protects everyone's rights by preventing dilatory motions. Members should decide what comes before the board.

Q: We are between sessions of a meeting that was adjourned to meet tomorrow. A controversial motion is on the floor, and we need to know who has a right to vote at the meeting on Friday. Our bylaws state that only members who are current in dues and who have attended at least three meetings in the previous twelve months can vote. The question is: Does the sign-in sheet for the first session on Wednesday serve as the sign-in for the second session? Or, if more qualified members attend, are they allowed to vote?

A: *An adjourned meeting is a legal continuation of a meeting. The meeting that happens tomorrow is therefore a legal continuation of the meeting held on Wednesday. It is not a second meeting. Therefore, the people who signed in at the Wednesday meeting are still considered present unless you mark them off the sheet as having left the meeting early. And, anyone coming to this meeting who wasn't at the meeting on Wednesday is signing in as someone who came in late to the meeting. Having a sign-in sheet entitled "Adjourned meeting" with Friday's date and then stapling it to the sign-in sheet of the Wednesday meeting may be wise.*

The rule for voting privileges at the adjourned meeting is the same as the rule at the regular meeting on Wednesday evening. The Friday meeting is not considered a separate meeting.

Based on the information given in your question, if someone did not come to the meeting on Wednesday evening but attends tomorrow and is current in dues and has attended at least three meetings in the previous twelve months, that member is allowed to vote. It is as if the person came in late. Would you allow latecomers to vote if this meeting were held all in one day? If so, they can vote at this adjourned meeting.

Q: We have received information that at an upcoming not-for-profit board meeting, some people plan to attend who are not duly elected but who are concerned. It seems logical that nonmembers cannot attend, because otherwise we would have a free-for-all at meetings. The organization's constitution is silent on the matter. Is there a source that answers this question?

A: *Robert's Rules of Order states that board meetings are customarily held in "executive session," which means that only the elected board members can attend.*

Do these members of the organization have a specific issue that they want to bring to the board? If they do, why not give them a hearing? After they've had their say, politely ask them to leave, or escort them graciously to the door, assuring them that the board will conscientiously consider their request and will make the board's decision known.

Another course of action is for the board to ask the members of the organization to put their concerns in writing. The board can then take up their concerns at another meeting.

If these people are curiosity seekers wanting to see what the board is up to, explain that the meeting is closed and is for board members only and that the full body of the organization will receive the board's report at the next regular membership meeting.

Usually the board is authorized to handle business between membership meetings, with the members having the right to override board decisions unless duties are specifically given to the board in the bylaws.

Q: Can the chair of a committee make a motion during the committee meeting?

A: *Yes, the chair can make motions, debate motions, and vote on motions. In committees, the chairman is usually the most active participant in the committee work. This is true for committees smaller than 12. If a committee is a public body, the rules may differ. If the committee is larger than 12, the chairman is more of a presiding officer at meetings, and the* *rules of formal meetings apply to committee work. That means that he or she can't make or debate motions and can vote only to make or break a tie vote, or in a ballot vote.*

Q: If a member of a board has a profound conflict of interest, should he or she leave the meeting during the time the area of conflict is under discussion? Is there a specific citation for a ruling?

A: *First you need a definition for conflict of interest. A conflict of interest is a question of direct personal or monetary interest that is not common to other members of the organization. However, if the member is being considered with other members in a motion or is being elected to office, he or she is allowed to vote. The general principle in parliamentary law is that when a member has a conflict of interest, he or she does not enter into the discussion or vote on the matter. However, there is no rule that says the member has to leave the room when others discuss the issue. The other principle of parliamentary law is that if the member is not allowed to vote, he or she is also not counted in the quorum. Be forewarned: If a member is not able to vote on an issue and his or her participation is needed for a quorum, members can't take a vote on the issue.*

MOTIONS

Q: Does a resolution need to have a second?

A: *A resolution is a formal way of phrasing a main motion. If a single member proposes it, it needs a second. If a committee of more than one votes to present a resolution to the membership, it does not need a second.*

Q: If a motion has been rejected, can members bring the same motion before the membership to vote on it again?

A: *A main motion that is defeated usually cannot be brought up again at the same meeting (unless someone who voted on the prevailing side moves to reconsider the vote, or unless time or* *circumstance change the motion). However, members can bring it up again at another meeting. This is called* renewing the motion.

Q: I have read many guides that tell you what to do but not exactly how to do it. For example, when someone makes a motion to do something, what are the exact words to say and what are the responses from the chair?

A: *When a person makes a motion, he or she should phrase it in the positive and say "I move to . . . " or "I move that . . . " and state what it is he or she wants to do.*

The chair says:

Chairman: It is moved and seconded that . . . . *[repeats the motion]* Is there any discussion?

If the motion does not get a second, the chair can ask for a second:

Chairman: Is there a second?

If no second is forthcoming, the motion is not before the assembly and the chair says:

Chairman: Because there is no second, the motion is not before the assembly. Is there further business?

Q: When a motion is made to table something and a second is made, does the full board then need to vote on the motion and the second? It is my interpretation that a vote is not needed when a motion is made and seconded to table something.

A: *A vote is taken on all motions made and seconded. The motion you asked about is the motion lay on the table. The correct procedure is to take a vote immediately on the motion to lay on the table; it is not debated. This motion should be used only to set business aside temporarily for more urgent business. If you want to "table it to the next meeting" or "to later in the meeting," the correct motion is* postpone the motion, *which needs a second and is debatable. To lay a motion on the table takes away the members' rights to debate without taking a two-thirds vote. It is an undemocratic motion unless used correctly. The member who makes the motion should give the reason for wanting to temporarily set aside the pending business. If the president does not agree that the business is urgent, the president can rule the motion out of order or restate the motion as the motion to postpone to a later time.*

Another important point about the motion to lay on the table is that it is recorded in the minutes, but the motion that has been temporarily put aside is not put on the agenda if it carries over to the next meeting. The motion is normally taken from the table during the same meeting. Because the members moved to put it on the table, the members are responsible for making the motion to take it from the table. The assembly must be careful that members don't use this motion as the motion to kill. If the intent is to kill the motion, the chair should rule it out of order. The proper motion to kill is postpone indefinitely.

Part V

GOVERNING DOCUMENTS

19

Various Types of Governing Documents

Without written and agreed-upon rules, organizations would be at the mercy of the majority's whims. A majority of those voting at a meeting could change the rules whenever those rules didn't suit certain goals. Over the centuries, there has evolved a way of structuring groups so that rights of the absent members, the minority, and each individual are protected. This structure is found in the governing documents of an organization.

The most familiar governing document is called the *constitution* or *bylaws*. This document brings the organization into being, defines its purpose, and specifies its powers and limitations. It includes provisions for change but makes change more difficult to adopt than the parliamentary motions to *rescind* and *amend something previously adopted*. This is not only to protect the rights of the minority and absent members, but to ensure the stability and continuity of the organization itself. The following sections explain the various governing documents that an organization may need.

THE CORPORATE CHARTER

An organization cannot act like a corporation unless it applies for corporate status from the state or federal government. In general, a corporate charter establishes the legal name, address, and object of the organization.

An organization needs to incorporate with the state in order to hold property, make legally binding contracts, sue or be sued as a society in its name, have a legacy left it, protect its members from personal liabilities incurred while performing their duties for the organization, provide for a legally recognized status, own a corporate seal, and provide for perpetual continuation as an organization.

An organization should hire a local attorney who is familiar with the laws in that state to draw up its incorporation papers. The corporate charter should include only the information necessary to get incorporated. The charter usually includes the name of the organization, where its headquarters are located (or its general field of operations), its object or purpose, and how the charter itself can be amended. It also may include the number of yearly meetings and designate a board of directors, whether the organization is nonprofit or profit, the amount of real estate it wishes authorization to hold, and its duration of term of existence. A lawyer can help the organization determine what it should include in the document.

When working with the attorney, the organization should provide the basic information. When the attorney finishes writing the draft, he or she should return it to the members for approval and suggested changes. When the final draft is completed, the attorney returns it to the members for signing the document. It is then sent to the secretary of state. In some states, the secretary of state also wants the organization's bylaws and other rules on file with the incorporation papers. The final papers may be referred to as *Articles of Incorporation, Certificate of Incorporation,* or *Articles of Association.* This is now a legal document and takes priority over the other documents of the organization. Therefore, bylaws or other governing documents can't adopt anything that is in conflict with the corporate charter. After the organization is incorporated, it is imperative that members don't simply put the corporate charter away in a file or vault somewhere and forget that it exists. The secretary should include it with the other governing documents of the society and refer to it when proposing any changes to other documents.

CONSTITUTION AND BYLAWS

The constitution or bylaws are the rules of a society relating to itself as an organization, and not the parliamentary rules that it follows. Having a constitution and bylaws as separate documents is not necessary; one document suffices, generally referred to as the *bylaws*. The bylaws define the primary characteristics of the organization, how it operates, and the relation of the assembly and individual members to the organization as a whole. It contains those rules that the society deems so important they can't be changed without previous notice and a specified large majority (for example, a two-thirds vote.) Chapter 20 explains bylaws in detail.

RULES OF ORDER

Every organization should adopt a parliamentary authority such as *Robert's Rules of Order*. But after an organization adopts a parliamentary authority, it may want to do some things differently than the authority advises. For example, an organization may want to have a different order of business than the authority recommends or different limits on debate. This is why organizations adopt *rules of order*. These rules relate to the orderly transaction of business and to the duties of officers in connection with conducting the business.

An organization may have long, involved ceremonies that must be performed in a certain order. It may have different orders of business for its different types of meetings. Or, it may have election rules that are unique. An organization should place anything of this nature in its rules of order. If members want to have electronic meetings or take a vote by e-mail, they should adopt rules of order to handle this special format. (The bylaws must establish the provision to have electronic meetings or vote by e-mail, but the procedures for accomplishing these things are put in the rules of order.)

An organization should not reinvent the wheel and include in this document things such as how to make a motion, how to preside, or other common parliamentary rules that a parliamentary authority outlines. By adopting a parliamentary authority, the members adopt sufficient rules of meeting procedures to help them solve their meeting problems. An organization adopts rules of order when it wants to do something different than the parliamentary authority. However, whatever the organization adopts should conform to common parliamentary law, which protects the rights of the minority and absent members.

Some city governments have adopted rules of order that concern various motions. One such rule concerns the motion to reconsider the vote. *Robert's Rules* states that members can make this motion only at the meeting in which the motion was adopted or lost. However, some cities have adopted rules that allow members to reconsider the motion at the next regular meeting. Other organizations may allow anyone to make the motion to reconsider the vote, rather than restricting that option to members who vote on the prevailing side of an issue.

Rules of order are sometimes mistakenly included in bylaws. The proper way to handle rules of order is to have them as a separate document, with its own heading, which is included in the same booklet as the bylaws. Rules of order usually provide for their own suspension at a meeting. This is no different than using the motion *suspend the rules* (see Chapter 9).

If an organization puts any rules of order in the bylaws, members need to know that any parliamentary rules in the bylaws, such as the order of an agenda, can be suspended. However, the other bylaws dealing with the structure, such as the appointment of organization committees, can't be suspended (unless the bylaws also provide for doing so).

Rules of order that are separate from the bylaws are adopted and amended by previous notice and a two-thirds vote. If no notice is given, then they can be adopted by the vote of the majority of the entire membership of the organization.

To adopt rules of order that are placed within the bylaws, the organization must follow its rules for amending the bylaws.

STANDING RULES

Another set of rules that organizations find helpful are *standing rules,* which concern the administration of the organization. A main motion brings them into being, and they remain in effect until rescinded or amended. A common standing rule sets the time for a meeting.

Because main motions establish these rules, a majority vote adopts them. They can be suspended for the duration of a meeting by a majority vote, and they can be rescinded by a two-thirds vote without previous notice or by a majority vote with previous notice. These rules remain in effect until the assembly rescinds them.

When an organization adopts motions that are for a lasting duration, the secretary should add them to a book entitled "Standing Rules." Many standing rules are adopted by *a resolution* instead of a main motion. The secretary should record each motion or resolution in its final version as adopted, as well as the date that the rule takes effect. If the rule is adopted by resolution, then the "Resolved, that" phrase is dropped when recording it in the book. If the rule is later rescinded, the secretary should strike it out and make a notation stating when it was rescinded. By keeping a record of these motions, each new administration knows what they are required to do. A list of standing rules keeps continuity in the organization so that new members do not need to perpetually ask long time members what to do and when.

If an organization does things "because that is always the way it has been done," the organization should write these customs down so that everyone knows what to do. A custom, whether it is written down or is a continual practice of the organization, becomes a force of law and needs a formal motion to rescind it, just as if the assembly had enacted it. Perhaps the assembly enacted a custom many years ago, but members have forgotten this fact.

Sometimes organizations have different names for their rules. Instead of naming the document "Standing Rules," they may call them "Guidelines" or "Policy Statements." To figure out what vote is needed to amend or rescind standing rules, use this principle:

- If the document or individual rule deals with parliamentary procedure, such as the order of an agenda or rules of debate, it is considered a rule of order. A two-thirds vote can suspend it for a meeting. A two-thirds vote and previous notice can change it.

- If the document or individual rule deals with administration, such as giving out awards for achievement, it is a standing rule. It can be suspended by a majority vote for a meeting. Members can rescind it without previous notice by a two-thirds vote or a majority vote with previous notice.

20

Bylaws

Bylaws are the most important document of the organization. Without bylaws, an organization would have no structure, and anarchy would rule. Bylaws state what rights the members have within the organization, how much power the assembly has to make decisions, and what limits of power are put on boards and officers. Bylaws determine the type of organization members have — democratic with powers residing in the assembly, or authoritarian with powers residing in the board and the officers. Those creating an organization need to carefully decide which format best suits the purpose of the organization. In some organizations, it is better to empower a board of directors to handle the affairs of the organization. In other organizations, it is better to let the assembly decide. However, most organizations are structured so that the power is balanced between officers and the assembly.

COMPOSITION OF BYLAWS

In defining the structure of the organization, most bylaws include the following topics in this order:

1. Name of the organization
2. Object or purpose
3. Members
4. Officers
5. Meetings
6. Executive board
7. Committees

8. Parliamentary authority

9. Amendments

Depending on the size of the organization and what it does, other topics may be needed. This is the basic structure for an organization, and putting these items in the bylaws saves the organization time. If there were no provision for meetings or committees, the assembly would have to make and adopt a motion every time it wanted to meet as an assembly or create a committee. If there were no provision for an executive board, the organization couldn't have one. By outlining the rules and requirements of members and officers, bylaws allow members a level playing field.

In drawing up bylaws, the first things an organization needs to decide are the organization's purpose for existing and who will have the power to make decisions. When these things are known, the following categories are easy to fill in with specific details.

Article I. Name
If an organization is incorporated, or if it has a constitution that states the organization's name, the bylaws do not include the name. This prevents the possibility of a conflict between the documents. Often an organization lists its name one way in the corporate charter and a different way in the bylaws. If you do have the name in two places, make sure that they agree.

Article II. Object
If the organization is incorporated, the corporation papers state the organization's object, which should not be stated again in the bylaws. The object should be concise (a single sentence) and state why the group exists and what it is organized to do. If the sentence is long, set off each thought with semicolons. The object sets limits on what business the members can bring before the assembly. If an organization wants to expand what it is doing and the object does not allow for this, members should amend the object to reflect its changing nature.

Article III. Members

This article usually has several sections that define who the members are, dues, and responsibilities.

Section 1. Classes of members.

Does your organization recognize various classes of members — active, inactive, and honorary? Bylaws should define the distinctions between these classes. Some classes of members may have more rights at meetings than others. The bylaws should state how one becomes a member of each class and if there are limitations on the number of members of each class.

Section 2. Eligibility for membership.

How does someone apply to be a member? Is there a test, a list of demands, or proficiency in a certain area that applicants must meet before they can apply? Are there other restrictions on who can join? For example, does the member have to reside in a certain geographical location? An organization must be careful not to discriminate if its membership is open to the general public.

Section 3. Dues or fees.

This section states the organization's dues structure, including the specific amount of dues. If dues are $45 a year, for example, only amending the bylaws can change this fee. Some bylaws state that the board of directors can set the dues yearly. However, if this is the case, the organization should stipulate some limitation to the amount of increase. Or, the bylaws can say that the board sets the dues every year but that members must ratify the amount. If there are different amounts of dues for different classifications of members, the bylaws state each amount.

This section of the bylaws also states when the dues are to be paid, when they are considered delinquent, to whom one pays the dues, what the procedures are for dropping a member for non-payment of dues, how a member can reinstate him- or herself, and any fines for late payment of dues.

Unless stated otherwise in the bylaws, an organization can't prevent a member who is late in paying dues from attending meetings or voting.

Likewise, members can't be assessed any additional amount of money unless stated in the bylaws. Therefore, if there is a one-time initiation fee or other assessments, the bylaws must state this information.

Section 4. Membership requirements.
Bylaws should define any requirement for staying a member. For example, some organizations have an attendance requirement. Other organizations may require that members serve on committees, attend regional conferences, or take educational classes.

Section 5. Disciplinary procedures.
Although this section of the bylaws may not be necessary, many organizations include it. Disciplinary procedures concerning members should be carefully thought out and written. Most parliamentary authorities include a chapter on this subject. Leaving discipline to the parliamentary authority instead of putting it in the bylaws may be wise.

Section 6. Resignation.
Some organizations have a provision explaining how to withdraw from the organization, as well as returning in good standing.

Article IV. Officers
This article lists all the officers in the organization, the duties of each office (if not too numerous), how officers are nominated and elected, and how to fill vacancies. The bylaws should list officers in the order of ranking, and classify directors as officers.

Section 1. Name the officers.
The first sentence of this section should name the officers in order of ranking. For example, "The officers of the organization are a president, vice president, secretary, treasurer, and three directors." The section can then state that the officers are to perform the duties outlined in the bylaws and parliamentary authority. If the duties are described in the bylaws, they should be briefly described for each office and designated

by sections. If the duties for officers are numerous, put them in a separate article. Organizations must take care not to omit any duties in the bylaws, because an omission can be interpreted to mean that a duty is not a requirement of that office. To solve this problem, the article can include the phrase "and such other duties applicable to the office as prescribed by the parliamentary authority adopted by the society."

Section 2. Nominations and elections.

This section should establish the nomination and election procedure. If a nominating committee handles nominations in the organization, the bylaws state who selects the nominating committee. The nominating committee is one committee that the president should not select or be a member of. It is usually best to have the members elect a nominating committee. This section of the bylaws should also state the duties of the committee. Do they select one candidate for each office or multiple candidates for each office? The wording of the bylaws decides how many members are nominated.

This section should also define how and when the election takes place, as well as describe the method of voting. Electing by ballot is usually best. If the bylaws do not provide for an exception to this method when only one candidate is nominated for each office, members must take a ballot vote. Some organizations state that if only one candidate is nominated, the members can take a voice vote. If the organization wants to take the vote by mail or e-mail or other electronic means, the bylaws must include this information. The bylaws must also state if the vote is something other than a majority vote.

Section 3. Eligibility.

The bylaws should state any eligibility requirements for each office.

Section 4. Term of office.

The bylaws should state term of office, when the term begins, and any term limits. If the bylaws do not state when the term begins, then as soon as officers are elected they take office. In the case of the president, as soon as the new president is elected, he takes over conducting the meeting. Instead of having this disruption, or having a newly elected president who is not prepared to preside, the bylaws should state that officers begin their terms after the meeting at which they are elected.

To ensure that there is always someone to serve in the office, the bylaws should state that officers "shall hold office for a term of . . . or [and] until their successors are elected." If no one is elected or there is a problem finding a nominee, the current officer remains in office until someone else is elected.

Having a rotation in office is also good. The bylaws may also state that a person can hold the same office only a certain number of consecutive terms.

Section 5. Removal from office.
The bylaws should contain a provision for removing a member from office. The provision can state that removal can occur for *cause* and then name the reasons to remove someone, or the removal can occur *without cause*. Removal from office should require a two-thirds vote. If the bylaws state that a person shall hold office for a term of so many years "*or* until the successor is elected," members can rescind the election. If the previous sentence says "*and* until the successor is elected," the only way to remove a member from office is to have a trial.

Section 6. Vacancies.
Including a section explaining how to fill vacancies is important. If an organization requires attendance at so many meetings, it may also include a provision for declaring a vacancy if an officer misses so many meetings. Because this is similar to removing someone from office, a two-thirds vote should adopt the vacancy declaration.

Article V. Meetings
This article sets the day of the meetings, the quorum of the meetings, the business conducted at meetings, and any provisions for calling special meetings.

Section 1. Meeting days.

The very first section of Article V should state the day that regular meetings will be held. For example, "There will be regular meetings on the third Thursday of every month." (The standing rules state the time of the meetings.) This section should also state which meeting is the annual meeting. For example, "The annual meeting is held the third Thursday of April." This section should also include guidelines concerning the business that members can transact at regular meetings and the annual meeting. For example, "At the annual meeting, members meet to conduct business, hear reports of committees and officers, and elect officers." The bylaws must specify if members must be notified of meetings, the method of notification (mail, e-mail, fax, telephone, and so on), and the time of notification. For example, "The secretary will mail out a call to the meeting 10 days prior to the meeting." The bylaws must also state if a vote other than a majority vote must adopt business.

Section 2. Quorum.

This section sets the quorum, which should be a number and not a percentage, for the meetings. The quorum should be the number of members that regularly attend meetings. For example, if an organization has 100 members and 20 members normally attend meetings, 20 should be the quorum. If the bylaws do not state a quorum, the quorum becomes a majority of the membership. However, members should not tie their hands by setting the quorum too high; if the quorum is set too high, nothing gets accomplished.

Section 3. Special meetings.

There are times when emergencies arise and members need to call special meetings. Members or officers can call special meetings only if a provision in the bylaws allows it. The bylaws should state who could call the meeting — officers and/or members. This section also states the procedure for calling the meeting. If the members want to call it, how many have to sign a petition to do so? If officers can call the meeting, who calls it and how? How many days notice do members need? Can the organization give the meeting notice by e-mail, fax, telephone, or mail, or a combination of all methods? The bylaws may state that no other business can be transacted except that for which the meeting was called. (This rule applies anyway, but having this in the bylaws is sometimes helpful because many people do not know this fact.)

Section 4. Cancellation of a regularly scheduled meeting.
Sometimes meetings need to be canceled because of weather or a national emergency. If the bylaws contain a provision for canceling meetings, it should indicate who is responsible for making the decision to cancel the meeting, how members are to be notified, and who has the right to reschedule the meeting.

Section 5. Electronic and other meetings.
If the organization wants to conduct any meetings by e-mail, online chat room, phone, or video conferencing, the bylaws must state this information. The rules of order should outline the procedure for holding these types of meetings (see Chapter 19).

Article VI. Executive Boards
Article VI creates a board. If the bylaws do not have this article, the officers of an organization can't act as the board. This article tells who the board members are, how they are elected, the total number of board members, the regular meeting day, the duties of board members, the quorum for board meetings, and other important information.

When writing this article, it is important to remember that the members can't revoke any duty specifically given to the board. However, if a duty hasn't been specifically given to the board in the bylaws, the membership can rescind it. If, for example, the bylaws state that the board shall sell or buy property, members can't complain if the board sells property without consulting the members, because the bylaws give the board this power. If the bylaws don't give the board a specific power, members can rescind any such action. In the case of buying and selling property, the bylaws should address who has this power. To preserve democracy, the members should decide who has what power whenever possible. If an organization meets quarterly, the board usually does not have that much power. As you set up your organization, be careful not to tie the members' hands by giving the board too much power.

Section 1. Board composition.

This section specifies how many members are on the board and how they become board members. Is the board composed of the officers of the organization? Are they elected from the membership? Are they board members by virtue of holding some office in the organization or outside of it? For example, the president-elect may be a board member by virtue of his office, or the mayor may be a board member by virtue of his office.

Section 2. Meetings.

This section states how often the board meets, what the quorum is, and what voting requirements are (if not a majority vote). Can the board call a special meeting? If so, who can call it? Who gives previous notice of the meeting? Can the notice be given by phone or e-mail? Can the board have e-mail meetings, telephone conference meetings, or video conference meetings? Are board meetings open to the membership? This section addresses all these issues. Include a provision for the board to change the day of the meeting if necessary.

A note about majority vote: In small boards, stating that all business transacted requires adoption by a *majority of the entire board* may be wise. Doing so protects absent members. For example, say a board has five members. If the quorum is three, and only three members attend a meeting, all three have to agree on something before it is adopted.

Section 3. Removal from office and vacancies.

Can the board remove one of its members? If a member is absent several meetings in a row, can the board members declare a vacancy by a two-thirds vote? If a board member resigns, can the board fill the vacancy or does the membership need to elect another member? This section addresses all these issues.

Section 4. Duties.
Specifically state the board's duties in this section. If the board has the power to appoint committees, make sure to include this information.

Other considerations
Some additional questions to ask as you set up provisions for a board include:

- Can a board make its own rules, providing they do not conflict with the organization's other rules?

- Do board members serve as ex officio members of committees?

- Does the board have power to spend money, enter into contracts, borrow money, purchase, and sell or lease property?

- Can the board represent the membership in dealing with the public, government agencies, and related organizations?

- Can the board hire and fire employees?

- Should board members be paid a salary?

Sometimes boards have an executive committee. The structure and duties of the executive committee are included in a separate article and have similar provisions.

Article VII. Committees
The bylaws identify all standing committees, which may include finance, auditing, program, social, and membership committees. This article states the number of members on each committee and describes the duties and responsibilities. It can also provide for rotation in office by indicating how long a person can serve on a given committee. Likewise, it should provide for the appointment of special, or *ad hoc*, committees. This section should also state who fills vacancies

and to whom someone submits a resignation. If there are eligibility requirements for certain committees, state them here. This article also indicates whether a committee has the ability to spend funds, and who gives it the authority to do so.

Each standing committee should have its own section giving its name, composition, duties, and manner of selection. If the president or another officer is to be an *ex officio* member of any committee, state this information here.

Article VIII. Parliamentary Authority

This article states which parliamentary authority and which edition of the authority the organization uses.

Article IX. Amending the Bylaws

This article provides a means for making changes in the bylaws. Amending the bylaws should require previous notice and a two-thirds vote.

Other Bylaw Provisions

Organizations may need to have other articles in the bylaws to meet their needs. The information in this chapter is just a basic outline for all organizations. Other clauses that your organization may want to include are a *dissolution clause,* which states what happens to the money or any property that the organization owns upon dissolving. For non-profit organizations, state law may require an *indemnity clause,* which provides legal exemptions from penalties or liabilities incurred by one's action in office. An attorney helping create a corporate charter can also help with this. If members are having a difficult time writing the bylaws, hiring a parliamentarian can be of great help.

When writing bylaws, keep the language simple and straightforward. Do not use legalese or duplicate words with slightly varying shades of meaning like "null and void" or "confirm and ratify." Write each sentence so that it is impossible to quote out of context. The complete meaning should be clear without making the reader refer to preceding or following sentences. Include exceptions or qualifications within the sentence to which they apply.

When an organization is brought into existence, the first bylaws should be simple and to the point and should include only what is necessary to begin functioning as an organization. As the organization grows and problems arise, the organization can amend the bylaws to meet its needs. Foreseeing all the problems that will arise or how the organization will develop is impossible. Therefore, members should periodically review their bylaws to see if they need changed. Reviewing the bylaws is an opportunity for members to be honest with themselves about whether the bylaws meet the organization's current needs.

Proposing amendments can usually solve most bylaw problems. However, over time an organization may make so many changes to the bylaws that a complete revision of the current bylaws is necessary.

REVISING THE BYLAWS

If an organization decides to revise the bylaws, it should appoint a large committee with the most interested and vocal people. The committee members should represent many viewpoints. Those members of the organization who would ask the most questions and propose many amendments at a bylaws meeting should also be appointed to the committee. This way, committee members can work out many disagreements at the committee level and not during the presentation to the entire membership.

Ask the entire membership to submit suggestions to the committee, and consider all suggestions carefully. There is no room for politics on the bylaw review committee. When the committee is done with the proposed revision, it needs to present the revision to the membership according to the amending procedure defined in the bylaws. Because a revision is a proposed replacement of the current bylaws, the organization should send a copy of the revision with a letter explaining the proposed major changes to the members.

The first thing members need to understand about a revision is that the current bylaws are not under consideration at all. If the revision is defeated, no changes to the current bylaws take place. If members like certain things in the revision but reject the revision as a whole, they have to propose the sections that they like as amendments to the current bylaws.

The second thing to remember about a revision is that it is like presenting new bylaws for the first time: Everything in the proposed revision is open to change by the membership, not just the changes that the committee proposes making to the previous bylaws.

Third, although not voted upon in this manner, the bylaw revision is usually considered, presented, discussed, and amended article by article. After all the articles are read, discussed, and amended, the revision as a whole is opened up for discussion and further amending. This way, if something in Article V is changed and it affects something in Article II, the members can return to Article II and fix it before voting on the amended revision.

Presenting a bylaw revision at a special meeting or series of special meetings is best. This way, members can consider the document carefully. At the first meeting, the chair should ask the bylaw committee chairman to give a report. At the end of the report, the chairman states, "By direction of the committee, I move the adoption of the bylaw revision." The chair then places the motion before the assembly and asks the bylaw committee chairman to read Article I and explain the changes and the reason for them. After this is done, the bylaw chairman sits down and the chair asks for discussion on Article I. Members can ask questions, discuss the article, and propose amendments. If any changes are proposed, the chair takes a vote on the amendment. If the amendment is adopted, it becomes part of the revision. When the members are finished with Article I, the chair asks the bylaw chairman to read Article II and explain the changes and the reason for them. The bylaw chairman sits down, and the chair asks the membership for discussion. Again the members can discuss, ask questions, or propose amendments. This same procedure continues for each article of the proposed revision.

After the members finish discussing the last article, the chair opens the amended revision for more discussion, debate, and amendments. When the members finish discussing and proposing amendments, the chair takes a vote on the revision as amended. This requires a two-thirds vote, which should be counted. Members can take the vote by ballot or take a rising counted vote. The secretary records the number of votes in the minutes. If the revision is adopted, it immediately replaces the bylaws. If it is defeated, the current bylaws remain as they are.

Sometimes members attach *provisos* (which state when a certain bylaw goes into effect) on certain provisions or on the entire revision. For example, if there is a change in the term of office that would affect current officers, the members can attach a proviso that says that this part of the document will become effective on a specific later date. You can find more information about the proviso motion later in this chapter.

AMENDING THE BYLAWS

When one change or a few changes to the bylaws are necessary, members can present these as individual amendments. Members should follow the procedure outlined in the bylaws for making amendments. Usually this requires giving the membership previous notice that a vote will be taken on an amendment, and it often requires submitting the amendment to the board or through a bylaws committee. If the amendment does not have to be submitted through a committee or board, the person submitting the notice should have another member sign it. This shows that two people want the amendment discussed. If no written notice is necessary, members can give notice orally at the previous meeting. The amendment then becomes a general order of business at the meeting during which it is proposed.

When giving notice that an amendment will be proposed, word the notice formally. For example, the notice can say, "To Amend Article III. Members, Section 2. Dues, by striking out $25.00 and inserting $50.00." If the notice requires mailing, state the original bylaw, the proposed amendment, and finally how the bylaw would read if the amendment were adopted. Many times organizations also include a reason for the proposed change.

Giving notice informs the membership that there is a limit to the proposed change. This is called the *scope of the notice*. It means that members cannot amend a bylaw beyond the scope of the notice, which protects the rights of the absent members. So at the meeting, members cannot propose a change below $25.00 or above $50.00, but they can propose a change between $25.00 and $50.00.

When a bylaw amendment appears on the agenda under general orders, a member must propose it as a formal motion, it must be seconded, and it is debatable. Members can also amend it within the scope of the notice. A majority vote adopts these amendments. For example, say an amendment was proposed to strike out $50.00 and insert $40.00, and it's adopted. Now the proposed amendment to the bylaws is to increase dues from $25.00 to $40.00. This is now presented to the assembly as the bylaw amendment, and it takes a two-thirds counted vote to adopt. The bylaw provision takes effect immediately if it is adopted, unless members vote that it takes effect later, which requires a proviso (discussed in the next section).

HELPFUL MOTIONS FOR BYLAW REVISION AND AMENDMENT

There are two helpful motions that members need to know concerning bylaws: *seriatim* (consideration paragraph by paragraph) and *proviso*.

Seriatim (Consideration Paragraph by Paragraph)

+ **Purpose:** To discuss and amend long documents, such as bylaws or a series of resolutions, one paragraph at a time (instead of considering the document as a whole).

◆ Needs a second.

◆ Not debatable.

◆ Amendable.

◆ Requires a majority vote to adopt.

◆ Cannot be reconsidered.

◆ **Result:** If adopted, the assembly considers the document one paragraph at a time. The chair begins with the first paragraph and takes up each following paragraph in order to the end of the document, instead of considering it as a whole document.

Normally, an organization should consider a revision of bylaws paragraph by paragraph. If the chair does not consider the revision this way, a member can make the motion *seriatim,* which calls for a paragraph-by-paragraph review of the bylaws until the entire document is discussed and amended. Members then vote upon the entire document.

Note: If the presiding officer decides to consider the document seriatim, but the members want to consider it as a whole, a member can make a motion to *consider as a whole.* The same rules as those stated for seriatim apply to this motion.

If, during the consideration of the document seriatim, a member makes the motion to *postpone indefinitely,* the chair states the motion but does not take debate or a vote until the entire phase of discussing paragraph by paragraph is complete. The chair doesn't take debate or a vote while *postpone indefinitely* is pending, because members can make motions of higher rank.

If members make the motions *refer to a committee, postpone,* or *lay on the table,* they are taken up immediately. If these motions are adopted, the bylaws are referred to a committee, put off to a later time, or laid on the table. When the document comes back to the assembly, members begin with the seriatim where they left off.

Members can apply motions to close debate or limit debate to the entire bylaws document or proposed amendments, but not to individual paragraphs.

Proviso

+ **Purpose:** To adopt another time when a bylaw amendment takes effect.

+ Needs a second.

+ Debatable.

+ Amendable.

+ Requires a majority to adopt.

+ Can be reconsidered.

+ **Result:** If adopted, instead of the bylaw taking effect immediately, it goes into effect at the time the proviso designates.

Proviso is an incidental motion that allows members to set a time in the future when a bylaw amendment will take effect.

There are three ways to handle a proviso:

■ First, while a bylaw amendment is pending, a member can make a motion to amend it by adding a clause such as "with a proviso that this amendment shall not go into effect until close of the annual meeting."

■ Second, while the bylaw amendment is pending, a member can make an incidental motion that it take effect at a specified time.

■ Third, if the transition from the current bylaws to the revision will be complicated and there are numerous provisos, they can be numbered on a separate piece of paper and attached to the revision. The motion to adopt the revision and provisos can be stated this way: "I move to adopt the revised bylaws with the provisos attached thereto."

Please note that when a proviso delays the time at which a bylaw amendment takes effect, the amendment becomes part of the bylaws document immediately. The proviso only delays the time it goes into effect; it doesn't alter the parliamentary rule that states that an amendment to the bylaws takes effect immediately when adopted. When the bylaw amendment is written into the bylaws and the amendment does not take effect for some time, place a footnote or other notation at the end of the amendment stating the time it does take effect.

SAMPLE BYLAWS

The following is an example of bylaws for an organization that is not incorporated.

BYLAWS
OF THE WHO DUNIT SOCIETY
OF GIG HARBOR

ARTICLE I
Name

The name of this society shall be the Who Dunit Society of Gig Harbor.

ARTICLE II
Object

The object of this society is to help private investigators and public law enforcement officials solve crimes, find missing persons, and promote courtesy and cooperation between private investigators and public law enforcement officials.

ARTICLE III
Members

Section 1. Application and Election. Anyone who is employed as a private investigator or for a public law enforcement agency and has been working in the field for two years shall be eligible for membership. Inquiries for application must be made to the secretary. Another member must sign the application and submit it to the secretary for presentation to the membership at the next regular meeting. A two-thirds vote will elect the candidate into membership.

Section 2. Dues. Dues are $40.00 a year and payable by January 31st of each year. If dues are not paid by January 31st, the member is considered delinquent and dropped from the rolls. If the person wishes to reapply for membership, he or she must pay his or her dues plus a fine of $15.00 by March 1st of the same year. After March 1st, the person will have to reapply for membership.

Section 3. Resignation. If a member wishes to withdraw from the organization and be in good standing, he or she must submit a letter to the secretary before January 31st and be current in his or her dues.

ARTICLE IV

Officers

Section 1. Officers. The officers shall be a president, vice president, secretary, and treasurer.

Section 2. Nominations and Elections. At the March meeting, members will elect a nominating committee of three to select a candidate for each office and report at the April meeting. Nominations from the floor will be allowed at the April meeting.

Section 3. Ballot Election and Term of Office. Officers will be elected by ballot for a term of one year or until their successors are elected. Officers take office June 1st.

Section 4. Limitations. Each person elected shall hold only one office at a time. Each person can serve two consecutive terms in the same office.

Section 5. Vacancies. If there is a vacancy in the office of president, the vice president will become the president. At the next regularly scheduled meeting, there will be an election for vice president. If there is a vacancy in any other office, members will fill the vacancy at the next regular business meeting.

Section 6. Removal from Office. Officers can be removed from office with or without cause by a two-thirds vote at a regular meeting where previous notice has been given.

ARTICLE V

Duties of Officers

Section 1. President. The president shall be responsible for conducting the meetings, attending one training session a year on parliamentary procedure, and planning the annual Christmas toy drive.

Section 2. Vice President. The vice president shall serve in the president's absence. He or she shall be responsible for having a program at each meeting.

Section 3. Secretary. The secretary shall be responsible for keeping the minutes, sending out the dues notices and delinquent slips, correspondence, and working with the other officers.

Section 4. Treasurer. The treasurer shall be responsible for collecting dues, giving the secretary information about who is delinquent, and paying bills upon membership approval.

Section 5. Other Duties. These officers shall perform the duties assigned to them in the bylaws or other acts of the society, and other such duties applicable to the office as prescribed by the parliamentary authority adopted by the society.

ARTICLE VI

Meetings

Section 1. Regular meetings. The regular meeting of this society is the first Thursday of the month. The annual meeting is the first Thursday in April. The annual meeting is for receiving reports, electing officers, and other business that shall arise.

Section 2. Special meetings. The president may call a special meeting; or, five members submitting a written request to the secretary can call a special meeting. Previous notice of the meeting shall be sent to the members at least three days prior to the meeting. The notice can be given by e-mail, postal mail, telephone, or fax.

Section 3. Quorum. The quorum shall be ten members of the society.

ARTICLE VII

Committees

Section 1. Social Committee. There shall be a social committee, which is responsible for planning the Fourth of July picnic and the Christmas party.

Section 2. Audit Committee. There shall be an auditing committee to audit the treasurer's books by the end of the year and report at the May meeting.

Section 3. Committee Selection. All committees will be elected at the annual meeting. Committees will have a minimum of four members.

Section 4. Other Committees. A majority vote of the membership can establish other committees.

Section 5. Quorum. Three members constitutes a quorum.

ARTICLE VIII

Parliamentary Authority

The rules contained in *Robert's Rules of Order: Simplified and Applied* shall govern meetings where they are not in conflict with the bylaws, rules of order, or other rules of the society.

ARTICLE IX

Dissolution

Previous notice and a two-thirds vote can dissolve this society. All outstanding bills will be paid, and the remaining money will be returned to the members or, by a vote of the members, can be given to a charity of their choice.

ARTICLE X

Amendment of Bylaws

These bylaws can be amended at any regular or special meeting providing that previous notice was given at the prior meeting in writing and then sent to all members of the society by the secretary. Previous notice can be sent by postal mail, e-mail, or fax.

Part VI

APPENDICES

Appendix A

Correct Parliamentary Terminology

This appendix shows the correct way to state a motion and the correct way for the presiding officer to repeat the motion to the assembly. Every motion listed in this book, from a main motion to motions that bring a question again before the assembly, is illustrated. The motions are listed in order of rank, beginning with the main motion.

MAIN MOTIONS

To obtain the floor say:

> *[rise]* Madam Chairman or Mr. Chairman; Madam President or Mr. President.

To make a motion say:

> I move that . . .

or

> I move to . . .

The chair states:

> It is moved and seconded that . . . . Is there any discussion?

343

VOTING

In taking the vote, the chair states:

> All those in favor say "Aye." Those opposed say "No."

In announcing the voice vote, the chair states:

> The ayes have it, and the motion is carried. We will be . . . , and *[give member's name]* will do it.

or

> The noes have it, and the motion is lost. We will not be doing . . . .

In taking a rising vote, the chair states:

> All those in favor please rise. Be seated. Those opposed please rise. Be seated.

In announcing a rising vote, the chair states:

> The affirmative has it, and the motion is carried. We will . . . , and *[give member's name]* will do it.

or

> The negative has it, and the motion is lost. We will not do . . . .

When a member doubts the result of a voice vote, the member calls out:

> Division.

or

> I call for a division.

The chair states:

> A division has been called for. All those in favor please rise.

Be seated. Those opposed please rise. Be seated. *[Announce the vote.]*

SUBSIDIARY MOTIONS

Postpone Indefinitely (Kill a Motion)

To make the motion to postpone indefinitely, a member states:

I move that the motion be postponed indefinitely.

The chair states:

It is moved and seconded to postpone the motion indefinitely. Is there any discussion?

The chair takes the vote:

All those in favor of postponing indefinitely say "Aye." Those opposed say "No."

Announcing the affirmative vote:

The ayes have it and the motion is carried. The motion is postponed indefinitely. That means it is killed for the duration of this meeting unless someone who voted in the affirmative moves to reconsider the vote. Is there further business?

Announcing the negative vote:

The noes have it and the motion is lost. Is there further discussion on *[the main motion; chair states what it is]*?

Amend

To make a motion to amend, a member says:

I move to amend the motion by adding at the end . . . .

or

I move to amend the motion by inserting . . . after . . . .

or

I move to amend the motion by striking out . . . and inserting . . . .

or

I move to amend the motion by striking out . . . .

The chair states the motion to amend:

It is moved and seconded to amend the motion by adding at the end . . . . If amended, the motion would read . . . . Is there any discussion on the proposed amendment?

or

It is moved and seconded to amend the motion by striking out . . . and inserting . . . . If amended, the motion would read . . . . Is there any discussion on the proposed amendment?

or

It is moved and seconded to amend the motion by striking out . . . . If amended, the motion would read . . . . Is there any discussion on the proposed amendment?

The chair takes a vote on amendments:

The question is on the adoption of the proposed amendment to add at the end . . . . All those in favor say "Aye." Those opposed say "No."

To announce the affirmative vote, the chair states:

The ayes have it, and the motion is amended. . . . will be added to the end. The question is on the adoption of the motion as amended. *[State the motion as amended.]* Is there any discussion?

To announce the negative vote, the chair states:

> The noes have it, and the amendment is lost. The question is on the adoption of the motion . . . . Is there further discussion?

Refer to a Committee (Commit)

To make the motion to commit, a member states:

> I move to refer the motion to the . . . committee, to do . . . and report back at the next meeting.

The chair states:

> It is moved and seconded to refer the motion to the . . . committee, to do . . . and report back at the next meeting. Is there any discussion on referring to a committee?

The chair takes a vote:

> All those in favor of referring the motion to the . . . committee say "Aye." Those opposed say "No."

In announcing the affirmative vote, the chair says:

> The ayes have it, and the motion is referred to the . . . committee to do . . . and report back at the next meeting. Is there further business? *[Or announce what the business is.]*

In announcing the negative vote, the chair says:

> The noes have it, and the motion is not referred to the . . . committee. Is there further discussion?

Postpone to a Certain Time

To make the motion to postpone, a member states:

> I move to postpone the motion to . . . *[state time or date or both, and if the motion is to be made a special order].*

The chair states the motion:

> It is moved and seconded to postpone the motion to . . . .
> Is there any discussion on postponing the motion?

The chair takes a vote:

> *[If the motion is a general order, it is a voice vote.]* All those in favor of postponing the motion, say "Aye." Those opposed say "No."

In announcing the affirmative vote, the chair states:

> The ayes have it, and the motion is postponed to . . . .
> Is there further business? *[Or announce what the business is.]*

In announcing the negative vote, the chair states:

> The noes have it, and the motion to postpone is lost. Is there further discussion on . . . .?

In taking the vote when the motion to postpone includes making the main motion a special order, the chair states:

> All those in favor of postponing the motion to . . . and making it a special order for . . . please rise. Be seated. Those opposed, please rise. Be seated. *[This motion requires a two-thirds vote for adoption.]*

In announcing the affirmative vote, the chair states:

> The affirmative has it, and the motion will be postponed to . . . and made a special order for . . . . Is there further business? *[Or announce what the business is.]*

In announcing the negative vote, the chair states:

> The negative has it, and the motion to postpone is lost. Is there further discussion?

Limit or Extend Debate

To make the motion to limit or extend debate, a member says:

> I move to limit debate to . . . .

or

> I move to extend debate to . . . .

The chair states the motion and immediately takes a vote:

> It is moved and seconded to limit debate to . . . . All those in favor please rise. Those opposed please rise. *[This motion requires a two-thirds vote to adopt.]*

In announcing the vote, the chair states:

> The affirmative has it, and debate is limited (or extended) to . . . . Is there further discussion?

or

> The negative has it, and debate is not limited (or extended) to . . . . Is there further discussion?

Close Debate (Previous Question)

To make the motion to close debate (previous question), a member says:

> I move the previous question.

or

> I move to close debate.

Note: Members can move the previous question on the immediately pending question, on all pending questions, or on consecutive pending questions.

The chair states:

> It is moved and seconded to close debate. If adopted, debate will cease on the pending question. All those in favor please rise. Be seated. Those opposed please rise. Be seated. *[This motion requires a two-thirds vote.]*

Or the chair can say:

> The question is on the adoption of the previous question. If adopted, debate will stop on the pending motion. All those in favor please rise. Be seated. Those opposed please rise. Be seated. *[This motion requires a two-thirds vote.]*

In announcing an affirmative vote on the previous question, the chair states:

> There is a two-thirds vote in the affirmative. Debate is closed. All those in favor of the pending motion say "Aye." Those opposed say "No."

In announcing a negative vote on the previous question, the chair states:

> There are less than two-thirds in the affirmative. The previous question is lost. Debate will continue. Is there further discussion?

Lay on the Table

To make the motion to lay on the table, a member must explain the reason for the motion. The member says:

> I move to lay the motion on the table because . . . .

The chair states the motion:

> It is moved and seconded to lay the motion on the table. All those in favor say "Aye." Those opposed say "No."

In announcing an affirmative vote, the chair states:

> The ayes have it, and the motion is laid on the table. *[The person who moved to lay on the table should be given the first opportunity to introduce new business.]*

In announcing a negative vote, the chair states:

> The noes have it, and the motion is lost. Is there further discussion *[if discussion is in order at that time]*?

PRIVILEGED MOTIONS

Call for the Orders of the Day

To call for the orders of the day, a member rises:

> Madam President (or Mr. President), I call for the orders of the day.

The chair states:

> The orders of the day are called for. The orders of the day are . . . .

To set aside the orders of the day by the initiative of the chair, the chair states:

> The orders of the day are called for. The orders of the day are . . . *[state what they are]*. The question is: Will the assembly proceed to the orders of the day? All those in favor of proceeding to the orders of the day please rise. Be seated. Those opposed please rise. Be seated. *[A two-thirds vote in the negative is needed to set aside the orders of the day. The vote must be a rising vote.]*

In announcing the affirmative vote, the chair states:

> The affirmative has it, and we will proceed to the orders of the day.

In announcing the negative vote, the chair states:

> There is a two-thirds vote in the negative, and the orders of the day are set aside. We will continue discussing . . . .

Raise a Question of Privilege

To raise a question of privilege, a member rises:

> Madam President (or Mr. President), I rise to a question of privilege concerning the assembly.

The chair responds:

> Please state the question. *[The question may be about conditions in the room, such as too hot, too cold, too noisy, too dark, and so on.]*

The chair rules on the question of privilege.

Recess

There are three ways to make the motion to recess:

> I move that the meeting recess until (a later time).

or

> I move to recess for 10 minutes.

or

> I move to recess until called to order by the chair.

The chair responds:

> It is moved to recess for 10 minutes. All those in favor say "Aye." Those opposed say "No."

In announcing the vote, the chair states:

> The ayes have it, and the meeting stands in recess for 10 minutes. *[one rap of the gavel]*

or

The noes have it, and we won't recess. Is there further discussion?

Calling the meeting back to order, the chair states:

The meeting will come to order. *[one rap of the gavel]*

or

The meeting will be in order.

Adjourn

In making the motion to adjourn, a member says:

I move to adjourn.

or

I move that the meeting adjourn.

The chair responds:

It is moved and seconded to adjourn the meeting. All those in favor say "Aye." Those opposed say "No." *[Announce the vote.]*

The chair announces the affirmative vote:

The ayes have it and the meeting will adjourn. *[Pause; look around to see if anyone is rising to do any one of the five things that are still appropriate at this time — see Chapter 8, "Adjourn."]* The meeting is adjourned. *[one rap of the gavel]*

The chair announces the negative vote:

The noes have it and the motion is lost. The meeting will not adjourn. Is there further business? *[or further discussion, depending on what was happening when the motion to adjourn was made]*

Fix the Time to Which to Adjourn

To make the motion to fix the time to which to adjourn, a member says:

> I move that when the meeting adjourns, it adjourn to meet at 8 p.m. tomorrow.

or

> I move that when this meeting adjourns, it stand adjourned to meet at 3 p.m. on Tuesday, May 1, at the town hall.

or

> I move that on adjournment, the meeting adjourn to meet at the call of the chair.

The chair responds:

> It is moved and seconded that when the meeting adjourns, it adjourn to meet at 8 p.m. tomorrow. All those in favor say "Aye." Those opposed say "No." *[Announce the vote.]*

The chair announces the affirmative vote:

> The ayes have it and the motion is carried. When this meeting adjourns, it will meet again tomorrow at 8 p.m. Is there further business? *[Or discussion, depending on what was happening when the motion was made. Or, if the motion to adjourn was pending when someone made the motion to fix the time to which to adjourn, the chair takes the vote on the motion to adjourn.]*

The chair announces the negative vote:

> The noes have it and the motion is lost. *[The chair returns to pending business.]*

INCIDENTAL MOTIONS

Point of Order

To make a point of order, a member states:

> Mr. President (or Madam President), I rise to a point of order.

The chair responds:

> Please state your point.

Parliamentary Inquiry

To make a parliamentary inquiry, a member states:

> Mr. President (or Madam President), I rise to a parliamentary inquiry.

The chair responds:

> Please state your inquiry.

Point of Information

To make a point of information, a member states:

> Mr. President (or Madam President), I rise to a point of information.

The chair responds:

> Please state your point.

Appeal from the Decision of the Chair

To appeal the chair's ruling, a member states:

> I appeal from the decision of the chair. *[This motion requires a second.]*

If the appeal is debatable, the chair states:

> The ruling of the chair is appealed. The chair ruled that . . .
> *[state the ruling and the reason for the ruling].* The question
> is, shall the decision of the chair be sustained? Is there any
> discussion?

In taking the vote on the appeal, the chair states:

> All those in favor of sustaining the chair's decision say
> "Aye." Those opposed say "No." *[Announce the vote.]* The
> ayes have it and the chair's decision is sustained. *[Announce
> the decision.]*

or

> The noes have it and the chair's decision shall not stand.

Object to Consideration of a Question

To object to considering the question, a member says:

> Mr. President (or Madam President), I object to the consid-
> eration of the question. *[This motion does not require a
> second.]*

The chair responds:

> The consideration of the question is objected to. Shall the
> question be considered? Those in favor of considering the
> question rise. Be seated. Those opposed to considering
> the question rise. Be seated. *[A two-thirds vote against con-
> sideration is needed to sustain the objection.]*

In announcing the vote (those in favor of considering the
question), the chair states:

> There are less than two-thirds opposed, and the objection is
> not sustained. The question is on the motion . . . .

In announcing the vote (those opposed to considering the question), the chair states:

> There are two-thirds opposed, and the question will not be considered. Is there further business?

Suspend the Rules

To suspend the rules, a member says:

> I move to suspend the rules and take up . . . . *[This motion requires a second.]*

The chair responds:

> It is moved and seconded to suspend the rules and take up . . . . All those in favor rise. Be seated. Those opposed rise. Be seated.

In announcing an affirmative vote, the chair states:

> There are two-thirds in the affirmative; the rules are suspended and we will take up . . . .

In announcing a negative vote, the chair states:

> There are less than two-thirds in the affirmative and the rules are not suspended. We will . . . .

MOTIONS THAT BRING A QUESTION AGAIN BEFORE THE ASSEMBLY

Reconsider

To reconsider the vote, a member says:

> I move to reconsider the vote on the motion . . . . I voted on the prevailing side. *[This motion requires a second.]*

If no other motion is pending, the chair responds:

> It is moved and seconded to reconsider the vote on the motion . . . . Is there any discussion? *[assuming the motion is debatable]*

If business is pending, the chair states:

> Will the secretary make a note that the motion to reconsider was made and seconded?

To call up the motion to reconsider, a member says:

> I call up the motion to reconsider the vote on the motion to . . . .

The chair responds:

> It is moved and seconded to reconsider the vote on the motion to . . . . Is there any discussion?

In taking the vote on reconsider, the chair states:

> All those in favor of reconsidering the vote on the motion . . . say "Aye." Those opposed say "No." *[Announce the vote.]*

Announcing the affirmative vote, the chair states:

> The ayes have it and the motion is carried. We will reconsider the vote on the motion to . . . . Is there any discussion? *[Members again debate the motion and take another vote.]*

Announcing the negative vote:

> The noes have it and the motion is lost. We will not reconsider the vote on . . . . It will be carried out.

Take from the Table

To take a motion from the table, a member says:

> I move to take from the table the motion . . . . *[This motion requires a second.]*

The chair responds:

> It is moved and seconded to take from the table the motion. . . . All those in favor say "Aye." Those opposed say "No."

In announcing the affirmative vote, the chair states:

> The ayes have it, and the motion is taken from the table. Is there any discussion?

In announcing the negative vote, the chair states:

> The noes have it, and the motion is not taken from the table. Is there further business?

Rescind

To make the motion to rescind, a member says:

> I move to rescind the motion that was adopted to . . . .
> *[This motion requires a second.]*

The chair responds:

> It is moved and seconded to rescind the motion that was adopted to . . . . Is there any discussion?

If no previous vote has been given, in taking the vote the chair states:

> Because no previous notice has been given, this requires a two-thirds vote to adopt. All those in favor please rise. Be seated. Those opposed please rise. Be seated.

If previous notice was given, the chair states:

> Because previous notice was given, this requires a majority vote to adopt. All those in favor say "Aye." Those opposed say "No."

If a two-thirds vote is required (and the vote was a rising vote), in announcing the affirmative vote, the chair states:

> There are two-thirds in the affirmative and the motion to rescind is adopted and the previous action . . . is rescinded.

If a majority vote is required (and the vote was a voice vote), in announcing the affirmative vote, the chair states:

> The ayes have it and the motion is carried. The previous action . . . is rescinded.

If a two-thirds vote is required (and the vote was a rising vote), in announcing the negative vote, the chair states:

> There are less than two-thirds in the affirmative and the motion is lost. The previous action stands as adopted.

If a majority vote is required (and the vote was a voice vote), in announcing the negative vote, the chair states:

> The noes have it and the motion is lost. The previous action stands as adopted.

Amend Something Previously Adopted

To amend something previously adopted, a member says:

> I move to amend the motion that was adopted at the last meeting to . . . by striking out . . . and inserting . . . .

The chair responds:

> It is moved and seconded to amend the motion that was adopted at the last meeting to . . . by striking out . . . and inserting . . . . If amended the action would be . . . . Is there any discussion on the proposed amendment?

The vote is taken and announced the same way as the motion to rescind. If no previous notice is given, the motion requires a two-thirds vote to adopt.

ADDITIONAL POINTERS FOR THE CHAIR

When a nondebatable motion is pending and a member rises to address the chair, the chair should say:

> For what purpose does the member rise?

When more than one motion is pending, the chair should state it this way when taking the vote on each motion:

> The question is on the adoption of the motion to . . . .

There are several correct phrases to use when taking the vote:

> As many as are in favor say "Aye." Those opposed say "No."

or

> All those in favor say "Aye." Those opposed say "No."

or

> The question is on the adoption of the motion to . . .

Appendix B

Meeting Script

Preparing the agenda is the very first step in getting ready to conduct the meeting. After the agenda is written down and the presiding officer knows what business is going to come up, the next step is writing a meeting script. The benefit of presiding from a meeting script is that all the presiding officer has to do is read it and follow any directions written on the script. Presiding officers don't get lost, the meeting goes smoothly, and less time is wasted.

In writing a script, write in complete sentences and put all directions of things to do in italics. Writing a meeting script is like writing a script for a play. This appendix provides an example — a general script that takes you through a complete order of business. It is easy to adapt this script to many kinds of meetings.

The outline of the agenda that you give to members might look like this:

Agenda for March Meeting

Pledge to the flag

Reading and approval of the minutes

Treasurer's report

Board report

Social Committee report

Elections and nominations

Unfinished business: donation to the Children's Museum

New business

Announcements

Adjournment

From this outline, the presiding officer writes the script.

Meeting Script for March Meeting

1. The meeting will come to order. *[one rap of the gavel]*

2. The members will rise and say the pledge to the flag.
    [Lead members in the pledge.]

3. The first business in order is the reading of the minutes.
    The secretary will read the minutes of the previous meet-
    ing. *[Sit down while the secretary reads the minutes.]*

    [After the secretary sits down, rise and ask] Are there any
    corrections? *[If no corrections, say]* The minutes are
    approved as read.

    [If corrections, then say] Is there any objection to making
    the correction? Are there further corrections? *[If none,
    say]* The minutes are approved as corrected.

4. The next business in order is the reports of the officers,
    the board, and committees. *[Reports of officers are given in
    the same order as the bylaws list the officers.]*

    The first report is that of the treasurer. May we have the
    treasurer's report? *[Sit down while the treasurer gives the
    report.]*

    [After the report, stand and ask] Are there any questions?
    [If questions, ask the treasurer to answer.]

    [When the report is finished, state] The treasurer's report is
    filed.

    The next report is that of the executive board. Mrs.
    Smith . . . . *[Sit down while report is given. After report,
    stand and say]* Are there any questions? *[If questions, ask
    chairman to answer; then state]* The report is filed.

    The next report is the report of the Social Committee.
    Mr. Jones . . . . *[Sit down while chairman gives report. Repeat
    the motion from the Social Committee to the assembly.]*

The question is on the adoption of the motion to have the Spring Banquet at Chez Paul on Friday, April 28th, at 7:30 p.m. at the cost of $15.00 per person. Is there any discussion? *[After discussion and any amendments, repeat the motion and take the vote.]*

All those in favor say "Aye." Those opposed say "No." *[Announce the vote and tell what the members have decided.]*

5. The next business in order is the nomination and election of officers. First we will hear the report of the nominating committee. The chair will then take nominations for each office from the floor. After nominations, we will vote on the officers by ballot. Will the chairman of the nominating committee give the report? Mr. Hall . . . . *[Sit down while the nominating committee reports; then repeat the nominations from the committee and ask for nominations from the floor for each office. Take the vote.]*

The nominating committee has nominated the following:

Janet Stacey for president

Eric Moen for vice president

David Haynes for secretary

Sarah Williams for treasurer

Are there any further nominations for president? *[If there are nominations from the floor, repeat them.]* Hearing none, nominations are closed for president.

Are there further nominations for vice president? *[If there are nominations from the floor, repeat them.]* Hearing none, nominations are closed for vice president.

Are there further nominations for secretary? *[If there are nominations from the floor, repeat them.]* Hearing none, nominations are closed for secretary.

Are there further nominations for treasurer? *[If there are nominations from the floor, repeat them.]* Hearing none, nominations are closed for treasurer.

The tellers will hand out the ballots. Members must put an *X* by the name of the candidate they want for a particular office. If you are writing in any of the candidates nominated from the floor, write the name under the office for which the person was nominated, and be sure to put an *X* in front of the name that you write in. Are there any questions concerning how to mark your ballot? *[Give members a few minutes to mark their ballots.]*

Will the tellers collect the ballots? *[Before the tellers leave the room, ask]* Has everyone voted who wishes to vote? *[Look around to see if anyone is calling for a teller.]*

The polls are closed, and the tellers will count the ballots. We will take a short recess while the ballots are being counted. This meeting stands in recess. *[one rap of the gavel]*

[When the tellers come in, call the meeting to order and announce the result of the vote. If any offices do not get a majority vote, you have to re-ballot for that office or offices.]

The meeting will come to order. *[one rap of the gavel]* May we have the report of the tellers' committee? *[Sit down while the tellers' committee gives the report. Then read it and announce the vote. Declare the winners; if no winners, take another vote.]*

6. The next business in order is unfinished business. The motion that was postponed to this meeting to give a $100 donation to the Children's Museum is now pending. Is there any discussion?

   [Be ready to handle any amendments or other subsidiary motions. Take a vote on each, and then a vote on the final motion.]

7. The next business in order is new business. Is there any new business?

8. *[Make any announcements.]* Our next meeting is next month on Tuesday, instead of Thursday, at 7 p.m. Remember to get your money to the Social Committee before next Thursday for the annual banquet. Are there further announcements? Is there further business?

9. *[Adjourn the meeting.]* If there is no objection, we will now adjourn the meeting. *[Pause; look around the room. If no one objects, say]* Hearing no objection, this meeting is now adjourned. *[one rap of the gavel]*

A special note about preparation: Before the meeting, call all those giving reports to see if they will be making motions at the end of their reports. If so, have the committee chairman or officer give the motion to you before you write the script.

If an officer makes a motion after his or her report, it needs a second. A committee of more than one does not need a second because the committee has already voted on presenting the motion. In that case, the presiding officer places it before the assembly this way:

> **Chairman:** The question is on the adoption of . . . . Is there any discussion?

After the script is prepared, stand up and read it aloud. You may find some awkward phrasing that you want to rewrite. Practicing aloud also familiarizes you with everything on the agenda and gives you confidence in presiding.

This written script, however, cannot prepare you for any unexpected things that may come up in the meeting. Leave blank spaces in the script where the members can bring up business or amend proposed motions. In the blank spaces, you can write down the motions that members make. If you don't leave blank spaces, put a blank sheet of paper on the lectern so you can write down motions that the assembly makes. Spend time reviewing the motions, the ranking of motions, and how to take the vote on several pending questions. Time spent in preparation makes you a better presiding officer and makes your meetings more efficient.

You can also give this script to the secretary to help him or her follow along, or you can give the secretary an agenda with everything in an outline form.

If you write your script using a computer, you can use the basic script outline for every meeting and make changes easily.

Appendix C

Sample Minutes

The following examples are minutes from two meetings: a regular meeting and an adjourned meeting.

MINUTES OF A REGULAR MEETING

Secretary: The regular meeting of Student Government was called to order April 10, at 3 p.m. by the president. The secretary was present. The minutes of the April 3 meeting were approved as read.

Because the treasurer had not arrived, the president proceeded to unfinished business. The motion to buy a computer and a laser printer not to exceed the cost of $1,000, which was postponed from the previous meeting, was taken up. Keith called for the orders of the day. The motion was lost. Members continued discussing the motion to buy a computer. After amendments, the motion to buy a computer and a laser printer not to exceed $2,000 was adopted as amended.

The treasurer gave his report.

Balance on hand as of April 3: $9,800.

Receipts from t-shirt sales: $200.

Expenditures for the bike-a-thon: $100.

Balance on hand as of April 10: $9,900.

The treasurer's report was filed.

The secretary presented a bill for $50 for photocopying. The members approved payment of the bill.

Mark moved to take from the table the motion to send five delegates to the state convention. The motion was adopted. Olivia moved to amend the motion by striking out "five" and inserting "two." Doc moved to refer the motion and its pending amendment to the finance committee to see what other funds are available. The previous question was ordered on all pending questions. The members voted to refer the motion and its amendment to the finance committee and report back at the next meeting.

Leslie, who voted on the prevailing side, moved to reconsider the vote on buying the computer and laser printer. The members voted to take a 15-minute recess. The meeting recessed at 3:45 p.m. and then reconvened at 4 p.m. The motion to reconsider the vote on buying the computer and laser printer was adopted. The motion to buy a computer and laser printer was carried. A division was demanded. The vote was retaken, and the motion to buy a computer and laser printer was lost.

Deadra moved that we lease a computer system from the Zone Corporation, not to exceed the specifications submitted in Proposal A.

Doc moved that when the meeting adjourns, it should adjourn to meet here tomorrow at 3 p.m. The motion carried. Doc moved to postpone the motion to lease a computer system to the adjourned meeting and make it the first item of business. The motion was adopted.

Byron moved to have a float in next year's homecoming parade.

Olivia raised a point of order that the motion to have a float in the homecoming parade was not within the scope of our bylaws. The chair ruled that the point was well taken. Byron appealed from the decision of the chair. The chair ruled that the motion was out of order because the purpose of our organization is to govern, not necessarily to participate in events. The chair's decision was sustained. The motion to have a float in next year's homecoming parade was no longer considered.

Leslie moved to adjourn. The motion was adopted.

Olivia gave notice that at the next meeting she would move to rescind Standing Rule Number 5, which states that we give $100 to Goofy Days.

The meeting adjourned at 4:30 p.m.

Jane Jones

Secretary

MINUTES OF AN ADJOURNED MEETING

When an assembly can't complete its business at the present meeting but must have it completed before the next regular meeting, a member can move to set the time for an adjourned meeting. This is helpful for groups that do not provide for special meetings in their bylaws. An adjourned meeting is a legal continuation of the current meeting. When the adjourned meeting is called to order, the assembly begins where it left off. However, the minutes of the meeting being continued are read and approved before beginning the business portion of the meeting. Members can make the motion to set an adjourned meeting when no quorum is present.

Following are the minutes of the adjourned meeting:

Secretary: The adjourned meeting of Student Government was called to order April 11 at 3 p.m. by the president. The secretary was present. The minutes of the April 10 meeting were approved as read.

The motion to lease a computer system that was postponed to the adjourned meeting was discussed. During the meeting, the treasurer received a note from the Dean's office that stated that all student activities offices will be getting a computer system by the end of the term. Deadra requested permission to withdraw the motion. Permission was granted by the assembly.

Mark moved that the meeting adjourn at 3:25 p.m. The previous question was ordered on the motion. The motion to adjourn at 3:25 p.m. was adopted.

Keith moved that the time of our meetings be changed to 7 p.m. Byron questioned the assembly's ability to change the time because it was established by a prior vote to be 3 p.m. The chair ruled that the procedure was proper. The procedure was the motion to "amend something previously adopted." Because no previous notice was given, the motion requires a two-thirds vote to adopt.

The chair adjourned the meeting at 3:25 p.m.

Jane Jones

Secretary

Appendix D

Steps in Making a Motion

1. Rise and address the chair:

   Madam President or Mr. President

   or

   Madam Chairman or Mr. Chairman

2. The presiding officer assigns you the floor by stating your name or nodding at you.

3. State the motion:

   I move to . . .

   or

   I move that . . . .

   Sit down after you make the motion.

4. The motion requires a second.

5. The presiding officer repeats the motion and places it before the assembly by stating:

   It is moved and seconded that . . . . Is there any discussion?

6. Members discuss the motion by rising, addressing the chair, and being assigned the floor.

7. The presiding officer takes a vote by stating:

   All those in favor say "Aye." Those opposed say "No."

8. The presiding officer announces the vote and whether the motion is adopted or defeated. If the motion is adopted, the presiding officer states the name of the person who will carry out the action.

The ayes have it, and the motion is carried. We will . . . .

or

The noes have it, and the motion is lost.

Appendix E

Ranking of Motions

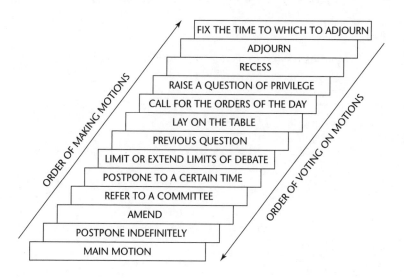

ORDER OF MAKING MOTIONS

ORDER OF VOTING ON MOTIONS

FIX THE TIME TO WHICH TO ADJOURN
ADJOURN
RECESS
RAISE A QUESTION OF PRIVILEGE
CALL FOR THE ORDERS OF THE DAY
LAY ON THE TABLE
PREVIOUS QUESTION
LIMIT OR EXTEND LIMITS OF DEBATE
POSTPONE TO A CERTAIN TIME
REFER TO A COMMITTEE
AMEND
POSTPONE INDEFINITELY
MAIN MOTION

Appendix F

A History

The term *parliamentary law* came from the English Parliament where it meant "the rules for carrying on the business of the Parliament." These rules evolved through a continuing process of development and precedent, similar to that of common law. They were brought to America with the early settlers who used them in their own legislative assemblies, and they further evolved. General parliamentary law or common parliamentary law of today has developed out of this legislative tradition.

Parliamentary law is used in *deliberative assemblies,* a term first used by Edmund Burke to refer to the English Parliament. It means a "group of persons meeting to make group decisions, to discuss and to determine a common course of action."

Under parliamentary law, a deliberative assembly can adopt any written rules of procedure. It can also add to or deviate from its own rules of procedure. *Rules of order* refers to a set of written parliamentary rules adopted by the assembly to conduct its business. These can be an existing set of rules especially composed by the assembly. *Parliamentary procedure* refers to the parliamentary law that a deliberative assembly follows, plus whatever additional rules of order the assembly may adopt for itself.

The origin of the English parliament is in the village assemblies of the Anglo-Saxon tribes that migrated to the British Isles in the fifth century A.D. In those days, freemen came together in a *village-moot* to make *bye-laws* for their village and to administer justice. Other larger deliberative assemblies of the day were the *hundred-moot,* a kind of district court of appeal, and the *folk-moot,* a still higher authority for arbitrating disputes. In Anglo-Saxon times, the folk-moot became the *Shire-moot,* later called the *Shire-court.*

After the Norman Conquest in 1066, the French administration developed a *Great Council* made up of feudal barons who advised the king. These were not truly democratic organizations because they were under the thumb of a king and a feudal system, but they formed the beginnings of a democratic parliament.

In the thirteenth century, the Great Council gradually evolved into the beginnings of the parliament that is known today. The barons who attended the king began to discuss with each other the *state of the realm* and the *king's business.* The parliament then began to include representatives of the shires and the boroughs (similar to counties and towns). These representatives were called the *commons.* Before long, they were in attendance at every parliament. Parliament was then separated into the *House of Commons* and the *House of Lords.*

During the next two centuries, procedures in the Parliament developed slowly and eventually were written down and published as part of a larger work by Sir Thomas Smyth in the sixteenth century. The first book about parliamentary procedures was *Lex Parliamentaria* by G. Petyt; it was a pocket manual prepared for members of parliament. This book enumerated some of the most fundamental principles of parliamentary procedure, such as:

- Take up business one subject at a time.
- Alternate between opposite points of view in debate.
- Require the chair to call for the negative vote.
- Keep personal attacks out of the debate.
- Debate only the merits of the question under discussion.
- Divide a question into two or more questions if appropriate.

Parliamentary procedure came to America in the seventeenth century when Virginia's House of Burgesses was founded in 1619. Other colonies founded governing assemblies based on their experiences in the old European countries from which they came. Eventually, their experiences led to the framing of state constitutions and state legislatures, which have their own rules of order.

In the eighteenth century, the restrictive policies of the British Empire caused American colonists to consider common resistance to the British colonial government. When the First Continental Congress convened in Philadelphia in 1774, its members already had enough parliamentary procedural experience to conduct business expeditiously. The Second Continental Congress framed the Declaration of Independence and declared war on the British colonial government. Existing state constitutions provided the material from which the Constitutional Convention of 1787 framed the U.S. Constitution. Through all of this turmoil, parliamentary procedures and rules were used to expedite business and to help resolve deep disagreements among the delegates. Out of this experience came the U.S. Constitution, which has been used as a model for other independent national constitutions worldwide. The usefulness of parliamentary procedure cannot be overemphasized in such a process because it enables many different representatives of widely varying points of view to come to a common agreement in the very difficult circumstances of a political revolution.

The first book about parliamentary procedure in America was Thomas Jefferson's *Manual of Parliamentary Practice,* published in 1801. Jefferson was serving as Vice President and Presiding Officer of the Senate. He observed that the Senate did not have a codified set of rules of order but rather allowed the presiding officer a wide discretionary power to make up rules as he went along. Jefferson saw that this power could easily be abused in the future, so he developed a set of parliamentary rules based on English works and documents regarding the procedures of the British Parliament. The Senate, state legislatures, other groups, and the House of Representatives adopted Jefferson's manual. (The House later developed its own unique set of procedural rules.)

The next book about parliamentary procedure was *Cushing's Manual,* which was a set of rules for voluntary organizations whose needs differed from legislative bodies. The meetings of small organizations were shorter, their delegates unpaid, and their business less voluminous, so a different set of rules was needed to accommodate such organizations. *Cushing's Manual* basically said that each organization should follow fundamental parliamentary law as outlined in the manual but should adopt its own rules of order appropriate to itself. While this idea was good in theory, it didn't have the practical effect of significantly helping new voluntary organizations. Many of them did not have the time, the expertise, or the will to develop their own set of parliamentary rules. Thus, there was still parliamentary confusion in organizations when Henry Robert arrived on the scene in the 1860s.

Appendix G

Who Was Henry Robert?

Henry Robert (1837–1923) was a West Point-educated United States Army officer. He became interested in parliamentary law when he was asked to preside at a meeting and didn't know how. After the meeting, he vowed to learn something about parliamentary law. He soon found that little information about the subject was applicable to small voluntary organizations. While he was stationed as an army officer in different parts of the country, he attended meetings and noticed that each organization was conducting meetings by its own set of rules. There were no universally accepted rules in existence. He saw that organizations would be better able to function and carry out their purposes if they had a universally recognized and accepted set of parliamentary rules. In researching the question, he obtained a copy of *Cushing's Manual,* Jefferson's *Manual of Parliamentary Practice,* and Barclay's *Digest of Rules and Practices of the House.* Seeing that these three standard works did not agree on the major points of parliamentary law, he began writing his own rules of order, a work he, at first, expected to be short.

In 1874, Robert had a few months to devote to writing his book of procedure. He envisioned a book that would be based on the rules of Congress but would be general enough for any society to adopt, while still allowing the society the latitude to make up and adopt for itself any special rules of order that it may need. He wrote the book during 1874 and 1875. When the manuscript was complete, he couldn't find a publisher, so he published it himself by hiring a printer to make 4,000 copies. The book was titled *Pocket Manual of Rules of Order for Deliberative Assemblies,* and it was 176 pages long. He did find a publisher, S. C. Griggs Company of Chicago, who retitled the book *Robert's Rules of Order.* The first edition of 3,000 copies (now a rare book) sold out in four months. A second edition, somewhat expanded and revised, came out in 1876, and a third edition was published in 1893. When the Griggs publishing company went out of business in 1896, the publishing rights were taken over by Scott, Foresman & Company, who held the publishing rights for 100 years until 1996.

Appendix H

National Organizations

There are two national organizations that provide information on parliamentarians and parliamentary procedures. If you are interested in becoming a parliamentarian, these organizations provide excellent guidance and also sell instructional materials. Each organization has a different requirement for membership, and both have local chapters that meet regularly. Interested parties are welcome to attend as guests. For those needing assistance with parliamentary procedure, these organizations have listings of registered and certified parliamentarians who organizations can hire in various capacities, such as convention parliamentarian, presiding parliamentarian, and bylaws consultant. These organizations can also suggest parliamentarians to give targeted workshops to your organization.

> The National Association of Parliamentarians
>
> 213 South Main Street
>
> Independence, MO 64050-3850
>
> 816-833-3892 or 1-800-627-2929
>
> e-mail: nap2@prodigy.net

> The American Institute of Parliamentarians
>
> P.O. Box 2173
>
> Wilmington, DE 19899
>
> 302-762-1811 or 1-888-664-0428
>
> e-mail: aip@aipparlipro.org

Appendix I

Motions That Take a Majority Vote

FIX THE TIME TO WHICH TO ADJOURN

ADJOURN

RECESS

LAY ON THE TABLE

POSTPONE TO A CERTAIN TIME

REFER TO A COMMITTEE

AMEND

POSTPONE INDEFINITELY

MAIN MOTION

CREATE A BLANK

REQUEST PERMISSION TO WITHDRAW
A QUESTION

TAKE FROM THE TABLE

RECONSIDER

RESCIND
(with previous notice)

AMEND SOMETHING ADOPTED
(with previous notice)

REOPEN NOMINATIONS OR THE POLLS

Appendix J

Motions That Take a Two-Thirds Vote

In general, a two-thirds vote is required for any motion that takes rights away from members. Such rights include the right to be informed of pending action, to conduct business by known and established rules, to debate, and to vote. The following motions require a two-thirds vote in all cases:

Previous Question (close debate)

Limit or Extend Debate

Close Nominations or Close the Polls

Object to the Consideration of a Question

Suspend the Rules

In some cases, a majority vote is sufficient when previous notice is given. The following motions take a two-thirds vote without previous notice or a majority vote with previous notice:

Rescind

Amend Something Previously Adopted

Discharge a Committee

Index

Robert McConnell Productions

P.O. Box 559, Gig Harbor, WA 98335 ~ USA
Phone: 1-800-532-4017 ~ Fax: 1-800-948-8463 ~ E-mail: info@parli.com
Web site: http://parli.com

VIDEOS FOR PARLIAMENTARIANS
1-800-532-4017

_____HOW TO CONDUCT A MEETING (32 min. VIDEO)
World's first video about conducting a meeting from beginning to end according to Robert's Rules of Order. Covers basic procedures: quorum, agenda, call to order, minutes, reports, unfinished business, new business, discussion, voting, and adjournment. Includes an audio cassette, a generic meeting script to help you perform like a pro, and an agenda planning guide. $74.50 +$6 S&H **$80.50 total.**

_____**Video cassette only $54.50+$6 S&H $60.50 total.**

_____**Audio cassette only $15+$5 S&H $20.00 total.**

_____COMO CONDUCIR REUNIONES (en Espanol) (46 min. VIDEO)
World's first video entirely in Spanish (this is not a voice-over) about conducting a meeting from beginning to end according to Robert's Rules of Order. Has same information as the video *How to Conduct a Meeting.* $74.50 +$6 S&H **$80.50 total.**

_____**Video cassette only $54.50+$6 S&H $60.50 total.**

_____**Audio cassette only $15+$5 S&H $20.00 total.**

_____PARLIAMENTARY PROCEDURE MADE SIMPLE (80 min. VIDEO)
Details how to make motions, amend motions, close debate, conduct committee and board meetings, take minutes, vote, and preside, and has an example meeting conducted according to Robert's Rules of Order. Every group, organization, and association should have a copy. $64.50+$6 S&H **$70.50 total.**

_____**Audio cassette only $20.00+$5 S&H $25.00 total.**

_____ALL ABOUT MOTIONS Pts 1 & 2 (140 min. VIDEO)
As a set, the *All About Motions* videos are a visual encyclopedia of virtually every motion in Robert's Rules of Order. Second video is a detailed meeting showing how many of the motions are used in an actual meeting. Each individual video cassette comes with a time coded booklet full of helpful additional information. $114.50+$6 S&H **$120.50 total.**

_____**Audio cassettes only $50.00 total ($25.00 each)**

_____NOMINATIONS AND ELECTIONS (65 min. VIDEO)
Explains and shows step-by-step nominating procedures and election procedures. Shows in detail how tellers' committee should hand out ballots, collect them, and count them. $69.95+$6.00 S&H **$75.95 total.**

_____**Audio cassette only $20.00+$5.00 S&H $25.00 total.**

FREE OFFER:
A list of the motions in Robert's Rules of Order entitled *Basic Parliamentary Information.* **You can take this handy quick reference sheet into your meetings, and use it to make any motion that is appropriate and in order. To receive this free offer, just call 1-800-532-4017.**

* All monies payable in U.S. dollars. Prices subject to change. All videotapes are subject to availability.